LABORATORY AND FIELD EXPERIMENTS IN MOTOR LEARNING

LABORATORY AND FIELD EXPERIMENTS IN MOTOR LEARNING

By

ROBERT N. SINGER, Ph.D.

Director, Division of Human Performance
Florida State University
Tallahassee, Florida

and

CONRAD MILNE, Ph.D.

Assistant Professor, Faculty of Physical Education
University of Western Ontario
London, Canada

With

Richard Magill, Ph.D.
Assistant Professor, Department of
Health and Physical Education
Texas A & M
College Station, Texas

Frank M. Powell, Ph.D.
Assistant Professor, Department of
Health and Physical Education
Furman University
Greenville, South Carolina

Lucien Vachon
Assistant Professor, Department of Physical Education and Psychology
University of Quebec
at Trois-Rivières

CHARLES C THOMAS · PUBLISHER
Springfield Illinois U.S.A.

Published and Distributed Throughout the World by
CHARLES C THOMAS · PUBLISHER
Bannerstone House
301-327 East Lawrence Avenue, Springfield, Illinois, U.S.A.

© 1975, by CHARLES C THOMAS · PUBLISHER
ISBN 0-398-03262-9
Library of Congress Catalog Card Number: 74 12024

*With THOMAS BOOKS careful attention is given to all details of manufacturing
and design. It is the Publisher's desire to present books that are satisfactory as to their
physical qualities and artistic possibilities and appropriate for their particular use.
THOMAS BOOKS will be true to those laws of quality that assure a good name and
good will.*

Printed in United States of America
M-3

Library of Congress Cataloging in Publication Data

Singer, Robert N.
  Laboratory and field experiments in motor learning.

  1. Physical education and training. 2. Motor learning. I. Milne, Conrad,
joint author. II. Title. [DNLM: 1. Motor skills—Laboratory manuals. WE25
S617L]
GV436.S54   613.7′1′0919   74-12024
ISBN 0-398-03262-9

Preface

Curricula in physical education are increasingly being developed along scientific lines. This trend is probably most apparent in that area concerned with the learning of skills (motor learning), where courses at both the graduate and the undergraduate levels are being added at a rapid rate in physical education programs throughout the country. Simultaneously, motor learning research laboratories are being developed to encourage research as well as to provide a medium for the application of techniques dealt with in the class situation.

As an outgrowth of topics typically handled in experimental psychology and the psychology of learning, physical education courses and laboratories in motor learning express the concerns of those more involved in the psychomotor domain. These laboratories do not often contain highly sophisticated equipment. Research in motor learning can occur in such designated formal laboratories or the field laboratories which include the gymnasium, athletic field, classroom or swimming pool. Learning phenomena of interest to the physical educator or coach can be effectively studied in both kinds of laboratories.

This laboratory manual is applicable to the laboratory or field situation. The purpose behind it is to present the layout for experiments that are simple to execute within the restrictions placed on class times and meetings. The manual is appropriate for courses dealing with motor learning, where experiments are assigned as class assignments. The experiments represent the kinds of learning phenomena of most general interest to the student of motor learning. The designs suggested permit students to easily observe the expected trends in the data while gaining the experience of directing an experiment.

The suggested experiments can encourage possible thesis, dissertation, or independent study projects. Every experiment contains an ample introduction and review of literature to provide the student with a reasonably adequate background to each study.

Furthermore, this manual has other unique features not found in other laboratory manuals. A laboratory experiment as well as a field experiment is suggested for each topic. This treatment enables experiments to be run without the presence of a formal laboratory and equipment, and shows laboratory as well as practical applications of research. Also, each laboratory experiment promotes the usage of basic apparatus which can be bought or made. Equipment illustrations and building instructions, illustrations of manufactured equipment and addresses of companies selling pertinent apparatus, and data recording sheets accompanies each unit.

It is hoped that the method of presenting each experiment will facilitate experimentation within the motor learning class and outside of it. And furthermore, the intent of these experiments is to promote a better understanding of the various aspects of motor learning and motor performance.

R. N. Singer

CONTENTS

Preface v
1. Experimental Design and Statistical Analysis 3
2. Learning Curves and Measurement 31
3. Bilateral Transfer 56
4. Knowledge of Results (Feedback) 68
5. Reaction Time and Movement Time 83
6. Massed and Distributed Practice 94
7. Task Generality Versus Specificity 106
8. Mental Practice 117
9. Whole and Part Practice Methods 127
10. Speed and Accuracy 138
11. Motivation 153
12. Inter-Task Transfer 160
13. Simple Reaction Time 170
14. Stress 179
15. Social Facilitation:
    Individual Versus Coacting Performance 196
16. Effects of Supplementary Cues 202
17. Human Abilities and Performance 211
18. Level of Aspiration 225
19. Fatigue 238
20. Kinesthetic Aftereffects 249
21. Overlearning and Retention 259
22. Short-Term Memory 270

LABORATORY AND FIELD EXPERIMENTS
IN MOTOR LEARNING

Chapter 1

EXPERIMENTAL DESIGN AND STATISTICAL ANALYSIS

INTRODUCTION

EXPERIMENTATION IS A MEANS by which we can better understand behavior and other areas of interest. One basic principle is to "design the experiment so that the effects of the independent variables can be evaluated unambiguously" (Underwood, 1957). This is not a simple matter since there is no one specific approach in the study of a scientific problem. The choice of the best appropriate strategy in studying a given problem cannot be overemphasized. The planning phase of an experiment is probably the more important step in conducting a scientific investigation, since it determines directly the results and interpretation.

The discussion on research designs that follows will be related to the experiments presented in the laboratory manual and in the typical context in which they will be conducted.

This chapter will contain the minimum research tools necessary to interpret and to statistically analyze the data obtained in the experiments presented in the manual. The reader will notice that only parametric statistical tests are presented to test the hypothesis pertaining to a particular experiment, although nonparametric statistical tests are more valid in the present context. This choice was made in order to permit students to familiarize themselves with the use and the interpretation of parametric statistics, which are found so often in the published motor learning research studies. The experiments in the manual call for extremely small numbers of subjects, arbitrarily chosen at that, for the sake of convenience.

RESEARCH DESIGN

The research designs which are suggested for the various experiments throughout the manual have been selected on the basis of simplicity and practicality. More appropriate research designs than those suggested can

3

be used in many cases. If the reader wants to conduct the following experiments in a more sophisticated manner than suggested, he may refer to a number of books that have been published in the area of research methods and experimental design.

Underwood (1957) presents a table in Chapter 4 of his book which illustrates the confoundings which he believes occur with greatest frequency when manipulating subject, task, or environmental variables. This table may help to focus attention to factors to consider during the first stages of planning of an experiment (Table 1). The tables presented by Campbell and Stanley (1963) which summarize the main sources of internal and external invalidity in experimental and quasi-experimental designs can be referred to for additional assistance.

Table 1

CONFOUNDINGS WHICH OCCUR WITH GREATEST FREQUENCY ACCORDING TO UNDERWOOD WHEN MANIPULATING A VARIABLE

(Underwood, 1957)

Variable Manipulated	Confounding Variable		
	Instructional & Environmental	Task	Subject
Instructional & Environmental	X		X
Task		X	X
Subject			X

The Pretest/Posttest One-group Design

Throughout the laboratory manual, a pretest/posttest one-group design is suggested for use in many occasions. The essentials of the design are as follows:

	Pretest	Treatment	Posttest
Experimental Group:	Yes	Yes	Yes

The subject is first given a pretest in order to evaluate his original level of performance on a specific task or test. A rest period is usually introduced after the pretest, which is followed by the administration of a particular treatment or condition. It is assumed that the observed difference between the mean of the trials on the posttest and the mean of the trials on the pretest represents an estimate of the treatment effects. Whether the observed difference between the pretest and the posttest is significant at the .05 or another selected significance level may be statistically tested with the one-tail one-sample t-test if change is expected to occur in one direction; otherwise, a two-tailed one-sample t-test should be used. This kind of design has many limitations and weaknesses. Nevertheless, it is convenient as far as the limited number of subjects tested is concerned, as suggested within the experiments in this laboratory manual.

The Pretest/Posttest Many Group Design

Another kind of design which is suggested in the laboratory manual is the pretest/posttest many group design. It implies that two or more groups of subjects are used, and that a same pretest and a same posttest is administered to all groups. In a two group research design, one group may serve as a control group where only the pretest and the posttest are administered, while the second group is administered a treatment before the posttest. More than one control group and one experimental group can also be used. Furthermore, if the comparison of the administration of different treatments is the only concern, the research design can be composed of only experimental groups. This pretest/posttest many group design is illustrated in Table 2, while Table 3 contains arbitrary numerical values assigned to each component of this design in order to facilitate its comprehension.

Table 2
A PRETEST-POSTTEST MANY GROUP DESIGN

Group	Pretest	Treatment	Posttest
Control	Yes	No	Yes
Experimental A	Yes	Yes: A	Yes
Experimental B	Yes	Yes: B	Yes
Experimental C	Yes	Yes: C	Yes

Table 3
A PRETEST-POSTTEST MANY GROUP DESIGN WITH ARBITRARY NUMERICAL VALUES AND WITH ADJUSTED VALUES OF THE POSTTEST, CONSIDERING PRETEST DIFFERENCE SCORES

Group	Pretest X	Treatment	Posttest Y	Posttest Y (adjusted)
Control	10	No	13	14
Experimental A	8	Yes: A	18	20
Experimental B	12	Yes: B	23	21
Experimental C	11	Yes: C	17	16

It is also assumed that subjects were randomly divided into groups to which a treatment was assigned at random. First of all, the assignment of subjects to groups and treatments to groups on a random basis permits the assumption of equivalence of groups in all respects before the administration of treatments, mainly if large sample sizes are used. On this basis, we should not expect large differences between groups when we administer a pretest. Examination of the pretest scores in Table 3 indicates that the group means are not the same. The next step would be to test if groups are significantly different at $P<.05$ on the pretest by using a one-way analysis of variance. If the groups are significantly different, at least one alternative may exist: to either randomly reassign subjects to groups until groups are not significantly different or to use a statistical model called analysis of covariance which will adjust the scores on the posttest by taking into account the predictive values of the scores on the pretest.

On the other hand, if the statistical test failed to show that groups are significantly different on the pretest, at least one alternative must be considered: One can either ignore the pretest and compare groups on the posttest alone with the analysis of variance or consider the pretest in order to obtain more interpretable and more refined results on the posttest. In that case, the analysis of covariance may be validly used if its assumptions are met. One argument in favor of the second choice, e.g. the use of the analysis of covariance, is that even if one degree of freedom is lost for the denominator of the fraction in comparison to the analysis of variance, it is probable that the consideration of the pretest will be accompanied with a decrease in the denominator value of the fraction. That is, a large F value will be obtained. Furthermore, the adjusted larger means on the posttest will give a clearer picture of the treatment effects.

Columns four and five of Table 3 may illustrate the conclusions that one experimenter could draw if the pretest is taken or not taken into account. From the posttest column, one item that can be noted is the close scores of experimental groups A and C. On the other hand, the observation of the column for adjusted means on the posttest as a function of pretest scores indicates that experimental groups A and B, or the treatment effects of A and B, have almost similar values. The scores of groups A and C are further apart. Conclusions in terms of trends are different depending upon consideration or non-consideration of pretest scores, or even if no significant differences are shown among them. Similar remarks could be made if a pretest is not given. An observed difference or the failure to observe a difference between groups on a final test may be either interpreted as being the results of treatment effects or the non-equivalence of groups before they were administered the treatment and the test. The intent of the preceding discussion was to sensitize you to some of the advantages and disadvantages of using a pretest and a control group.

Counterbalanced Designs

The use of a counterbalanced design is suggested in some laboratory experiments because of its appropriateness or on the basis of practicality (when only a small group of subjects is available and when dividing the available group of subjects into sub-groups is not possible or is meaningless). In this design, the experimental control is achieved by entering all subjects into all treatments. Suppose you administer two movement time tests consisting of depressing a button at the onset of a visual stimulus and at the onset of an auditory stimulus. Also, suppose you administer sixty trials under each condition to each subject. Evidently, if you administered the movement time test to a visual stimulus first, practice on the first test may influence the subject's performance on the second test (auditory stimulus movement time).

Unless this situation is of experimental interest, some strategies should be used to counterbalance these effects. One alternative would be to assign the order of administration of both tests to each subject on a random basis. Another approach would be to assign a subject a constant order, e.g. test one—test two, and to a second subject, test two—test one, and so on for all subjects. If more than two measurements are taken on many occasions on the same subjects, it is important to use a counterbalancing situation meeting the requirement that each test precedes and is preceded equally often by each other test. As an example, assume we have three tests, *A, B,* and *C,* given to all subjects. The basic pattern could be: *ABC; BCA; CAB; CBA; BAC; ACB,* etc. . . . Comparisons could then be made by averaging the scores obtained on each test.

STATISTICAL ANALYSIS

The interpretation of the results of a study depends upon the control of the systematic effects of the confounding variables so that the effects of the independent variables can be clearly evaluated. If the comparison of treatment effects is interpretable, then statistical tests of significance are used to test whether or not the obtained difference rises above the random fluctuations to be expected in cases of no true difference for samples of that size. The issue of statistical procedures is tied to experimental design, and in sophisticated research, both are taken into account jointly in the design of experiment.

Statistical models widely used in research and appropriate for the laboratory manual are presented next. A simple procedure will be suggested for computing the standard deviation of a sample mean, the Pearson product moment correlation, the one sample *t*-test, the one-way analysis of variance for two or more independent means, and the two by two analysis of variance to test an interaction hypothesis.

Variability—Standard Deviation (S.D.)

Suppose you administer a two-hand coordination test once to a group of thirty subjects. A mere observation of the thirty obtained scores is not too informative. How can you summarize these thirty scores in a simple manner? What is the average value (mean) of the group? What is the variability around the mean? The mean is obtained by adding the thirty scores and by dividing the sum by thirty, e.g. the number of observations. One method of obtaining an overall value of all deviations from the mean is called the standard deviation. It tells you, among other things, the range in which approximately 68 per cent of the thirty scores scatter around the mean. A simple method for calculating the standard deviation from the raw scores is presented after the discussion on the relationship between two sets of scores.

Relationship—Pearson Product-Moment Correlation *(r)*

In a typical correlational situation, there are measurements available on two variables, or on one variable measured on two occasions, for each individual in a group. For example, suppose that IQ and the ability to high jump are measured in a group of thirty students. We may be interested in evaluating the way intelligence as measured by an IQ test is related to performance in the high jump. If high IQ values are associated with high jump values, and vice versa, a positive correlation between the variables exists. It indicates that for your sample, in general, the higher the IQ of an individual, the greater his performance in the high jump will be. On the other hand, if there are no apparent consistencies between the scores of the subjects on both variables, a correlation coefficient close to zero will be observed, which indicates a low or non-existent linear relationship between IQ and the height reached in the high jump. And a negative correlation would be obtained if large values of one variable are associated with small values of the other, and vice versa. It would inform us that the higher the IQ, the lower is performance in the high jump. As a correlation coefficient approaches $+1$ or -1, we have a high relationship, respectively positive and negative, while as it approaches zero, we have a low or non-existent relationship between two variables.

In general, it is of importance to determine if the obtained correlation coefficient from a sample is really different from zero in order to know if the two variables are related or not. If they are truly related, the second question is how much are they related. At least two criteria may be used to interpret the degree of relationship between two variables: (1) We can compare them to the correlation coefficients obtained in related studies and discuss it in that context, or (2) we can use the traditional method which says that only correlation coefficients higher than .70 should be considered as meaningful in the interpretation of relationships, since the square of .70 equals .49 which is an index that informs us that there is 49 per cent of commonality between the two variables. Subtracting .49 from unity then gives an estimation of the specificity of the two tests considered simultaneously. The term *specificity* also includes error. In some instances, only correlation coefficients significantly higher than .70 may be of interest ($r > .70$ at $P.01$). The interpretation of correlations, whether statistically or subjectively, must be considered according to the type of data collected and the relationships examined. Before concluding this section, you must remember that there are many types of statistical correlations, and the Pearson product moment correlation, although the most widely used, is not always appropriate. Some assumptions have to be met for using it.

Computation of S.D. and *r*.

A simple method of calculating the standard deviation or the correlation coefficient directly from the raw scores is presented here. The following steps are appropriate for computing the product moment correlation coefficient and to obtain the standard deviation of both sets of scores. However, one may follow steps 1, 2, 3, 11, 12 and 15, and omit steps 4, 5, 6, 7, 8, 9, 10, 13 and 14, to calculate the standard deviation of the mean of a given set of raw data particularly if the correlation coefficient is not appropriate or not of interest. You can follow the derivation of each number in Table I-4.

The steps are:

1. Add the raw data in ① to get ΣX.
2. Square ΣX to get $(\Sigma X)^2$.
3. Divide $(\Sigma X)^2$ by N to get $\dfrac{(\Sigma X)^2}{N}$.
4. Add the raw data in ② to get ΣY.
5. Square ΣY to get $(\Sigma Y)^2$.
6. Divide $(\Sigma Y)^2$ by N to get $\dfrac{(\Sigma Y)^2}{N}$.

7. Multiply ΣX (step 1) by ΣY (step 4) to get $[(\Sigma X)\ (\Sigma Y)]$.

8. Divide $[(\Sigma X)\ (\Sigma Y)]$ by N to get $\dfrac{(\Sigma X)\ (\Sigma Y)}{N}$.

9. Multiply each X in ① by the corresponding Y in ② to get XY, and enter in ③ .

10. Add XY in ③ to get ΣXY.

11. Square each X value in ① to get X^2, and enter in ④ .

12. Add X^2 in 4 to get ΣX^2.

13. Square each Y value in ② to get Y^2, and enter in ⑤ .

14. Add Y^2 in ⑤ to get ΣY^2.

15. By substitution, you get:

$$rxy = \frac{\text{step } 10 - \text{step } 8}{\sqrt{[\text{step } 12 - \text{step } 3]\ [\text{step } 14 - \text{step } 6]}}$$

$$\text{S.D. }_x = \frac{\sqrt{\text{step } 12 - \text{step } 3}}{N - 1}$$

$$\text{S.D.}_y = \frac{\sqrt{\text{step } 14 - \text{step } 6}}{N - 1}$$

An illustration of the preceding steps is given in Table 4. Suppose you administer a test called *X* and a test called *Y* to a group of five subjects. You want to know the mean, the standard deviation for each test, and the correlation coefficient between them. After Table 4, a model of a computation sheet is included to serve you in analyzing the results of the laboratory experiments.

Differences

A usual attempt in motor learning research is to determine whether there is a significant difference between the means of task scores of groups or between the means on a task administered to subjects on two different occasions. It is important to differentiate between these two situations since different statistical tests are valid for independent and for related means. In the first case, a two-sample *t*-test or the analysis of variance are usually appropriate; while in the second situation, a one-sample *t*-test or a repeated measures analysis of variance design are more valid. It must also be mentioned that the two-sample *t*-test and the analysis of variance yield the same results when two independent means are compared without specifying the expected directionality of the difference. The same holds true for the one-sample t-test and the one-sample multivariate analysis of variance design. For this reason, we will present only the procedures for computation of the analysis of variance, omitting those necessary for the two-sample t-test. As a first step, let us consider the one-sample t-test.

The One-Sample t-*test*

Suppose you measure time-on-balance on a stabilometer (balance platform) on one occasion. The next five days, the subjects practice balancing on a regulation balance beam according to a distributed practice schedule. One day after the training period, you again measure your subjects on the stabilometer. At this point, it is of interest to verify statistically whether practice upon the balance beam was beneficial for balancing upon the stabilometer. We would compare the two measurements taken on the stabilometer before and after balance beam practice with the one-sample t-test. Because the subjects' performance on the posttest is probably related to their performance on the pretest, the one-sample t-test is chosen instead of the two-sample t-test or the analysis of variance. Furthermore, as performance is more likely to improve with practice, e.g. from pretest to posttest, than to decrease, you may expect that a one-tail one-sample t-test is appropriate to test if improvement was significant or not.

The difference between a one-tail and a two-tailed t-test is as follows. In using a two-tailed t-test, the directionality of the expected difference is not hypothesized before conducting an experiment. It is appropriate to use when an investigator does not know, after searching through the related literature or applying logic, if the administration of a treatment between a pretest or a posttest will contribute to increased or decreased performance on the posttest. In that case, the null hypothesis is that pretest equals posttest, as compared to the alternate hypothesis that pretest does not equal posttest:

$$H_0: U_1 = U_2$$
$$Alt.H: U_1 \neq U_2$$

However, when the directionality of the effects of a treatment can be hypothesized, the one-tail t-test is more valid. In that case, the hypotheses are:

$$H_0 = U_1 \leq U_2$$
$$Alt.H = U_1 > U_2$$
$$or$$
$$H_0 = U_1 \geq U_2$$
$$Alt.H = U_1 < U_2$$

Table 4   Example Data for Computations

Subject Number	Variable X	Variable Y	Product XY	Square X^2	Square Y^2
	①	②	③	④	⑤
1	1	8	8	1	64
2	2	11	22	4	121
3	3	6	18	9	36
4	2	8	16	4	64
5	2	7	14	4	49
N=5	Σ X: 10 $\bar{X}$: 2.0 $(\Sigma X)^2$: 100	Σ Y: 40 $\bar{Y}$: 8.0	Σ XY: 78	ΣX^2: 22	ΣY^2: 334

$$r_{XY} = \frac{78 - \left[\frac{(10)\ (40)}{5}\right]}{\sqrt{\left[22 - \frac{(10)^2}{5}\right]\left[334 - \frac{(40)^2}{5}\right]}}$$

$$= -.38$$

$$S.D._X : \sqrt{\frac{22 - \frac{(10)^2}{5}}{5-1}} = .71$$

$$S.D._Y : \sqrt{\frac{334 - \frac{(40)^2}{5}}{5-1}} = 1.87$$

$$S.D._X = \underline{.71} \qquad\qquad S.D._Y = \underline{1.87}$$

Subject Number	Variable X	Variable Y	Product XY	Square X^2	Square Y^2
	①	②	③	④	⑤
1					
2					
3					
4					
5					
6					
7					
8					
9					
10					
11					
12					
13					
14					
15					
16					
17					
18					
19					
20					
21					
22					
23					
24					
25					
N=	ΣX : $\bar{X}$: $(\Sigma X)^2$:	ΣY : $\bar{Y}$: $(\Sigma Y)^2$:	ΣXY :	ΣX^2 :	ΣY^2 :

$$r_{XY} : \frac{\Sigma XY - \left[\dfrac{(\Sigma X)(\Sigma Y)}{N}\right]}{\sqrt{\left[\Sigma X^2 - \dfrac{(\Sigma X)^2}{N}\right]\left[Y^2 - \dfrac{(\Sigma Y)^2}{N}\right]}}$$

$$S.D._X : \sqrt{\frac{\Sigma X^2 - \dfrac{(\Sigma X)^2}{N}}{N-1}}$$

$$S.D._Y : \sqrt{\frac{\Sigma Y^2 - \dfrac{(\Sigma Y)^2}{N}}{N-1}}$$

S.D. $_X$: _____   S.D. $_Y$: _____

The null hypothesis (H_o) specifies that the pretest is equal to or smaller than the posttest, while the alternate hypothesis (Alt.H) says that the pretest is greater than the posttest. The critical values for the rejection of the null hypothesis are not the same (see Table 13) and the one tail t-test has more chance of rejecting a null hypothesis than a two-tailed test, if we assume identical validity.

A simple procedure to compute the one sample t-test is provided in Table 5. Follow the derivation of each number in Table 5. The steps are:

1. For ease of computation, write the set of data with larger values in ① , and the second set of data in ② , in keeping the data in their original pairs.
2. Subtract each score in ① by the corresponding score in ② to get Y − X = Z, and enter in ③ with the appropriate algebraic sign.
3. Square each Z in ③ , to get Z^2, and enter in ④ .
4. Add the scores in each column (① , ② , ③ , and ④) to get ΣY, ΣX, ΣZ, ΣZ^2, and enter in ⑤ .
5. Write the number of observations of each set of scores in columns ① and ② in ⑥ .
6. Divide ΣY and ΣX of columns ① and ② by N in ⑥ , to get Y and X, and enter in ⑦ .
7. Square ΣZ in ⑤ below column ③ , to get $(\Sigma Z)^2$, and enter in ⑧ .
8. Notice that ΣZ^2 appears in ⑤ below columns ④ .
9. By substitution, t = step 6:

$$\frac{\overline{Y} - \overline{X}}{\sqrt{\dfrac{(\text{step 5}) (\text{step 8}) - \text{step 7}}{N^2 (N - 1)}}}$$

10. According to your hypotheses, and the alpha level chosen (probably .05), you look at Table 13 to know the critical value for the rejection of the null hypothesis. The number of degrees of freedom (d.f. for denominator) is N − 1.

In our example, N − 1 = 5 − 1 = 4; then, according to Table 13, the critical values for rejection of the null hypothesis are 2.13 for a one-tail one-sample t-test and 2.78 for a two-tailed one-sample t-test. A one-tail test seemed appropriate, and the obtained Y value was 6.0. We can reject the null hypothesis in favor of the alternate hypothesis $U_1 > U_2$, e.g. Y>X, with alpha set at .05.

One-way Analysis of Variance and Two-sample t-test

A method for testing hypotheses about the difference between two independent means is the two-sample t-test. A limitation of the t-test

Table 5 **Example of Computation of a One Sample I-Test**

	Posttest	Pretest		
	Y ①	X ②	Y−X=Z ③	Z² ④
	8	1	+7	49
	11	2	+9	81
	6	3	+3	9
	8	2	+6	36
	7	2	+5	25
⑤ Σ	40	10	30	200
⑥ N	5	5		
⑦ $\bar{Y}$ and $\bar{X}$	8.0	2.0		
⑧ $(\Sigma Z)^2$			900	

$$t = \frac{\bar{Y} - \bar{X}}{\sqrt{\dfrac{N(\Sigma Z^2) - (\Sigma Z)^2}{N^2(N-1)}}} = \frac{8-2}{\sqrt{\dfrac{5(200)-900}{25(5-1)}}}$$

$$= \frac{6}{\sqrt{\dfrac{1000-900}{100}}} = \frac{6}{1}$$

$$= 6.0$$

technique is that it cannot be used validly with more than two means. Suppose you want to test a hypothesis on the differences among four group means. In this case, a technique called analysis of variance must be used. Furthermore, the analysis of variance can be used on two groups and the results are exactly the same as doing a two-sample *t*-test. In that special case, in finding the square root of the obtained *F* ratio, the results are the same as in the *t*-test ratio and then you may use it either as a one-tail or a two-tailed *t*-test. Because of this, the procedures to compute the one-way analysis of variance will be presented, omitting those to calculate the two-sample *t*-test. It is assumed that the reader will be able to transform the *F* ratio to the *t*-test ratio, if it is of interest.

SUBJECT NUMBER	POSTTEST Y	PRETEST X	Y — X: Z	Z^2
	①	②	③	④

⑤   Σ

⑥   N

⑦ $\bar{Y}$, $\bar{X}$

⑧ $(\Sigma Z)^2$

$$\underline{t} : \frac{\bar{Y} - \bar{X}}{\sqrt{\dfrac{N\ (\Sigma Z^2)\ -\ (\Sigma Z)^2}{N^2\ (N-1)}}}$$

Suppose you have four groups of subjects with five observations made on each one. The following tables illustrate the obtained scores and the computation of the one-way analysis of variance. The steps are as follows:

1. Add the raw data in ①, ②, ③, and ④, to get ΣX, and enter in ⑥. (Table 6)
2. Write the number of observations made in each group in ⑤.
3. Divide each Σ in ⑥ by the corresponding N in ⑤, to get X, and enter in ⑦.
4. Square each Σ in ⑥, and enter in ⑧.
5. Square each original value in ①, ②, ③, and ④, and add them for each group to get ΣX^2, and enter in ⑨.
6. Add all N in row ⑤, and enter in ⑩.
7. Add all Σ in row ⑥, and enter in ⑪.
8. Add all X in row ⑦, divide the sum by the number of groups, and enter in ⑫.
9. Add all $(\Sigma)^2$ in row ⑧, and enter in ⑬.
10. Add ΣX^2 in row ⑨, and enter in ⑭.
11. By substitution, plug the appropriate values in the sum of Squares Table (Table 7), and execute the proper calculations, to get ⑮, ⑯, and ⑰.
12. Enter the values of ⑮, ⑯, and ⑰ in the Anova Table (Table 9).
13. Find the number of degrees of freedom (df) for ⑮ by subtracting one from the number of groups.
14. Subtract the number of groups from the total number of subjects to get df for ⑰.
15. As a check value, find df for ⑯ by subtracting one from the total number of subjects. It should equal the sum of degrees of freedom for ⑮ and for ⑰.
16. Divide each sum of squares (SS) by the corresponding df to get Mean Squares (MS) and enter under Mean Squares (MS).
17. Divide "Column MS" by "Within MS" to get the *F* ratio for the comparison of all groups simultaneously.
18. Where lies the difference? A test for simultaneous statistical inference may be used, whether the overall *F* ratio is significant or not, but in the context of the laboratory manual, you may probably compare groups in a pair-wise manner with the one-way analysis of variance or the two sample *t*-test, starting with the larger mean differences. To illustrate this, we rewrite the data in Table 6, corresponding to groups I and II, in order to test the difference between these two means. (The same steps as before are undertaken).

Table 6

	Group I ①	Group II ②	Group III ③	Group IV ④	Total	
	1 (1)	8 (64)	4 (16)	2 (4)		
	2 (4)	11 (121)	5 (25)	3 (9)		
	3 (9)	6 (36)	6 (36)	4 (16)		
	2 (4)	8 (64)	7 (49)	5 (25)		
	2 (4)	7 (49)	8 (64)	6 (36)		
⑤	5	5	5	5	20	⑩
⑥	10	40	30	20	100	⑪
⑦	2.0	8.0	6.0	4.0	5.0	⑫
⑧	100	1600	900	400	3000	⑬
⑨	22	334	190	90	636	⑭

Table 7   Sum of Squares Table

1	2	3
Columns	Total	Within
$\dfrac{⑬/⑤ - ⑪^2}{⑩}$	$\dfrac{⑭ - ⑪^2}{⑩}$	$\dfrac{⑭ - ⑬}{⑤}$
⑮	⑯	⑰

Table 8

Example:	1	2	3
	$\dfrac{3000}{5} = 600$	$636 = 636$	$636 = 636$
	$\dfrac{-(100)^2}{20} = 500$	$\dfrac{-(100)^2}{20} = 500$	$\dfrac{-3000}{5} = 600$
	⑮ 100	⑯ 136	⑰ 36

Table 9   Anova Table

	Source	SS	df	MS	F
⑮	COLUMN (Between-Groups)	100	3	33.33	
⑰	WITHIN	36	16	2.25	14.81
⑯	TOTAL	136	19		

Table 10

		Group I	Group II	Total	
⑤	N =	5	5	10	⑩
⑥	Σ =	10	40	50	⑪
⑦	X =	2.0	8.0	5.0	⑫
⑧	$(\Sigma)^2$ =	100	1600	1700	⑬
⑨	ΣX^2 =	22	334	356	⑭

Table 11   Sum of Squares Table

	1		2		3	
$\dfrac{1700}{5}$	340	356	356	356	356
$\dfrac{(50)^2}{10}$	250	$\dfrac{(50)^2}{10}$	250	$\dfrac{1700}{5}$	340
	⑮ 90		⑯ 106		⑰ 16

Table 12   Anova Table

	Source	SS	df	MS	F	t
⑮	Column	90	1	90		
					45	6.71
⑰	Within	16	8	2		
⑯	Total	106	9			

Group I		Group II		Group III		Group IV		Total
X 1	X^2	X 2	X^2	X 3	X^2	X 4	X^2	
ΣX:								
N:								
$\overline{X}$:								
$(\Sigma X)^2$:								
ΣX^2:								

SUM OF SQUARES		
COLUMNS	TOTAL	WITHIN
(13) / (5) Minus (11)² / (10:) (15:)	(14:) Minus (11)² / (10:) (16:)	(14:) (13) / (5) (17:)

ANOVA TABLE				
Source	SS	df	MS	F
COLUMN : (15)				
WITHIN : (17)				
TOTAL : (16)				

Table 13
CRITICAL VALUES OF THE *t* DISTRIBUTION, AND OF THE *F* DISTRIBUTION, $P < .05$.

df for denom	t distribution one tail	two tailed	F distribution df for numerator		
	Q	2Q	1	2	3
2	2.92	4.30	18.51	19.00	19.16
3	2.35	3.18	10.13	9.55	9.28
4	2.13	2.78	7.71	6.94	6.59
5	2.01	2.57	6.61	5.79	5.41
6	1.94	2.45	5.99	5.14	4.76
7	1.89	2.36	5.59	4.74	4.35
8	1.86	2.31	5.32	4.46	4.07
9	1.83	2.26	5.12	4.26	3.86
10	1.81	2.23	4.96	4.10	3.71
11	1.80	2.20	4.84	3.98	3.59
12	1.78	2.18	4.75	3.88	3.49
13	1.77	2.16	4.67	3.80	3.41
14	1.76	2.14	4.60	3.74	3.34
15	1.75	2.13	4.54	3.68	3.29
16	1.75	2.12	4.49	3.63	3.24
17	1.74	2.11	4.45	3.59	3.20
18	1.73	2.10	4.41	3.55	3.16
19	1.73	2.09	4.38	3.52	3.13
20	1.72	2.09	4.35	3.49	3.10
30	1.70	2.04	4.17	3.32	2.92
40	1.68	2.02	4.08	3.23	2.84

In using the analysis of variance, determine if the groups compared are significantly different. No directionality is involved as in the two-tailed two-sample t-test. In a two-group design, the comparison of the obtained t or the obtained F with the appropriate critical value in Table 13 will indicate if we have failed or not failed to reject the null hypothesis, e.g. $U_1 = U_2$. In looking at the two means, you can determine the directionality of the differences. To obtain the t value, you find the square root of the obtained F value. In our example (Table 12), $F = 45$, then $t = 6.71$. If a one-tail test is of interest, we look in the appropriate column of Table 13 with $N_1 + N_2 - 2$ degrees of freedom, here $= 8$, and we compare the critical value 1.86 to the obtained t value 6.71. Then we conclude that we can reject the null hypothesis in favor of group II. On the other hand, if a two-tailed t-test had been used, the critical value would have been 2.31, and the same conclusion would have been drawn. Also, if the F ratio had been considered ($F = 45$) with the number of groups compared simultaneously minus one, here $2 - 1$, as the degrees of freedom for the numerator, and the total number of subjects minus the number of groups, e.g. $10 - 2$, as degrees of freedom for the denominator, a ratio of 5.32 would be necessary to reject the null hypothesis. The same results as with the two-sided t-test are obtained.

At this point, let us consider Table 9 where four group means are compared simultaneously. The F ratio was 14.81, with 3 degrees of freedom for the numerator, and 16 degrees of freedom for the denominator. Table 13 reveals a critical value of 3.24, and we can, therefore, reject the null hypothesis, with alpha set at .05. In this case, the rejection of the null hypothesis only tells us that at least two group means are significantly different. Nothing is said about which group means and how many of them are different. This is why, after having obtained a significant F when more than two group means are compared simultaneously, one needs to further analyze the data with a simultaneous statistical inference test (Bonferroni t statistics, Scheffé, Tukey, for example) or, in the present context, by repeating analysis of variance or two-sample t-test on two-group means at a time, proceeding from the larger group mean differences to the smallest. It may also happen that the overall F is not significant, but that at least two-group means are significantly different. The overall F says little about the F for a pairwise comparison, and for this reason, is usually of little interest in an experiment.

If the obtained t value in our example had been lower than 2.13, we would have failed to reject the null hypothesis: $Y = X$ at $P.05$. Notice that the equality of Y and X is not implied when one fails to reject the null hypothesis. It only says that they are not significantly different. A computation sheet is included after Table 12.

Interactions: 2 x 2 analysis of variance

Suppose an investigator is interested in evaluating the combined effect of distribution of practice and distance visual perception ability on the immediate level of performance of the set shot in basketball, using naive subjects to undertake the task. It would be informative to know whether the combination of these two variables produces greater or lesser effects than the variables considered singly. The two levels of the distance perception dimension could consist of shooting either with both eyes open or with only one eye open. On the other hand, the distribution of practice dimension could consist of continuous practice vs. distributed practice.

In summary, the treatment combinations in this experiment may be represented in the following manner:

Table 14

		Levels of Distance Perception	
		I (one eye)	II (two eyes)
Levels of distribution of practice.	I (continuous)	Group I: Cell 1: Continuous—one eye $n_1 = 5$	Group II: Cell 2: Continuous—two eyes $n_2 = 5$
	II (distributed)	Group III: Cell 3: Distributed—one eye $n_3 = 5$	Group IV: Cell 4: Distributed—two eyes $n_4 = 5$

In order to simplify the calculation, the same number of subjects is assigned to the four groups. But this is not a necessary condition. The following steps can serve to compute a 2 x 2 ANOVA from raw data:

1. Find the sum of the obtained scores for each cell, square each individual score and sum them to get ΣX^2.

Table 15

Example:	1	(1)	8	(64)
	2	(4)	11	(121)
	3	(9)	6	(36)
	2	(4)	8	(64)
	2	(4)	7	(49)
$\Sigma =$	10	22	40	334
	4	(16)	2	(4)
	5	(25)	3	(9)
	6	(36)	4	(16)
	7	(49)	5	(25)
	8	(64)	6	(36)
$\Sigma =$	30	190	20	90

Then ΣX cell $_1 =$ $\Sigma X_1 = 10$ and $\Sigma X^2 = 22_1$
                                 $\Sigma X_2 = 40$ $\Sigma X^2 = 334_2$
                                 $\Sigma X_3 = 30$ $\Sigma X^2 = 190_3$
                                 $\Sigma X_4 = 20$ $\Sigma X^2 = 90_4$

2. Enter ΣX of each cell in ① of Table 16.
3. Add the scores of each column and each row, and enter in ② .
4. Add the number of subjects of each column and of each row, and enter in ③ .
5. Divide each Σc and Σr ② by their respective N in ③ , and enter in ④ , where c refers to column and r to row.
6. Square each Σc and each Σr ② , to get $(\Sigma c)^2$ and $(\Sigma r)^2$, and enter in ⑤ .
7. Divide each $(\Sigma c)^2$ and each $(\Sigma r)^2$ in ⑤ by their respective Nc and Nr in ③ , to get $\dfrac{(\Sigma c)^2}{Nc}$ and $\dfrac{(\Sigma r)^2}{Nr}$, and enter in ⑥ .
8. Square the value in cell 1 and divide it by its number of subjects. Repeat for cell 2, cell 3, and cell 4.
9. Add cells' values in a column wise and in a row wise manner, and enter in ⑦ .

Example: $\dfrac{(10)^2}{5} + \dfrac{(30)^2}{5} ; \dfrac{(40)^2}{5} + \dfrac{(20)^2}{5} ; \dfrac{(10)^2}{5} + \dfrac{(40)^2}{5} ; \dfrac{(30)^2}{5} + \dfrac{(20)^2}{5}$.

10. Add Σc or Σr values, and enter in ⑧ .
11. Add Nc or Nr values, and enter in ⑨ .
12. Divide ⑧ by ⑨ , and enter in ⑩ .
13. Square ⑧ and divide by ⑨ , and enter in ⑪ .
14. Add $\dfrac{(\Sigma c)^2}{Nc}$ in ⑥ , and enter in ⑫ .
15. Add $\dfrac{(\Sigma r)^2}{Nr}$ in ⑥ , and enter in ⑬ .
16. Add values in column ⑦ , and enter in ⑭ .
17. Add values in row ⑦ and enter in ⑮ .
18. Add Σx^2 found in step 1, and enter in ⑯ .
19. Substitute in the sum of squares table the values found in the preceding steps (Table 17).
20. Subtract the first value by the second one in a column wise manner, and enter successively in ⑰ , ⑱ , ⑲ , ⑳ , ㉑ , ㉒ , at the bottom of Table 17.
21. By substitution, plug the appropriate score in the SS columns (Table 18).
22. Find the number of degrees of freedom in computing: Number of columns minus one, number of rows minus one, the product of the preceding degrees of freedom, and the total number of subjects minus the number of cells. As a check value, the df of *total* is the

total number of subjects minus one. Verify if the sum of the column for df equals this value (Table 18).

23. Divide SS by the corresponding df (Table 18).
24. Find the F value for the interaction, dividing *interaction MS* by *Within MS* (Table 18).

Table 16

	1 Distance Perception (Colums)		2 Σc	3 Nc	4 $\bar{X}c$	5 $(\Sigma c)^2$	6 $\frac{(\Sigma c)^2}{Nc}$	7
	I	II						
(1) Practice Rows — I	10, $n_1 = 5$	40, $n_2 = 5$	50	10	5.00	2500	250	340
(1) Practice Rows — II	30, $n_3 = 5$	20, $n_4 = 5$	50	10	5.0	2500	250	260
(2) Σr	40	60	(8) 100					
(3) Nr	10	10		(9) 20				
(4) $\bar{X}r$	4.0	6.0			(10) 5.0			
(5) $(\Sigma r)^2$	1600	3600				(11) 500	(12) 500	
(6) $\frac{(\Sigma r)^2}{Nr}$	160	360				(13) 520	(14) 600	
(7)	200	400				(15) 600	(16) 636	

Table 17   SUM-OF-SQUARES TABLE

① COLUMNS	② ROWS	③ CELLS	④ INTERACTION	⑤ TOTAL	⑥ WITHIN
⑬ minus ⑪	⑫ minus ⑪	⑭ or ⑮ minus ⑪	⑲ minus ⑰ + ⑱	⑯ minus ⑪	㉑ minus ⑲
⑰ =	⑱ =	⑲ =	⑳ =	㉑ =	㉒ =

SUM-OF-SQUARES TABLE : Example.

① COLUMNS	② ROWS	③ CELLS	④ INTERACTION	⑤ TOTAL	⑥ WITHIN
520 − 500	500 − 500	600 − 500	100 − 20	636 − 500	136 − 100
⑰= 20	⑱= 0	⑲= 100	⑳= 80	㉑= 136	㉒= 36

Table 18   ANOVA-TABLE : Example.

Source	SS	df	MS	F(df)
COLUMNS (c)	⑰ = 20	1	20	
ROWS (r)	⑱ = 0	1	0	
INTERACTION (c) (r)	⑳ = 80	1	80	
WITHIN	㉒ = 36	16	2.25	35.55(1, 16)
TOTAL	136	19		

re = Table 15

X	X²	X	X²

M ___ ___   M ___ ___

X	X²	X	X²

M ___ ___   M ___ ___

re = Table 16

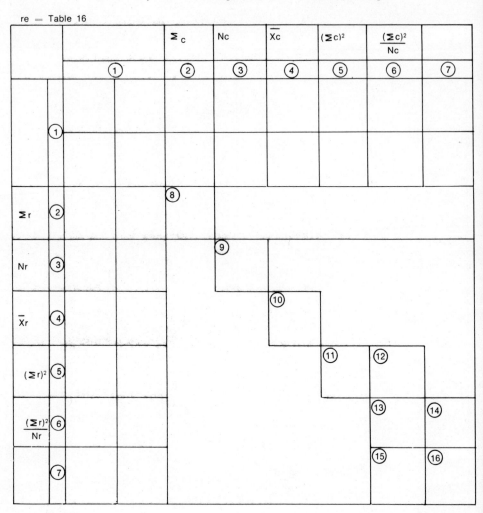

Table 17   SUM-OF-SQUARES TABLE

① COLUMNS	② ROWS	③ CELLS	④ INTERACTION	⑤ TOTAL	⑥ WITHIN
⑬ minus ⑪	⑫ minus ⑪	⑭ or ⑮ minus ⑪	⑲ minus ⑰ + ⑱	⑯ minus ⑪	㉑ minus ⑲
⑰=	⑱=	⑲=	⑳=	㉑=	㉒=

① COLUMNS	② ROWS	③ CELLS	④ INTERACTION	⑤ TOTAL	⑥ WITHIN
⑰ =	⑱ =	⑲ =	⑳ =	㉑ =	㉒ =

Table 18　　　　　　　　ANOVA-TABLE: Example.

Source	SS	df	MS	F(df)
COLUMNS (c)	⑰ =			
ROWS (r)	⑱ =			
INTERACTION (c) (r)	⑳ =			
WITHIN	㉒ =			
TOTAL				

REFERENCES

Alexander, H. and Brozek, J.: Components of variation and the consistency of repeated measurements. *RES Q Am Assoc Health Phys Educ, 18*:152, 1947.

Baumgartner, T. A.: Estimating reliability when all test trials are administered on the same day. *Res Q Am Assoc Health Phys Educ, 40*:222, 1969.

Baumgartner, T. A.: The applicability of the Spearman-Brown prophecy formula when applied to physical performance tests. *Res Q Am Assoc Health Phys Educ, 39*:847, 1968.

Baumgartner, T. A. and Sullivan, W. J.: A comparison of correlational methods. *Res Q Am Assoc Health Phys Educ, 42*:3, 1970.

Berger, R. A.; and Sweney, A. B.: Variance and correlation coefficients. *Res Q Am Assoc Health Phys Educ, 36*:368, 1965.

Brewer, J. K. and Jones, B. J.: An analysis of the power of statistical tests reported in the Research Quarterly. *Res Q Am Assoc Health Phys Educ, 43*:23, 1972.

Campbell, D. T. and Stanley, J. C.: *Experimental and Quasi-experimental Designs for Research.* Chicago, Rand-McNally, 1963.

Elashoff, J. D.: Analysis of covariance: a delicate instrument. *Am Educ Res J, 6*:383, 1969.

Feldt, L. A. and McKee, M. E.: Estimation of the reliability of skills tests. *Res Q Am Assoc Health Phys Educ, 29*:279, 1958.

Haggard, E. A.: *Intraclass Correlation and the Analysis of Variance.* New York, Dryden Press, 1958.

Heise, D. R.: Separating reliability and stability in test-retest correlation. *Am Sociol Rev, 34*:93, 1969.

Hollander, M. and Wolfe, D. A.: *Nonparametric Statistical Methods.* New York, Wiley, 1973.

Johnson, H. G.: An empirical study of the influence of errors of measurement upon correlation. *Am J Psychol, 57*:52, 1944.

Kehneman, D. and Tversky, A.: Belief in the law of small numbers. *Psychol Bull, 74*:105, 1971.

Kroll, W.: A note on the coefficient of intraclass correlation as an estimate of reliability. *Res Q Am Assoc Health Phys Educ, 33*:313, 1962.

Liba, M.: A trend test as a preliminary to reliability estimation. *Res Q Am Assoc Health Phys Educ, 33*:245, 1962.

Lord, F. M. and Novick, M. R.: *Statistical Theories of Mental Test Scores,* Reading, Massachusetts, Addison-Wesley, 1968.

Miller, R. G. Jr.: *Simultaneous Statistical Inference,* New York, McGraw-Hill, 1966.

Morrison, D. F.: *Multivariate Statistical Methods,* New York, McGraw-Hill, 1967

Slater-Hammel, A. T.: Statistical model and experimental procedures. *Res Q Am Assoc Health Phys Educ, 39*:2, 1968.

Stanley, J. C.: General and special formulas for reliability of differences. *J Educ Measurement, 4*:249, 1967.

Terrace, H. and Parker, S.: *Psychological Statistics,* Unit 14, California, Individual Learning Systems, 1971, p. 20.

Traub, R. E.: A note on the reliability of residual change scores. *J Educ Measurement, 4*:253, 1967.

Underwood, B. J.: *Psychological Research,* New York, Appleton-Century-Crofts, 1957, p. 96.

Winer, B. J.: *Statistical Principles in Experimental Design,* 2d ed., New York, McGraw-Hill, 1971.

Chapter 2

LEARNING CURVES
AND MEASUREMENT

ILLUSTRATIONS DEALING WITH learning scores either for an individual or a group of subjects can serve many functions. A graphical representation of the stages of learning of a specific task may shed some light on the functioning of processes involved in learning. This is the main interest of investigators in learning research. Furthermore, from a practical point of view, it can indicate to a teacher of physical activity the degree to which an individual or a group has improved due to planned practice after a specified period of teaching. It can also reveal how long (e.g. trials, days) it takes to read a criterion of skill. Learning, over learning, retention, relearning, transfer effects, and other phenomena can all be represented with what is currently called a learning curve.

The intent of this chapter is to present some topics and current issues related to learning curves. It is hoped that both the beginning student and the advanced scholar will acquire some meaningful information in the following material.

LEARNING AND PERFORMANCE

Distinctions between learning and performance are made by many authors (Singer, 1972; Gagné, 1970; Dunham, Jr., 1971). It has been generally accepted that the observed performance of an individual is the best available indice of learning. No direct means are presently available to quantify amount of learning. Choice of the most valid dependent measure, research design, and statistical analyses contribute to our knowledge about learning. In studying learning, it is important to keep in mind that it is possible to learn without any change in performance as it is possible to observe change in performance with no learning taking place. Performance can be influenced by many factors other than learning effects, and so may represent in some instances the interplay of many variables, such as change in internal states of the learner not directly related to learning processes or temporary environmental influences.

The quantification of a motor skill or a sport skill is a necessary condition to determine the level of execution of a performance attained by an individual at a given stage of practice.

During practice, internal processes and external influences interact to produce changes in level of performance of a skill. The variations in performance of an athlete from trial to trial, or from day to day, or week to week, have been perceived by most of us. A problem is then raised with respect to the explanation of variations in performance and with respect to the increased performance level with meaningful practice.

At this point, it seems that at least two basic kinds of information can be obtained from quantitative and/or qualitative data of an individual's performance: the level of performance and the amount of learning. Basically, this difference must always be made in the interpretation of data from an individual's performance. Sometimes we may ask if a change in the level of attainment in a task is a manifestation of variations in performance or of learning or both of them. Some ways to answer this question will be presented later in this chapter.

The representation of learning and of variations in performance or learning can be illustrated graphically in a figure. It is usually called either a performance curve or a learning curve. This terminology is often used interchangeably. From the preceding discussion, it seems that the appellation *performance curve* should be arbitrarily used when improvement in performance is not significantly evident from the data. With the same logical thinking, a learning curve would usually denote a significant improvement in performance due to practice.

GRAPHICAL REPRESENTATION

The graphical representation of performance or of learning can be made in various ways. On the abscisse line (horizontal line) you can have marks that correspond to each trial or each set of five trials, or to each second or each ten seconds. The ordinate line marks (vertical line) can represent various units of measurement presented along an appropriate scale. For example, number of attempts, time-on or time-off target, number of degrees, percentage, and some standardized scores may correspond to the ordinate line. The graphical representativeness of a phenomenon depends on its nature and the importance of the interval between units for the study. The investigator has the responsibility to choose the relative dimensions of a graphic in order that it illustrates the results of the study in accord with reality. Care must be taken not to emphasize too much of a slight change in performance that is not significantly meaningful, for interpretation purposes.

For a general criterion with respect to proportions of a table, it is usually suggested that the ordinate be about two-thirds the length of the abscisse.

The procedures used for the construction of a frequency distribution can be adapted to the drawing of a performance or learning curve. However, the shape of the curve will probably differ. Also, instead of people, such measures as trials will be represented in the learning curve. The confidence interval of each point of interest on the learning curve can also be represented on the graph.

What is currently called a learning curve can represent various phenomena related to learning and relative degrees of learning. Practice can be given on a task for a given amount of time or trials, or until a criterion (learning) or 50 percent over a criterion (overlearning) is attained. It can also be given in a matter of minutes, hours, days, or weeks. Learning can be inferred within a session, or after a practice session, the next day or next week. This last solution is usually preferred as more indicative of true levels of learning (Carron, 1971) at least when such temporary depressants as fatigue or massed practice are being examined. Furthermore, one may notice a period of no improvement during practice, which has been called a plateau. Sometimes, when practice on a task is given for two successive days, the initial level of performance on the second day may be higher than the final level of performance on the first day without any practice period between these sessions. This phenomenon is usually called reminiscence, and it may also be evident within a practice session when a relatively long rest interval is given between blocks of trials. The reverse can also be observed, and then it is usually called warm-up decrement (Schmidt, 1972).

Many other phenomena can be inferred or studied from a learning curve. Someone may be interested in the rate of learning, in abilities and learning, in prediction of later learning level, among other things. Related to learning is the phenomenon of retention. It is important to know to what extent learning of a task is retained over a period of seconds, minutes, weeks, months, or years. Without any retention, we cannot talk of learning. A concern may also exist with respect to relearning after an interval of time without practice.

Suppose one administers fifteen trials to a group of subjects on a new motor task, such as a mirror tracing task, and plots the scores of trials one-two, five-six, nine-ten, and fourteen-fifteen in a graph. (See graph A.)

In this case, a linear curve represents improvement in performance as practice proceeds. It illustrates a linear relationship between practice effects and performance. (See graph B.)

However, the form of the performance curve may also be positively accelerated as well as negatively accelerated (quadratic trend). (See graph C.)

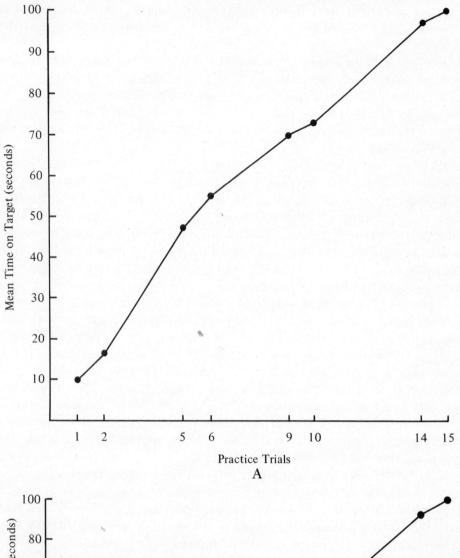

Practice Trials

A

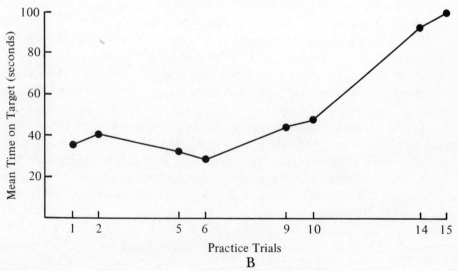

Practice Trials

B

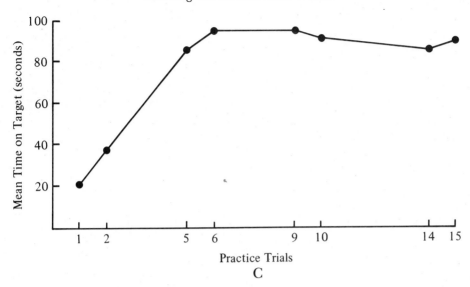

C

Another typical learning curve is an S-shaped curve (cubic trend) such as illustrated below, (See graphs D and E):

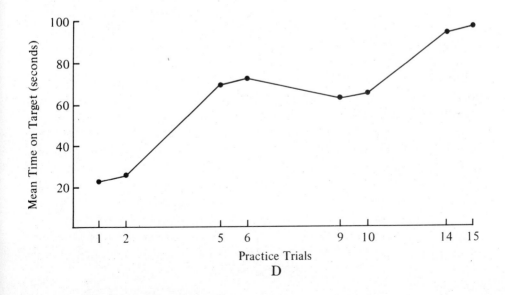

D

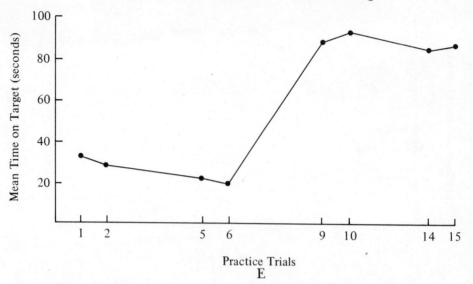

Practice Trials
E

The typical learning curves just presented illustrate different kinds of relationships between practice effects and performance on a new task. In practice the performance curve is likely to approximate one of the pre-ceding typical learning curves instead of to replicate them exactly. Then, if an investigator is interested in knowing the nature of the relationship between practice effects or other treatment effects and performance, tests for trends can be conducted.

Another kind of information that can be included in a graph is the area around the obtained group mean scores where new group mean scores could fall if the experiment was replicated. This information can be given through confidence intervals on each obtained group mean scores plotted in the graph. Suppose you build a confidence interval: c[lower bound<trial n<upper bound] = .995 for each of eight trials. For example, on trial one, if you obtain: c[20<trial 1 = 25<30] = .995, and on trial five, if you obtain: c[20<trial 5 = 30<40] = .995 you may plot the results as in graph F.

From this graph, you can conclude that the performance curve is positively accelerated (quadratic trend), and that learning is not signifi-cant from trial one to trial ten because the intervals on each of these trials show that the lower limit of the confidence interval of trial ten includes, in great part, the area of the confidence intervals on the trials preceding it. On the other hand, if trials fourteen and fifteen are compared to preceding trials, it can be noticed that the lower bound of the interval of trials fourteen and fifteen does not include values of the upper bound of the confidence intervals of the preceding trials. It can then be said that a significant amount of learning has occurred from trials nine and ten to trials fourteen and fifteen. Similar conclusions would have been obtained

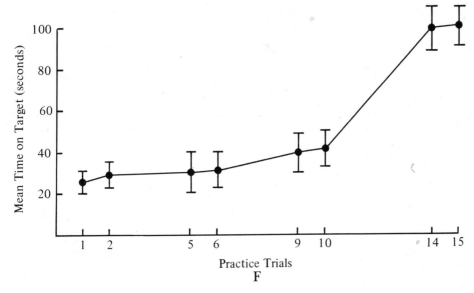

Practice Trials

F

if significance tests comparing trials nine and ten, and trials fourteen and fifteen had been conducted.

Some investigators may also be interested in illustrating the change in total variability as practice goes on. A similar graph to the preceding one can serve this purpose. Instead of building confidence intervals on each trial, the investigator computes the standard deviation of each group mean score appearing in the graph, and plots the upper limit (mean + standard deviation) and the lower limit (mean − standard deviation) around each mean on the graph. This kind of graph represents scores where 68 per cent of the subjects' scores in the group fall around the group mean. Many other techniques exist for illustrating change in performance as practice proceeds, but the techniques just mentioned seem the more usual.

Trial data obtained from an individual may be plotted as a learning curve, or a group mean curve may be plotted. Questions have been raised about similarities and dissimilarities between individual learning curves and group mean curves. Can we generalize from a group mean to a given individual curve? Or only to most individual curves?

INDIVIDUAL CURVES VS. GROUP CURVES

The appropriate interpretation and understanding of group curves is the concern of learning researchers. Questions about the validity of inferences from curves of functional relationships based on averaged data have been raised by Sidman (1952). This writer has shown that ". . . given a mean curve, the form of the individual curves is not uniquely specified." Sidman also suggested that ". . . the mean curve does not provide the information necessary to make statements concerning the function for the individual." Researchers in learning are used to computing mean curves and depend upon averages for groups of individuals to determine functional relationships since they have limited control over behavioral variability. The group curve will remain one of our most useful devices both for summarizing information and for theoretical analysis provided adequate interpretations are made.

The principal point to be made is that "as any mean score for a group of organisms could have arisen from sampling any of an infinite variety of populations of scores, so also could any given mean curve have arisen from any of an infinite variety of populations of individual curves" (Estes, 1956). Therefore, states Estes, inference from mean curve to individual curve is hazardous, and it is risky to determine the effect of an experimental treatment upon rate of learning, for example. Caution in handling averaged data must be taken in the testing of hypotheses about individual functions.

As a first step, Estes suggests that we recognize that the effects of averaging are not unpredictable and are not necessarily artifacts. Given any specified assumption about the form of individual functions, we can proceed to deduce the characteristics to be expected of an averaged curve and then to test these predictions against obtained data. The task would be to test the one hypothesis under consideration.

In testing theories against averaged data, (a) the form of the learning curve or (b) the slope parameter of the learning curve may be of interest. In studies involving the form of the learning curve, the question should be: Is the form of the mean empirical curve in accord with the assumption that the individual functions are of a given form, instead of assuming that the form of a mean curve reflects the form of individual curves? The problem is to determine for any given function what testable prediction can be made concerning the mean curve for a group.

In studies involving the slope parameter, the assumption is usually made that if the function obtained for an individual is $y = f$ (d, a, b, . . .), then the function describing the mean curve for a group of organisms should be a curve of the same form with parameters equal to the means of the corresponding individual parameters. Since this assumption may not be true, it requires recognizing the instances in which the assumption holds and not holds in order to determine what information about parameter values is obtainable from the mean curve. Estes considered three types of mathematical functions to deal with the previous problems. Since the detailed presentation of classification of functions as presented by Estes would be out of context here, the reader is invited to consult the Estes' paper for further information.

RATE OF LEARNING

Subjects do not learn a task at the same rate. Some individuals reach the terminal level very rapidly, while others may take much time. Some investigators (e.g. Woodrow, 1938) have been interested in the relationships between ability level and rate of learning. In general, they found no significant relationships between these learning parameters.

Woodrow administered thirty-nine days of practice in each of seven tasks to fifty-six subjects. His study suggested the nonexistence of a general improvement factor. A general ability to learn seems not substantiated by research findings.

Jones (1972) suggests that we distinguish between the rate process and terminal process. Improvement would be the difference between the first and the last trials and would not involve exclusively the rate process, but also plateaus (Woodrow, 1946). The pure rate process would be "the difference between initial score and initial score as estimated from final score" (Jones, 1972). "Terminal trials have to stabilize so as to be free of the rate process," states Jones.

PLATEAUS

Do plateaus appear for some or all types of motor tasks during practice? This is a controversial issue. In some motor tasks, plateaus might be apparent while in others no such evidence might be shown.

A general definition of plateaus could be "the periods of non-progress" (Kao, 1937), e.g. a situation where practices do not result in significant gain. Plateaus do not necessarily exist, and as a result, few universal criteria serve to identify them.

Batson (1916) in a toss and catch two balls task, in a rolling a ball to a mark task, in a rolling a ball on an inclined board task, and in a timing task, did not find any plateaus manifested. In a task which included a toss and catch of two rubber balls Peterson (1917) reported similar results. However, Trow and Sears (1927) found evidence in favor of the existence of plateaus when conflicting methods were used in a card sorting task.

Kao (1937) suggested the distinction between a plateau in a group mean curve and in an individual mean curve. Even if he did not observe a plateau from group means, he mentioned that individual differences may be hidden. For some learners, improvement may last longer than for others. Some may show no plateau; others may show long or short periods of plateau.

In 1919, Chapman and Hills observed twenty individual curves on typewriting over periods of practice of 180 hours. Most subjects did show short plateaus rather than long plateaus. In one experiment involving a ringball game Smith (1930) found evidence of plateaus for each of the nine subjects under study. Similar evidence was found in rolling a ball with a knitting needle on an inclined plane task in a second study (Smith, 1930). From an experiment dealing with the transcription of words into shorthand, he added that the periods of arrested progress were not characteristic of any particular stage in the aquisition of skill but seemed rather to be scattered promiscuously among the curves. Smith observed also that plateaus seemed temporary in general.

The observation of a plateau within a learning curve does not mean that learning does not occur during a plateau. As was said before, there is no pure measure of learning, and performance is presently the best index of an inference of learning. The choice of a valid criterion score as an inference of level of performance is one of the most basic problems in the study of learning. A lack of validity of a criterion score related to learning may result in a plateau. As a hypothesis, suppose accuracy and speed of a movement are measured. These dependent measures do not describe all aspects of the quality of movement execution. It may be that when a plateau occurs, as derived from quantitative measures, individuals are placing emphasis in that aspect of the execution which is not being measured. In this case, a plateau is observed, but in fact, learning occurs with respect to elements which are not considered in the dependent measure. Mechanical analysis might be of some help to quantify the quality of movement.

Factors that may contribute to the controversial issues on plateaus may arise from the type of curve chosen to illustrate learning (Peterson, 1917), the nature of the criterion score (Peterson, 1917), the nature of the learning task (Kao, 1937), and also upon the nature of the learner (Kao, 1937).

Although plateaus in learning seem not to be a well established fact in research, current arguments about the possible causes of plateaus are:
1. The division or shift of attention of a learner to separate elements of a task (Batson, 1916; Smith, 1930; Kao, 1937).
2. Changes in the physical or psychological state of the learner (Smith, 1930; Kao, 1937).
3. Introduction of a new factor to a task (Smith, 1930).
4. The level of ability necessary to meet the learning requirements at one stage of learning may be insufficient and hinder learning (Smith, 1930).
5. The disruptive influence of environmental factors (Smith, 1930).
6. The resulting effects of automatization and learning (Kao, 1937) and choice of strategies (Kao, 1937).

7. The difficulty of a task and its ceiling level (Smith, 1930).

Until this point, discussion has centered around plateaus in terms of group means or individual mean curves. However, it may be of interest to look at plateaus with respect to individual differences, i.e. plateaus of the differential process (Jones, 1972).

DIFFERENTIAL STABILIZATION

The term *differential stabilization* is used by Jones (1972) to denote trial variances remaining the same during two-three trials of a given practice period. The concept is similar to a plateau in the study of mean changes. The criterion suggested by Jones to infer differential stabilization, when scores are analyzed from a superdiagonal matrix, is the observation of small (r<.01 or .02) or no differences among correlations within a set of trials, and of stable correlations along the rows with the last trials within equally narrow limits. (A large sample size is probably assumed here.) As long as correlations keep changing along the rows as more and more trials are recorded, stabilization will not be reached.

In order to illustrate differential stabilization one may calculate the standard deviation of scores at each trial of a practice period and plot the results as a learning curve. Another way would be to use the variances instead of the standard deviations as the ordinate values. The standard deviation squared gives the variance. Other ways, such as the building of confidence intervals on intra-class correlation coefficients are suggested by Haggard (1958). Furthermore, for synthesis purposes, a mean curve and a variance curve can both be plotted in a same graph. Plateaus may be observed both for means and for variances. Jones (1972) mentioned that such a correspondence between trial mean and trial variance is generally found.

Can we infer the existence of a plateau in a one-group design? Can a deceleration observed in a learning curve be considered as a plateau? In a one-group study of learning curves, it seems rather difficult to find a plateau, since extraneous variables can affect the learning curve and are not under control with such a research design. The observation of a plateau would necessitate the absence of effects from other internal and external processes than practice effects.

SPECIFICITY AND GENERALITY OF LEARNING CURVES

For a long time an S shape curve served to illustrate the course of learning, in motor learning as well as in verbal learning. However, a number of studies did not confirm the existence of such a typical curve of learning. From the results obtained in several sets of experiments, Batson (1916) concluded that there was no typical curve for all types of learning. In a typewriting task, Chapman and Hills did not find a typical curve of improvement among twenty individual curves (Chapman and Hills, 1919).

However, Kao (1937) suggested the existence of a typical curve of motor skill. It would consist of rapid improvement at the beginning of practice. Dunham (1971) investigated the relationship between performance on a mirror tracing task and a pursuit rotor task. In both tasks, a significant improvement was observed ($P<.01$); however, the relationship between performance change for the two tasks was represented by a correlation of .04. Correlations between the two tasks were computed for each of the twenty-four days of practice, and showed only four of the twenty-four correlations significantly different from zero. The amount of generality and specificity contained in the correlations for each day's practice was obtained by employing the formula: $r^2 + k^2$. r^2 denotes generality, while k^2 denotes specificity and error. As a result, in five of the twenty-four days, an amount of generality between 32.8 and 49.7 per cent was observed. For other days, generality was between 17.1 per cent and 0.2 per cent, thus suggesting a probable high degree of specificity, as defined in this study (Dunham, 1971). Intercorrelations were low between learning tasks, such as the wall volley, ball bounce, and target toss (Brace, 1941). Brace suggested that there are probably different types of motor learning, such as sport-type skills, stunt-type skills, or rhythm-type skills. Studies on the identification of tasks that show similar and dissimilar courses of learning for a specified group of persons are needed to add knowledge on the specificity and the generality of learning curves in motor learning. More practical would be to know the course of learning for most students for each motor skill taught in school in order to understand and to plan the process of learning. If teaching a specific skill until a criterion is reached is one aim of a program, the knowledge of the number of hours or of trials it takes to reach the criterion, including periods of slow and rapid increase in performance level, would help to systematically plan teaching. Motivational techniques and special practice techniques could be used during slow improvement stages.

VALIDITY OF A LEARNING TASK

Sports and games that are commonly taught may not be convenient as learning tasks. Difficulty of obtaining adequate measures during practice, the level of knowledge and execution of a learner before being provided with practice on a task, and the level of task difficulty are some factors to be considered in the choice of a learning task. A medium level of task difficulty, high reliability with few trials, novelty, and the ability of subjects to master a task in a reasonable time period might be an appropriate combination when considering the selection of a learning task.

For example, Brace (1941) found fair reliability coefficients for a wall test, a ball bounce test and a target toss task when computed on the basis of the first six trials, and a high rate when computed on the basis of thirty trials. The choice of a task involving the consideration of blocks of thirty trials each may not be of practical use in some instances, e.g. laboratory studies, for reasons of economy of time and energy.

Some of the criteria that might be applied to the choice of a learning task are:

1. Normality of distribution of scores at each trial.
2. Validity of the learning task. Can it be used to reflect the intended learning processes one wants to study? What is its face validity, its content validity, its concurrent validity, and even its predictive validity? These questions can be asked according to the interest of the investigators.
3. Equivalence of stability or predictability from block to block of trials, or from pretest to posttest (Kroll, 1967) of the criterion scores (blocks or trials mean).
4. Sufficient validity of the criterion scores related to what a person wishes to measure.
5. Consideration of task difficulty. A medium level of difficulty is suggested to avoid ceiling effects.
6. Practical considerations such as the amount of time or number of trials it takes performance to stabilize, availability and maintenance of equipment, cost, precision, and so forth.

PREDICTION OF FINAL LEVEL OF LEARNING

It is important to be able to predict the final attainment of an individual on a task after practice from short administered pretests or other criteria (Cronbach, 1970). When a selection of members of a team must be made, or a selection of manual workers for high precision and speed tasks, a prediction equation might be informative to indicate the probability that a person will fit a specific job or a specific sport-skill after a given amount of practice. By prediction equation, it is meant an equation where covariates are assumed to be fixed, and dependent variables randomly distributed. Unfortunately, few prediction studies show us definitive evidence in this matter. One approach could be to use a prediction equation for a task in the population of interest, and to build a confidence interval on the basis of the risk one wants to take in predicting performance of a new individual taking selection tests. For instance, Welch (1963) found that a good multiple correlational prediction of individual attainment in a free-standing ladder task after n days of practice required using initial skill estimates combined with learning scores that cover at least the first $n/2$ days of practice.

INDIVIDUAL DIFFERENCES AND LEARNING CURVES

Until now, topics related to individual differences were presented, but not elaborated upon. That some individuals learn faster than others for a particular task, or reach higher levels of performance, or adopt different strategies for learning a task are examples of differences among individuals within a group. These differences can be distinguished from an individual's trial to trial variations in performance. Here you will notice that we question how practice affects variability (total variance) (Carron and Leavitt, 1969). The total variance is partitioned between the true score variance (individual differences) and intravariability (variability within an individual), as suggested by Haggard (1958). Carron and Leavitt mentioned, relative to the problem of intra and intervariance, that it is only to the extent that the variation within individuals is small as compared to the variation between individuals, that individual differences assume importance. If there is a low stability of performance from trial to trial, it is difficult to ascertain individual differences. The relative importance of individual differences during the course of learning merits consideration. A decrease in true score variance means that with practice, individuals become more nearly alike in a specific skill, while a decrease in intravariance means that subjects are becoming more stable in their own individual performances. Haggard (1958) has suggested techniques on how to partition the total variance.

Jones (1972) proposed the following suggestions to analyze or score individual differences:

1. Determine the critical dimensions of individual differences.
2. Find how the differential process that accompanies learning breaks down.
3. Decide how acquisition should be analyzed.
4. Construct or use valid tests that measure the intended processes.

It should be noted that processes are the central point and that reference tests are not first chosen to later find what they represent.

Fruchter and Fleishman (1967) proposed multiple ways to analyze individual differences, and have critiqued the use of the intercorrelation matrix for such purposes, interpreting previous studies and inferring that differential composition of a task varies from trial to trial, and different abilities may be involved at different stages of practice. These authors favor the use of factor analysis models. One approach proposed would be to administer a reference battery of aptitude tests to a sample, followed by the administration of practice on a task, and then to determine the factors that should be extracted from the battery and the trials together. An alternative procedure would be to factor the variance-covariance matrix or the correlation matrix and then to examine the loadings of reference ability and skill tests of established factor content on the factor space spanned by the learning trials. A three-mode factor analysis is another method that could be used where more than one kind of measure per trial is taken. Another approach suggested by Fruchter and Fleishman is to take simultaneously many dependent measures at each trial, during p-trials, and to find the factor loadings which represent the data from which the functions or common elements which are important for proficiency at the different periods or stages of learning are inferred.

As it is evident, various approaches have been used to analyze individual differences. Other statistical models could also be used, such as cluster analysis and principal components analysis. Each might yield important information.

What happens to individual differences with practice on a specific motor task?

Carron and Leavitt (1969) tested thirty boys, aged between ten and twelve, on a stabilometer and administered six days of practice to subjects (twelve trials: thirty-second work/thirty-second rest schedule). They found that stability of performance and individual differences decreased with practice. They obtained results similar to those in the Henry and Welch study with freshman college women as subjects. The Meyers' study showed no appreciable change in stability of performance or intervariability on the Bachman ladder climb task with high school girls as subjects (Meyers, 1965). With the pursuit rotor, Lersten (1966) noted an increase in individual difference and in stability of performance with sixty practice trials. Additional practice did not affect either inter or intravariance.

From this short review of literature, it is apparent that more studies are needed to clarify the process of individual differences and learning.

CRITERION MEASURES OF LEARNING

In learning research, measures are often recorded as a matter of convenience rather than based on theoretical grounds. This is done despite the distinction between the basic processes of learning and performance.

An example of an arbitrary choice of response measures in learning is the use of a dichotomous score as an indicant of an underlying process which is assumed or known to be normally and continuously distributed (Bahrick, Fitts, and Briggs, 1957). Success or failure, or the number of errors made on a pursuit rotor, are examples of dichotomous scores. The arbitrary choice of a cutoff point in the dichotomizing of continuous response distributions can impose contraints upon the shape of resulting learning curves and can lead to misleading interpretations. The illustration of this point by Bahrick, Fitts, and Briggs was made with the use of time-on-target scores as indicants of the level of skill attained in tracking tasks. Time-on-balance on a stabilometer, or time-on-a-pathway as in a mirror or maze-tracing task, are also submitted to these restraints.

The same performance, when scored with different target-tolerance standards, may result in different learning curve shapes. This implies that if we study learning on several versions of a task which differ in difficulty, it may be of interest to take into account the change in sensitivity of our measure between the versions, or at different stages of the learning process within a version (Bahrick, Fitts, and Briggs, 1957).

Otherwise we may conclude in favor of treatment effects at one stage of training and not at other stages, or on a simple-task version and not on a difficult-task version, when, in fact, we are dealing with artifacts produced by the non-linearity of our measures (Bahrick, Fitts, and Briggs, 1957).

Studies suggest that criterion measures at one point where subjects are 50 per cent on target are sensitive to variations as well as to treatment effects. A task with 10 per cent or 90 per cent on-target scores would have poor sensitivity, and it would be difficult to demonstrate the effect of any independent variable upon performance (Bahrick, Fitts, and Briggs, 1957). Also, if the initial performance level is 12 per cent on target, while at another stage of practice it is about 50 per cent, this last performance is in a more sensitive range of the performance measure, and may result in artifacts. "Artifacts in the interpretation of results occur primarily when attempts are made to test for interaction effects or to interpret functional relations over an extended range of task difficulty or over an extended period of learning" (Bahrick, Fitts, and Briggs, 1957).

In order to counteract these problems, one possible approach would be the simultaneous recording of scores for several criterion targets or the recording of the complete amplitude distribution of error. It must be added that the criterion targets should be about medium difficulty in order to avoid biases due to ceiling effects.

Bahrick, Fitts, and Briggs mentioned that low correlations among various indicants of presumably the same learning process in a tracking task have been found by Fitts, Bennett, and Bahrick (1956). For certain gross comparisons, intended only to determine the presence or absence of a significant effect, different types of scores may be adequate. More research studies are needed on the various problems related to task difficulty such as those mentioned by Fitts, Bennett, and Bahrick.

The specificity of task difficulty levels could be investigated by selecting at random from a population of cutoff points a sample of criterion performance points. Performance scores on each cutoff point could then be compared in using the one sample multivariate T^2 and appropriate contrasts. Furthermore, the linearity of subjects' performance on cutoff points equidistant on the basis of a physical scale could be investigated by using the one sample multivariate T^2 for performing tests for a linear trend, a quadratic trend, or a cubic trend. Similar approaches were used by Vachon et al. (1973) to investigate the linearity and specificity of task difficulty of performance on a stabilometer task. Conclusions were in favor of a linear relationship between task difficulty and performance, and in favor of specificity of low levels of task difficulty.

Sometimes arbitrary combinations of many different indices of learning are used in the study of learning. As an example, accuracy may be divided by speed and this ratio becomes a criterion score of level of performance. Ehrlich (1943) critiqued such a procedure on a validity basis related to measure learning of a task and suggested the use of independent treatments instead of compound score, unless data are available on the validity of such a compound score. In general, we may say that it is more difficult to interpret a compound score than a component score. The more elements a score represents, the harder its interpretation. Even a component score, as the number of errors on a stabilometer, seems difficult to interpret. What do number of errors measure? Probably not the same thing as time-on-balance since they show low intercorrelations between them.

MEASUREMENT OF LEARNING: FORMULAE

Various formulae have been used by scholars to determine the amount of learning demonstrated in their experiments. Improvement is sometimes measured as the difference between the first and the last trials (Woodrow, 1946; Cronbach and Furby, 1970). This can lead to fallacious conclusions since such scores are systematically related to any random error of measurement (Cronbach and Furby, 1970). McCraw (1955) compared eight methods of scoring tests in a rope skip test and a mirror target toss test. In general, low or negative intercorrelations among most of these methods of scoring were obtained. However, lack of presentation of data on the stability of performance on the initial score or on the final score, and the nonconsideration of a control group in these formulae, suggested severe limitations of these methods of scoring and their intercorrelations. The consideration of a control group is necessary in order to isolate practice effects from undesired effects, caused by the passage of time, for instance. Brace (1941) presented as criterion measures of learning, the number of trials required to perform the task correctly, the total score on all trials, the per cent of possible gain method, the difference in per cent of gain method, and the gain divided by the initial score method. Correlation coefficients of .55, .80, and of .73 between the following methods of scoring learning were reported: the total score method, the per cent of possible gain, and difference between initial and final per cent of gain.

CRITERION SCORES IN A LEARNING CURVE

Let's assume a valid method of measuring learning is used. The next step is to choose data from which a statistical analysis will be computed. Are we going to use each trial as dependent measures, or blocks of two trials, or blocks of five trials? How do we define *true score* (Lord and Novic, 1968)?

Ehrlich (1943) suggested that we analyze learning curves in experiments involving speed and accuracy from three points of view: initial status, rate of learning, and maximum end points. Gulliksen (1942) proposed learning ability and initial competence as parameters of learning curve. McCraw (1955) proposed that the measurement of improvement should be made in terms of where the individual is at the beginning of the practice period and of the relative difficulty for improvement. That warm-up trials must be discarded and that consideration should be given to the maximum performance no matter where it occurs after the initial score were among his propositions. Harris (1963) mentioned that one estimate of the true average change of a group is the difference between the average initial score and the average final score. From another point of view Kroll (1967) was in favor of the use of the average of trials as the criterion score mainly if no significant trend exists among trials, and if the trials mean is a better predictor of true performance than individual trials. The use of an analysis of variance design for repeated measures with tests for trends were suggested by Kroll. He stated that if there is a trend effect, one can assess its magnitude and consider it in some ways when using these trials as criterion score. In general, it seems that the use of the average of trials as the criterion score should be considered only if it is justified to do so. Otherwise, each trial should be considered as a criterion score, either as covariate(s) or dependent measure(s). One question is: Is it preferable to use the mean of n trials as covariate or to use the n trials as covariates? The same question applies to dependent variables. It seems evident that multivariate techniques are particularly appropriate to cope with such problems. At this point, questions about the stability, the reliability, or the predictability of the criterion measure(s) can be raised. The use of the mean of n trials as criterion score is often justified on the basis of stability or predictability. However, the use of n trials independently as simultaneous dependent criterion scores is probably more valid provided the n trials selected are representative of the population of trials. Multiple correlation and the one-sample multivariate prediction analysis can serve to determine the choice of criterion scores. The criterion with higher predictability of trials scores should be retained.

Fruchter and Fleishman (1967) proposed a procedure called "the trials by measure design." Several independent measures of learning for each trial over the same learning period would be factor analyzed to determine trials to be included within each block. They applied factor analysis to a learning curve and three factors were extracted and rotated. They found, mainly as factors: initial trials, final trials, and middle trials. Each factor also had low loadings on other factors. This procedure is, however, not likely to find identical results if different models and/or different criteria are used, and if if the covariance matrix or the correlation matrix is factor analyzed. If one wants to factor analyze his data, the canonical factor analysis model is suggested.

STATISTICAL ANALYSES OF LEARNING CURVES

The appropriate statistical analysis of a learning curve is a complex matter. One of the more frequently used statistical models is the univariate analysis of variance with repeated measures on the last dimension. Another approach is the determination of gain in learning from initial score(s) to final score(s) in using a true gain method (McNemar, 1958) or a true residual gain method (Cronbach and Fury, 1970; Dubois, 1957; Traub, 1967; Glass, 1968; Davis, 1971). The use of univariate t-tests for comparing groups on each trial is also currently used. This is appropriate if the trial stability is high enough. In general, the nature of the hypotheses you wish to test determines the statistical models that should be used in the analysis of your data.

With the purpose of simplifying the following presentation of suggestions on how to analyze learning curves, assume we have two groups of fifty subjects each to which nine trials were administered on a learning task. Suppose also that one group was designated as the control and the other, experimental.

One may be interested to know if there was a treatment by trials interaction. The ANOVA with repeated measures is currently used for this purpose in spite of the difficulties of defining the exact nature of the error term in the equation of this model. It must be underlined that the two sample-one factor multivariate T^2 can serve also to test this hypothesis with more validity. If this last approach is used, one may conduct the analysis with the group vectors composed of eight correlated trials, substracting the last four trials from the first four trials.

We may also want to know if a significant amount of learning has occurred from the first to the last trial(s). The one sample multivariate T^2 could be applied to each group, comparing correlated trials one and nine, or trials one, two and eight, nine. It may also be interesting to investigate the linearity of each of the learning curves. Again, you may use the one sample multivariate T^2 and investigate for linear, quadratic, and cubic trends in building the appropriate contrasts. The criterion measures selected may be trials one, five, and nine, or one, two, five, six, eight and nine, or any other combination you wish to use. You can also do it in using univariate tests such as presented in Winer's book (1971). If the interest is toward knowing if groups are significantly different on some selected trials, e.g. trials eight and nine, the two sample multivariate T^2 can be used to make these comparisons. It must be emphasized that multivariate and univariate t-tests are two different statistical models. In general, it seems that multivariate techniques are more appropriate to investigate learning than are univariate techniques.

One may also wish to know if it is possible to predict final trials on a motor task from scores, for instance, on the Cattel 16 Personality Factor Test. In this last example, a multivariate predictor model could be run to see if a significant prediction equation within this model exists at the probability level selected.

The predictors previously mentioned can also be used as covariates if the analysis of covariance, univariate or multivariate, is used. One of the problems associated with the analysis of covariance is the assumption of linearity, which is not likely to be met in many situations. The best fit of the relationship between the covariate(s) and each dependent variable can be found, but if it is significantly different from linearity, then we have no test to verify the parallelism of the slopes. The use of non-standard models of analysis of covariance must then be investigated.

Another interest may be on change in intra or intervariance with practice on a task. The analysis of variance model and the intraclass correlation technique, which are typically used, have been mentioned before. It should be noted that the intraclass correlation is a univariate statistic and is particularly appropriate for repeated measures on the same subjects. By contrast, the Pearson product-moment correlation is a bivariate statistic and its use is mainly appropriate for correlations between two different variates. The use of a confidence interval on the intraclass correlation coefficient can help to draw conclusions on change of individual variability with practice on a task.

Some researchers are also interested in knowing the components of a learning curve. The principal axis factor analysis technique from the correlation matrix was typically used to identify such components (Fruchter and Fleishman, 1967). However, if one decides to use factor analysis for such purposes, the canonical factor analysis model should be considered. The use of principal components analysis should also be considered as a better choice than factor analysis. The approach that seems more convenient to identify stages of learning on a task is probably the one sample multivariate T^2.

It is not possible to summarize in a few pages all the appropriate ways to analyze a learning curve with respect to all possible interests of investigators in motor learning. However, the preceding summary can probably bring the reader's attention to some potential ways to analyze data in a motor learning experiment. Before concluding, let's discuss briefly the problem of simultaneous statistical inferences. Before conducting an experiment, the hypothesis(es) to be tested in one experiment are selected in relation to the main problem(s) under study. The investigator selects the probability of falsely rejecting at least one null hypothesis, assuming they are all true (the alpha level for his experiment may be set at the .05 level), and then be decides on the alpha assigned to each hypothesis tested. Suppose one interaction hypothesis, four tests on the significance of correlation coefficients, and twenty tests (univariate and multivariate) of significance for differences among means are of interest in the experiment. In this case, twenty-five hypotheses constitute the natural family for this investigation. One can then split the alpha of his experiment (.05) into twenty-five equal alpha levels (.002), and attribute an alpha of .002 to each hypothesis tested for significance. One could also select an alpha of .001 for each hypothesis on means, an alpha of .005 for each hypothesis on correlation coefficients, and an alpha of .01 for the interaction hypothesis. The sum of them also gives an alpha of .05 for the experiment (Miller, 1966).

In many published investigations, the alpha for the experiment is unfortunately forgotten, and sometimes it is even greater than unity. It is hoped that more investigators will pay some attention to it in the near future when statistically analyzing their data and interpreting them. The use of the Bonferroni t statistics should also be used more often when doing simultaneous statistical inferences because in many experiments, testing all possible hypotheses is not of interest due to the great generality in application. Also, it competes with most simultaneous techniques with respect to the length of the intervals it gives. In general, an investigator should investigate and select the simultaneous technique that provides a shorter interval with respect to the alpha selected for the experiment (Miller, 1966). Measuring learning in the appropriate manner is not simple. Researchers should be aware of contemporary knowledge in measurement and statistics and take it into account when analyzing data. Otherwise, either inappropriate conclusions are made or incomplete information is drawn from the data. In addition, it is of great importance to measure learning with the most valid and available research tools in order to properly develop theories in motor learning.

REFERENCES

Bahrick, H. P., Briggs, G. E., and Fitts, P. H.: Learning curves—facts and artifacts. *Psychol Bull, 54*:3, 1967.

Bakan, D.: A generalization of Sidman's results on group and individual functions and a criterion. *Psychol Bull, 51*:63, 1954.

Batson, W. H.: Acquisition of skill. *Psychol Monogr, 21*:3, 1916.

Bereiter, C.: Using tests to measure change. *Personnel and Guidance J, 41*:6, 1962.

Bloom, B. S.: *Stability and Change in Human Characteristics.* New York, Wiley, 1964.

Bogartz, R. A.: The criterion method: Some analyses and remarks. *Psychol Bull, 64*:1, 1965.

Brace, D. K.: Studies in the rate of learning gross bodily motor skills. *Res Q Am Assoc Health Phys Educ, 12*:181, 1941.

Brian, C. R. and Goodenough, F. L.: Certain factors underlying the acquisition of motor skills by pre-school children. *J Exp Psychol, 12*:127, 1929.

Bryan, W. L. and Harter, N.: Studies on the telegraphic language: The acquisition of a hierarchy of habits. *Psychol Rev, 6*:345, 1899.

Bunderson, R. V.: *Transfer Functions and Learning Curves: The Use of Ability Constructs in the Study of Human Learning.* Educational Testing Service, Princeton, 1964.

Buxton, C. E.: Reminiscence in the acquisition of skill. *Psychol Rev, 49*:191, 1942.

Buxton, C. E.: The status of research in reminiscence. *Psychol Bull, 40*:313, 1943.

Buxton, C. E. and Henry, C. E.: Retroaction and gains in motor learning. *J Exp Psychol, 19*:616, 1936.

Carron, A. V.: *Laboratory Experiments in Motor Learning.* Englewood Cliffs, Prentice-Hall, 1971.

Carron, A. V. and Leavitt, J. L.: Effects of practice upon individual differences and intra-variability in a motor skill. *Res Q Am Assoc Health Phys Educ, 39*:3, 1969.

Chapman, J. C.: The learning curve in typewriting. *J Appl Psychol, 3*:252, 1919.

Courtis, S. A.: *The Measurement of Growth.* Ann Arbor, Brumfield and Brumfield, 1932, p. 155.

Cronbach, L. J. and Furby, L.: How we should measure "change" or should we? *Psychol Bull, 74*:1, 1970.

Damarin, F., Messick, S. A., and Tucker, L. R.: A base free measure of change. *Psychometrika, 31*:457, 1966.

Davis, F. B.: *Estimation of differences between equivalent scores on forms of the same test administered to the same individual or group.* Philadelphia, University of Pennsylvania. (Mimeographed material, 1972)

Davis, F. B.: The assessment of change. In Bliesmer, E. L. and Kingston, A. J. (Eds.): *Tenth Yearbook of the National Reading Conference for Colleges and Adults.* Milwaukee, Marquette University Reading Center, 1961, p. 86.

Davis, F. B. and Murphy, H. D.: A note on the measurement of progress in remedial reading. *Peabody J Educ, 271*:108, 1949.

Dubois, P. H. and Manning, W. H.: The measurement of learning. *Technical Report,* Number 6, Office of Naval Research, Contract Number 816 (02), 1958.

Dunham, P.: Communications: learning and performance. *Res Q Am Assoc Health Phys Educ, 42*:3, 1971.

Ehrlich, G.: A method of constructing learning curves for a motor skill involving total body speed and accuracy. *J Appl Psychol, 27*:494, 1943.

Estes, W. R.: The problem of inference from curves based on group data. *Psychol Bull, 53*:2, 1956.

Fleishman, E. A. and Hempel, W. E. Jr.: Changes in factor structure of a complex psychomotor test as a function of practice. *Psychometrika, 19*:239, 1954.

Gagné, R. M.: *The Conditions of Learning.* 2d ed., New York, Holt, Rinehart and Winston, 1970.

Gates, G. S.: Individual differences as affected by practice. *Arch Psychol, 8*:1, 1922.

Glass, G. V.: Response to Traub's note on the reliability of residual changes scores. *J Educ Measurement, 5*:265, 1968.

Grant, D. A.: Analysis-of-variance tests in the analysis and comparison of curves. *Psychol Bull, 53*:2, 1956.

Greene, E. B.: An analysis of random and systematic changes with practice. *Psychometrika, 8*:1, 1943.

Greene, E. B.: Practice effects on various types of standard tests. *Am J Psychol, 49*:67, 1937.

Harris, C. W. (Ed.): *Problems in Measuring Change.* Madison, University of Wisconsin Press, 1963.

Harris, C. W. (Ed.): *Problems in Measuring Change,* 2d ed., Madison, University of Wisconsin Press, 1967.

Hayes, K. J.: The backward curve: A method for the study of learning. *Psychol Rev, 60*:269, 1953.

Henry, F. M.: "Best" versus "average" individual scores. *Res Q Am Assoc Health Phys Educ, 38*:317, 1967.

Henry, F. M.: Influence of measurement error and intra-individual variation on the reliability of muscle strength and vertical jump tests. *Res Q Am Assoc Health Phys Educ, 30*:155, 1959.

Henry, F. M.: Reliability measurement error and intra-individual differences. *Res Q Am Assoc Health Phys Educ, 30*:21, 1959.

Henry, F. M. and Welch, M.: Individual differences in various parameters of motor learning. Unpublished manuscript, Berkeley, University of California.

Hilgard, E. R. and Smith, M. B.: Distributed practice in motor learning: A score changes within and between daily sessions. *J Exp Psychol, 30*:136, 1942.

Hills, M. E. and Chapman, J. C.: Positive acceleration in improvement in a complex function. *J Exp Psychol, 1*:494, 1919.

Jones, M. B.: A two-process theory of individual differences in motor learning. *Psychol Rev, 77*:353, 1970.

Jones, M. B.: Differential processes in acquisition. In Bilodeau, E. A. (Ed.): *Principles of Skill Acquisition.* New York, Academic Press, 1969.

Jones, M. B.: Individual differences. In Singer, Robert N. (Ed.): *The Psychomotor Domain: Movement Behavior.* Philadelphia, Lea & Febiger, 1972, p. 119.

Jones, M. B.: Practice as a process of simplification. *Psychol Rev, 69*:4, 1962.

Jones, M. B.: Rate and terminal processes in skill acquisition. *Am J Psychol, 83*:222, 1970.

Kao, Dji-Lik: Plateaus and the curve of learning in motor skill. *Psychol Monogr, 49*:3, 1937.

Keller, F. A.: The phantom plateau. *J Exp Behav, 1*:1, 1958.

Kientzle, M. J.: Properties of learning curves under varied distributions of practice. *J Exp Psychol, 36*:3, 1946.

Kroll, W.: Reliability theory and research decision in selection of a criterion score. *Res Q Am Assoc Health Phys Educ, 38*:3, 1967.

Lersten, K. C.: Inter and intra-individual variations during the progress of motor learning. Unpublished doctoral dissertation, Berkeley, University of California, 1966.

Linn, R. L. and Werts, C. E.: Path analysis, psychological examples. *Psychol Bull, 74*:3, 1970.

Lord, F. M.: A paradox in the interpretation of group comparisons. *Psychol Bull, 68*:304, 1967.

Lord, F. M.: Elementary models for measuring change. In Harris, C. W. (Ed.): *Problems in Measuring Change.* Madison, University of Wisconsin Press, 1963.

Lord, F. M.: Further problems in the measurement of growth. *Educ Psychol Measurement, 18*:437, 1958.

Lord, F. M.: The measurement of growth. *Educ Psychol Measurement, 16*:421, 1956.

Lord, F. M. and Novick, M. R.: *Statistical Theories of Mental Test Scores.* Massachusetts, Addison-Wesley, 1968.

McCraw, L. W.: A comparison of methods of measuring improvement. *Res Q Am Assoc Health Phys Educ, 22*:191, 1951.

McCraw, L. W.: Comparative analysis of methods of scoring tests of motor learning. *Res Q Am Assoc Health Phys Educ, 26*:440, 1955.

McDonald, R. P.: The theoretical foundations of principal factor analysis, canonical factor analysis, and alpha factor analysis. *Br J Math Stat Psychol, 23*:1, 1970.

McNemar, Q.: On growth measurement. *Educ Psychol Measurement, 18*:47, 1958.

Merrill, M.: The relationship of individual growth to average growth. *Hum Biol, 3*:37, 1931.

Morrison, D. F.: *Multivariate Statistical Methods.* New York, McGraw-Hill, 1967.

O'Connor, E. F.: *Extending classical test theory to the measurement of change.* C.S.E. Report 60, Los Angeles, Center for the Study of Evaluation, 1970.

Peterson, J.: Experiments in ball-tossing: the significance of learning curves. *J Exp Psychol, 2*:178, 1917.

Reed, H. B. and Zinszer, H. A.: The occurrence of plateaus in telegraphy. *J Exp Psychol, 33*:130, 1943.

Reynolds, B.: The effects of learning on the predictability of performance. *J Exp Psychol, 44*:189, 1958.

Runnels, L. K. et al.: Near perfect runs as a learning criterion. *J Math Psychol, 5*:362, 1968.

Savin, H. B. and Stevens, J. C.: On the form of learning curves. *J Exp Anal Behav, 5*:15, 1962.

Schmidt, R. A.: Experimental psychology. In Singer, Robert N. (Ed.): *The Psychomotor Domain: Movement Behavior.* Philadelphia, Lea & Febiger, 1972.

Seal, H. L.: *Multivariate Statistical Analysis for Biologists.* New York, Wiley, 1964.

Sears, R. A. and Trow, W. C.: Learning plateau due to conflicting methods of practice. *J Educ Psychol, 18*:43, 1927.

Seashore, R. H.: Work methods: an often neglected factor underlying individual differences. *Psychol Rev, 46*:123, 1939.

Seashore, R. H. and Seashore, S. H.: Individual differences in simple auditory reaction times of hands, feet and jams. *J Exp Psychol, 29*:342, 1941.

Sidman, M.: A note on functional relations obtained from group data. *Psychol Bull, 49*:263, 1952.

Singer, R. N.: *Coaching, Athletics and Psychology.* New York, McGraw-Hill, 1972.

Smith, L. E. and Whitley, J. D.: Larger correlations obtained by using average rather than "best" strength scores. *Res Q Am Assoc Health Phys Educ, 34*:2, 1963.

Smith, M. D.: Periods of arrested progress in the acquisition of skills. *Br J Psychol, 21*:24, 1930.

Smith, P. C. and Taylor, J. G.: An investigation of the stage of learning curves for industrial motor tasks. *J Appl Psychol, 40*:142, 1956.

Snoddy, G. S.: Learning and stability. *J Appl Psychol, 10*:1, 1926.

Stake, R. F.: Learning parameters, aptitudes and achievements. *Psychometric Monogr,* 1961, p. 9.

Viteles, M. S.: The influence of training on motor test performance. *J Exp Psychol, 16*:556, 1933.

Woodrow, H.: Factors in improvement with practice. *J Psychol, 7*:55, 1939.

Woodrow, H.: Interrelations between measures of learning. *J Psychol, 10*:49, 1940.

Woodrow, H. A.: The ability to learn. *Psychol Rev, 53*:147, 1946.

Chapter 3

BILATERAL TRANSFER

INTRODUCTION

A YOUNG BASKETBALL PLAYER is told that he must learn to dribble and shoot with either hand if he is to become a successful player. A soccer player is told similarly that he must be able to shoot well with either foot. Although the most desirable method for developing the use of either hand or either foot for these skills may be specific practice with both hands or feet, it is not always possible to devote sufficient time to both limbs to develop them. The question arises then whether it is possible to improve the skill of one hand or foot by practicing with the other hand or foot. An affirmative response to this question could help the instructor or coach better plan his practice time to incorporate this approach. It could also aid the learner by allowing him to spend his time in practice more profitably.

The ability of an individual to more easily learn a particular skill with one hand or foot after it has been learned with the opposite hand or foot is generally termed bilateral transfer or cross-education. Another way to express the definition of bilateral transfer was given by Walters (1955) as the gain in strength or skill of an unpracticed extremity through training of its contralateral muscle group.

The discovery of this phenomenon is by no means new. The first experimentation with bilateral transfer is usually credited to Scripture in 1894. From that time through the first-third of this century, bilateral transfer was a very popular area of study. Results of those experiments were rather consistent. Cook (1936) stated that with a few minor exceptions, probably due to chance error, all experimenters in the field of bilateral transfer had found some positive transfer.

Various skills have been tested in bilateral transfer experimentation. Such skills as tapping, mirror tracing, rotary pursuit, line drawing, and juggling have been used to indicate that bilateral transfer effects may be realized for both gross and fine motor skills. These experiments were not only concerned with determining if bilateral transfer does in fact occur but also between which limbs and in which direction. Ammons (1952) summarized these findings and suggested that transfer of proficiency would be greater for hand-to-hand or foot-to-foot than hand-to-foot or vice versa. Concerning direction of transfer, most studies have found that the amount of transfer is greater from preferred limb to nonpreferred limb (e.g. Swift, 1903; Ewert, 1926; Koch, 1933).

Since those early studies, other questions concerning bilateral transfer have been raised and examined. The question of practice schedule, i.e. the best practice schedule to achieve maximum bilateral transfer, was studied by Allen (1948). He found that performance was better after the subjects practiced alternately with one hand and then the other than when they practiced with both simultaneously. Walters (1955) considered the effect of overload in training for transfer and concluded that the greatest transfer effects were obtained in overload. Feedback and bilateral transfer were discussed by Laszlo (1971). She found that no or very limited peripheral feedback, i.e. visual, auditory, tactile, and kinesthetic, yielded positive transfer for the preferred hand but not for the nonpreferred hand.

The reason bilateral transfer occurs is perhaps the most intriguing question concerning this phenomenon. Ammons (1958) suggested that *common elements* are involved in the transfer process. That is, transfer occurs from limb to limb because of certain common elements of a skill. Some of the identifiable aspects of skilled performance which have been designated as common elements and thus facilitate bilateral transfer are: cues from verbal self-instruction; visual cues; complex perceptual adjustments; formulated principles for efficient performance of the task; familiarity with the nature of the task; past learning of highly similar skills, and feelings of confidence. As with other learning phenomena, such as inter-task transfer, retention, and practice effects, bilateral transfer effects vary from individual to individual and from task to task. Thus the same effects of amounts of transfer should not be expected for everyone or for every skill.

Generally, bilateral transfer experiments follow a basic design. Two groups are used, one experimental, the other a control group. The experimental group follows this procedure: test nonpreferred limb; practice preferred limb; test nonpreferred limb. The control group receives both tests but has no practice with the preferred hand; thus: test nonpreferred limb; no practice; test nonpreferred limb.

Task selection is an important consideration when testing for bilateral transfer. Since familiarity with the nature of the task and past learning of a highly similar skill can affect the amount of bilateral transfer, it is recommended that novel tasks, that is tasks which are unfamiliar to the subjects and tasks that are relatively difficult for the subject, be used in bilateral transfer experiments. Although the experimenter wants to control for these factors in order to obtain general results concerning whether or not bilateral transfer occurs and to what extent, the teacher or coach, on the other hand, would want to take advantage of these factors to allow for maximal transfer for a student learning a skill.

Thus it can be expected that training for bilateral transfer will produce transfer from the trained to the untrained limb. However, the amount of that transfer will be dependent on a number of factors involving the individual being trained and the skill being taught.

GENERAL RESEARCH FINDINGS

Some of the more conclusive findings concerning bilateral transfer are:
1. Gain in skill can usually be expected in an untrained limb following training of its contralateral muscle group.
2. Transfer of proficiency is generally greater for hand-to-hand or foot-to-foot than for hand-to-foot or vice versa.
3. The amount of transfer is generally greater from preferred limb to nonpreferred limb than from nonpreferred to preferred limb.
4. Alternating practice from limb to limb will usually produce a greater amount of transfer from limb to limb than will massed practice on one limb.
5. Amount of transfer from limb to limb varies according to individuals and types of tasks.

REFERENCES

Allen, R. M.: Factors in mirror drawing. *J Educ Psychol, 39*:216, 1948.

Ammons, R. B.: Le Mouvement, In Steward, G. H. and Steward, J. P. (Eds.): *Current Psychological Issues,* New York, Holt, Rinehart and Winston, 1958.

Ammons, R. B. and Ammons, C. H.: Bilateral transfer of rotary pursuit skill. *Am Psychol, 6*:294, 1951. (Abstract of paper presented at 59th Annual APA convention, Chicago, Ill., 1951).

Ammons, R. B., Ammons, C. H., and Morgan, R. L.: Transfer of skill and decremental factors along the speed dimension in rotary pursuit. *Percept Mot Skills, 6*:43, 1956.

Barch, A. M.: Bilateral transfer of warm-up in rotary pursuit. *Percept Mot Skills, 17*:723, 1963.

Bell, A. H.: Bilateral transfer of work decrement effects as a function of lengths of rest. *Percept Mot Skills, 9*:181, 1959.

Cook, T. W.: Studies in cross education. I. Mirror tracing the star-shaped maze. *J Exp Psychol, 16*:144, 1933.

Cook, T. W.: Studies in cross education. II. Further experiments in mirror tracing the star-shaped maze. *J Exp Psychol, 16*:679, 1933.

Cook, T. W.: Studies in cross education. III. Kinesthetic learning of an irregular pattern. *J Exp Psychol, 17*:749, 1934.

Cook, T. W.: Studies in cross education. IV. Permanence of transfer. *J Exp Psychol,* *18*:255, 1935.

Cook, T. W.: Studies in cross education. V. Theoretical. *Psychol Rev, 43*:149, 1936.

Ewert, P. H.: Bilateral transfer in mirror-drawing. *Pedagogical Seminary J Genet Psychol, 33*:235, 1926.

Frion, A. L., and Gustafson, L. M.: "Reminiscence" in bilateral transfer. *J Exp Psychol, 43*:321, 1952.

Grice, G. R., and Reynolds, B.: Effect of varying amounts of rest on conventional and bilateral transfer "reminiscence." *J Exp Psychol, 44*:247, 1952.

Hellebrant, F. A.: Cross education: Ipsilateral and contralateral effects. *J Appl Physiol, 4*:136, 1951.

Koch, H. L.: A study of the nature, measurement, and determination of hand preference. *Genet Psychol Monogr, 13*:117, 1933.

Laszlo, J. I., and Baguley, R. A.: Motor memory and bilateral transfer. *J Motor Behav, 3*:235, 1971.

Laszlo, J. I., Baguley, R. A., and Bairstow, P. J.: Bilateral transfer in tapping skill in the absence of peripheral information. *J Motor Behav, 2*:261, 1970.

Munn, N. L.: Bilateral transfer of learning. *J Exp Psychol, 15*:343, 1932.

Rockway, M. R.: Bilateral reminiscence in pursuit-rotor learning as a function of amount of first-hand practice and length of rest. *J Exp Psychol, 46*:337, 1953.

Schrecker, K. A.: Approximate ambidexterity. Why and How? *J Sports Med Phys Fitness, 8*:44, 1968.

Sitts, F. D. and Olson, A. L.: Action potentials in unexercised arm when opposite arm is exercised. *Res Q Am Assoc Health Phys Educ, 29*:213, 1958.

Swift, E. J.: Studies in the psychology and physiology of learning. *Am J Psychol, 14*:201, 1903.

Ulich, E.: Transfer of training related to finger-dexterity. *Percept Mot Skills, 17*:274, 1963.

Walker, L. C., DeSoto, C. B., and Shelly, M. W.: Rest and warm-up in bilateral transfer on a pursuit rotor task. *J Exp Psychol, 53*:394, 1957.

Walters, C. E.: The effect of overload on bilateral transfer of a motor skill. *Phys Ther Rev, 35*:567, 1955.

Wieg, E. L.: Bilateral transfer in the motor learning of young children and adults. *Child Dev, 3*:247, 1932.

LABORATORY EXPERIMENT

PURPOSE. To consider whether bilateral transfer does occur between hands and whether the amount of that transfer is greater from preferred hand to nonpreferred hand or vice versa.

EQUIPMENT. Purdue Hand Precision Test (PHPT), Model 4201A.

Interval timer

Timer

Impulse counter

See the Appendix of this chapter for further information concerning these pieces of equipment. If an interval timer is not available, a stop-watch may be used to time the duration of each trial and rest period.

Other laboratory equipment such as the pursuit rotor, star tracing task, and the Minnesota Dexterity Test, could be readily adapted for use in this experiment. Scoring techniques would need to be modified to fit the task selected although the same experimental design could be applied.

PROCEDURE. Divide the class into four groups by randomly assigning each student to a group by means of a table of random numbers. Two of these groups will be experimental groups while two will act as control groups. The groups will differ in the hand used for the pretest and the interpolated activity done between the pre and posttests. These groups will follow the following sequence of events (note: PH = preferred hand, the hand normally used by the subject for such tasks as writing or throwing; NPH = nonpreferred hand).

	Pretest	*Practice*	*Posttest*
Group 1	1 trial with NPH	8 trials with PH	1 trial with NPH
Group 2	1 trial with NPH	no practice, rest for four minutes	1 trial with NPH
Group 3	1 trial with PH	8 trials with NPH	1 trial with PH
Group 4	1 trial with PH	no practice, rest for four minutes	1 trial with PH

The equipment should be assembled as described in the Appendix to consider both the time off-target and the number of hits scored. Set the speed indicator of the PHPT to the middle position. The interval timer should be set to operate the PHPT on a fifteen-second-on and fifteen-second-off interval.

The subject should be seated comfortably in front of the PHPT. All other equipment should be kept from his view. No knowledge of results should be given to the subject following each trial.

The subject should be given the stylus in the hand to be used for trial one and instructed that he is to try to hit every target that appears on the PHPT wheel in consecutive order by following the rotary shutter. Scoring is according to the number of hits but subjects are penalized for having the stylus in contact with any part of the wheel except for the targets.

A trial will last fifteen seconds with a fifteen-second rest between trials. If the subject is in either of the control groups, Groups 2 or 4, he should be instructed that following one trial, there will be a four-minute rest before the next trial. Each subject will take approximately five to six minutes for testing, depending on how much time is needed for instructions.

The number of hits and time off target for each subject for every trial should be recorded. The score for each trial is calculated by the following formula: Trial score = Number of hits − Time off target (to the nearest second).

For class purposes, so that every class member has an opportunity to be both experimenter and subject, it may be desirable to rotate from subject to experimenter. Thus after a subject has been tested, he becomes the experimenter for the next subject and so on. It should be remembered however that this is only an instructional device and that in the course of actual experimentation, the experimenter should remain the same for all subjects in this type of experiment.

RESULTS. Record the score for each subject for each trial on the score sheet provided in this section. Subtract trial one from trial ten and place this difference score as a positive or a negative number. Record this difference score on the data sheet. Calculate the mean and standard deviation for each group by using these difference scores as the dependent measure.

The purpose of this experiment was two-fold: first, to determine if transfer did in fact occur between the practiced and the nonpracticed hand, and second to determine which direction, PH to NPH or NPH to PH, produced a greater amount to transfer.

To answer the first question, calculate the percentage of transfer that occurred between the experimental group and its own control group. It should be noted at this point that many different methods have been developed to determine amounts of transfer in these type of experiments. The percentage method is being used here since it provides a relatively easy and valid measure of transfer.

To calculate percentage of transfer, use the following formula:

E = experimental group difference score mean
C = control group difference score mean

$$\frac{E - C}{E + C} \times 100$$

The percentage obtained from this method will indicate the relative amount of transfer that occurred. This percentage should be calculated for each of the two experimental-control conditions, i.e. Groups 1 and 2 and Groups 3 and 4. If a positive percentage is obtained in these two conditions, it can be concluded that positive transfer occurred from NPH to PH and from PH to NPH.

This method, however, simply reports whether or not the transfer was positive or negative and the relative amount of transfer that occurred. A further analysis might be considered to determine whether or not that amount of transfer was significant or simply due to chance. Two independent *t*-tests could be calculated, one between Groups 1 and 2, the other between Groups 3 and 4. The difference scores for each group should be used in the calculation of these tests.

To answer the second question raised, i.e. which direction, PH to NPH or NPH to PH, produced the greater amount of transfer, one of two methods can be used. The first method is simply to look at the percentage of transfer figures. Which one is larger? This method however does not indicate whether or not the difference between those percentages is real or due to chance. Therefore, the second method would be more valid. This analysis involves an independent t-test using the differences between the groups as the dependent measures. Thus, subtract the control group scores from the experimental group scores for Groups 1 and 2 and compare them to Groups 3 and 4 differences. The results will indicate whether the improvement due to the bilateral transfer phenomenon was greater from NPH to PH or PH to NPH. Thus if the Group 1-2 difference scores are significantly larger than those for the Groups 3-4 condition, it would be concluded that transfer was greater from PH to NPH.

FIELD EXPERIMENT

PURPOSE. To determine the effect of practice with the preferred foot (PF) of a kicking accuracy task on the performance of the nonpracticed foot, i.e. the nonpreferred foot (NPF).

EQUIPMENT.
soccer ball
soccer goal
heavy twine or thin rope
eye-hooks

This experiment is designed to be done out-of-doors. It could be modified for in-door use by marking a wall in the gymnasium in such a way as to resemble a soccer goal.

PROCEDURE. Assign four students to an experimental group and four students to a control group by means of random assignment. The experimental group and control group will be differentiated in this experiment by the presence or absence of a practice session between the pre- and posttests.

The two groups of subjects in this experiment will follow the following sequence of events:

	Pretest	Practice	Posttest
Experimental Group	1 trial (NPF)	8 trials	1 trial (NPF)
Control Group	1 trial (NPF)	10 min. rest	1 trial (NPF)

The task to be used in this experiment involves marking a soccer goal by means of heavy twine or thin rope so that the following target areas are formed. (The point value for each target area is indicated.)

3′	3′	3′	12′	3′	3′	3′	
5	4	2	0	2	4	5	3′
4	3	1	0	1	3	4	4′
5	4	2	0	2	4	5	3′

A trial in this experiment consists of five kicks at the goal. These kicks should be from the penalty kick spot, which is twelve yards from the center of the goal. Mark this spot with an X. The total of the five kicks will be the score for the trial.

The time between kicks should only be the amount of time needed to place a ball on the X. Trials should continue from one through ten for the experimental group with a one-minute rest period between trials five and six.

In order to facilitate the administering of this experiment, it is suggested that at least two soccer balls be used so that one ball may be placed in position for the subject while the other ball is being retrieved. Thus at least two people other than the experimenter should be used to administer the test to each subject, one to retrieve the kicked ball and the other to set-up the ball to be kicked.

Should the ball hit a rope and not enter the goal, that kick should receive a point value equal to the higher of the two point values of the point area divided by the rope that was hit. A score of zero should be given to any kick for which the ball does not enter the goal. A kicked ball may enter the goal by way of a bounce, a roll, or in the air.

RESULTS. Record the point values for each kick on the score sheet provided. Transfer the score for each subject for trials one and ten to the data sheet. Calculate the gain score for each subject by subtracting trial one from trial ten. A correlated *t*-test for each group may then be calculated to determine if the gain in performance from trial one to trial ten was significant. This will then indicate whether or not improvement occurred within each group due to the practice, or lack of it, with the preferred foot.

To determine whether or not the improvement, or gain scores, between groups was significant, calculate an independent *t*-test using the mean gain scores of each group. If the experimental group gain is significantly greater than the control group gain, it will indicate that the improvement of the experimental group was greater than that of the control group and was due to the practice between the pre- and posttest. Thus bilateral transfer occurred as a result of training.

Table 23
LABORATORY EXPERIMENT: BILATERAL TRANSFER DATA ANALYSIS SHEET

For each subject, * make a score sheet similar to the following:
Name_____   Group_____

Trial	Hand	No. Hits	—	Time off target (sec.) = Score
1	____	____		____	____
2	____	____		____	____
3	____	____		____	____
4	____	____		____	____
5	____	____		____	____
6	____	____		____	____
7	____	____		____	____
8	____	____		____	____
9	____	____		____	____
10	____	____		____	____

Difference Score = Trial 10 − Trial 1 =   ____

*If the subject was a control group member, no score will be recorded for trials 2-9.

LABORATORY EXPERIMENT :   BILATERAL TRANSFER DATA ANALYSIS SHEET

Record the Difference Score (D) (from the score sheet) for each subject :

<table>
<tr><th colspan="3">Group 1   (PH to NPH)</th><th colspan="3">Group 2   Control</th></tr>
<tr><th>S</th><th>D_1</th><th>D_1^2</th><th>S</th><th>D_2</th><th>D_2^2</th></tr>
<tr><td>1</td><td></td><td></td><td>1</td><td></td><td></td></tr>
<tr><td>2</td><td></td><td></td><td>2</td><td></td><td></td></tr>
<tr><td>3</td><td></td><td></td><td>3</td><td></td><td></td></tr>
<tr><td>4</td><td></td><td></td><td>4</td><td></td><td></td></tr>
<tr><td>5</td><td></td><td></td><td>5</td><td></td><td></td></tr>
<tr><td>6</td><td></td><td></td><td>6</td><td></td><td></td></tr>
<tr><td>ΣD</td><td></td><td>ΣD_1^2</td><td>ΣD_2</td><td></td><td>ΣD_2^2</td></tr>
<tr><td></td><td>$\bar{D}_1$</td><td></td><td></td><td>$\bar{D}_2$</td><td></td></tr>
</table>

% of transfer $\dfrac{\bar{D}_1 - \bar{D}_2}{\bar{D}_1 + \bar{D}_2}$ X 100 _____ %

<table>
<tr><th colspan="3">Group 3   NPH to PH</th><th colspan="3">Group 4   Control</th></tr>
<tr><th>S</th><th>D_3</th><th>D_3^2</th><th>S</th><th>D_4</th><th>D_4^2</th></tr>
<tr><td>1</td><td></td><td></td><td>1</td><td></td><td></td></tr>
<tr><td>2</td><td></td><td></td><td>2</td><td></td><td></td></tr>
<tr><td>3</td><td></td><td></td><td>3</td><td></td><td></td></tr>
<tr><td>4</td><td></td><td></td><td>4</td><td></td><td></td></tr>
<tr><td>5</td><td></td><td></td><td>5</td><td></td><td></td></tr>
<tr><td>6</td><td></td><td></td><td>6</td><td></td><td></td></tr>
<tr><td>$\Sigma D_3 =$</td><td></td><td>$\Sigma D_3^2 =$</td><td>$\Sigma D_4 =$</td><td></td><td>$\Sigma D_4^2 =$</td></tr>
<tr><td></td><td>$\bar{D}_3 =$</td><td></td><td></td><td>$\bar{D}_4$</td><td></td></tr>
</table>

% of transfer $\dfrac{\bar{D}_3 - \bar{D}_4}{\bar{D}_3 + \bar{D}_4}$ X 100 _____ %

To calculate the *t*-tests, use the formulas found in Chapter 2 and follow the instructions in the results section of the laboratory experiment of this chapter.

FIELD EXPERIMENT : BILATERAL TRANSFER DATA SHEET

Record the total scores for each subject for the trials indicated :

Experimental Group

Subject	Total score on Trial 10	Total score on Trial 1	Gain (G)	G^2
1				
2				
3				
4				

$\Sigma G=$ _____ $\Sigma G^2=$ _____

$\bar{G}=$ _____

Control group

Subject	Total score on Trial 2	Total score on Trial 1	Gain (G)	G^2
1				
2				
3				
4				

$G=$ _____ $G^2=$ _____

$\bar{G}=$ _____

FIELD EXPERIMENT : BILATERAL TRANSFER DATA SHEET

For each subject in the *Experimental group,* make a score sheet similar to the following :

Subject ___(Name)___   Group ___(E or C)___

Foot	Trial	Kick 1	Kick 2	Kick 3	Kick 4	Kick 5	Total Trial Score
NPF	1	___ +	___ +	___ +	___ +	___ =	___
PF	2	___ +	___ +	___ +	___ +	___ =	___
PF	3	___ +	___ +	___ +	___ +	___ =	___
PF	4	___ +	___ +	___ +	___ +	___ =	___
PF	5	___ +	___ +	___ +	___ +	___ =	___
PF	6	___ +	___ +	___ +	___ +	___ =	___
PF	7	___ +	___ +	___ +	___ +	___ =	___
PF	8	___ +	___ +	___ +	___ +	___ =	___
PF	9	___ +	___ +	___ +	___ +	___ =	___
NPF	10	___ +	___ +	___ +	___ +	___ =	___

For each subject in the Control Group , make a score sheet similar to the following :

Subject ___(Name)___   Group ___(E or C)___

Foot	Trial	Kick 1	Kick 2	Kick 3	Kick 4	Kick 5	Total Trial Score
NPF	1	___ +	___ +	___ +	___ +	___ =	___

— — - - - - - - - - - - - - - -10 MINUTE REST _ - - - - - - - - - - - - - - - - - - - — — -.

Foot	Trial	Kick 1	Kick 2	Kick 3	Kick 4	Kick 5	Total Trial Score
NPF	2	___ +	___ +	___ +	___ +	___ =	___

APPENDIX

PURCHASED EQUIPMENT. The Purdue Hand Precision Test may be purchased from:

Lafayette Instrument Co.
Bypass 52 & N. 9th St. Road
Lafayette, Indiana 47902

The Purdue Hand Precision Test consists of a rotating shutter, variable speed control, and hand stylus. A friction clutch is provided to prevent damage to the stylus when a subject is unable to keep pace with the rotating shutter. The speed control provides a continuously variable shutter speed from 30 to 60 RPM. Three measures may be recorded with this instrument: (1) the total number of correct responses, (2) the total number of attempts, and (3) the total time that the stylus is in contact with the base plate or shutter, i.e. total error time.

CONSTRUCTED EQUIPMENT. The marking off of the soccer goal used in the field experiment may be easily accomplished by using threaded eye-hooks that can be screwed into the goal posts of the soccer goal and into the ground. Tie the thin ropes used to mark off point areas onto these eye-hooks.

If soccer goals are not available, the experiment could be modified to use volleyball standards or portable high-jump standards that could be used to mark off target areas as indicated for this experiment.

Chapter 4

KNOWLEDGE OF RESULTS
(FEEDBACK)

INTRODUCTION

KNOWLEDGE OF RESULTS (KR) has been extensively investigated, including various delays of KR, frequencies of KR, and types of KR. One of the problems with research in this area is that different terms referring to the same learning phenomenon have been used by a variety of learning researchers. Some investigators use the terms KR and reward interchangeably; others use KR and reinforcement as equivalents, while more recent researchers refer to KR as feedback. Psychomotor research specialists such as the Bilodeaus and Fitts and Posner tend to favor the term feedback over KR although each places strict qualifiers on their definitions. Although there are theoretical distinctions between the terms knowledge of results and feedback, for our purposes the terms will be used here synonymously.

Knowledge of results includes the various kinds of information which the individual receives about his performance. This information may consist of various forms visual and proprioceptive feedback or comments made by a coach or teacher as to the qualitative aspects of the performance.

Holding's (1965) diagramatic classification indicates the kinds of KR that exist and the comparisons that can be made in KR research. For example, is verbal or nonverbal (kinesthetic or visual) KR more effective in motor learning? Are different skills (continuous or discrete, fine or gross, simple or complex) influenced in the same manner when a particular KR or combination of them is introduced? Will the stage of learning, or skill level of the individual, suggest a more appropriate form of KR?

Intrinsic KR is a natural consequence of the movement itself, i.e. it occurs as a result of one's own action. This may be exemplified by seeing the ball go through the hoop in basketball shooting or feeling the adequacy of a gymnastic movement. Another form of intrinsic KR related to performance in basketball shooting may be the proprioceptive information from various sensory receptors from the muscles and joints as to the

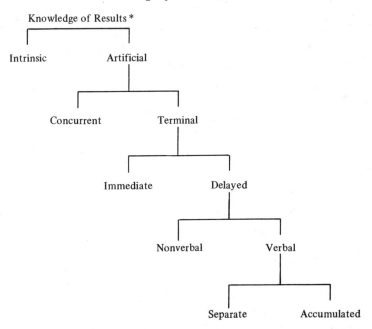

force and rate of movement of the shooting arm and the position of the body during execution. The accomplishment of higher levels of performance requires a greater reliance on intrinsic cues by the subject. Extensive practice under the appropriate conditions will aid in this development.

Artificial KR is the information the subject receives from an external source as to the effectiveness of his actions. Information provided by the coach as to the analysis of his basketball shot would constitute artificial or augmented feedback for the basketball player. Video tape replays of an intricate dive would be another form of artificial KR.

Conflicting evidence has been reported in this area of research with as many studies showing null effects as beneficial effects on the use of artificial or augmented KR. Several researchers have suggested that artificial or augmented feedback may not elicit a different response habit but instead motivate the subjects to do better. Smode (1958), doing research with augmented feedback, found that groups that had received augmented feedback on their first day trials continued to perform at a higher level than the control groups even when the augmented feedback was withdrawn on the second day. One may hypothesize from this study that in certain tasks augmented feedback may improve the level of motivation and thereby influence performance.

---

* Only the artificial branch has been delineated for clarity. The student is directed to Holding's text *Principles of Training* (1965) for further discussion.

Anyone who has watched a major track meet would be sure to see coaches along the track's edge passing on *lap times* to their runners as they speed past. This knowledge of lap performance enables the runner to check his lap pace or level of performance set for him by his coach.

GENERAL RESEARCH FINDINGS

Some of the more conclusive findings in the area of KR are as follows:

1. Findings indicate that with simple motor skills such as line drawing and tapping, immediate KR is generally beneficial. In more complex tasks interference in the form of other responses, positioned between the main response and KR, may cause decrements in performance. The rate of learning has been found to decrease according to the number of trials in which KR was delayed.

2. Investigations on frequency of KR have indicated that learning depends upon the presence of KR and its absolute rather than relative frequency. Few studies on rather selective tasks have demonstrated that continuous KR was more beneficial than intermittent KR in skill acquisition.

3. The need for KR in maintaining and improving performance level has been verified in that performance does not improve without KR; performance improves with KR, and performance deteriorates or shows no improvement when KR is withdrawn. Many motor learning researchers would agree that knowledge of results or feedback is the strongest and most important variable affecting performance and learning.

REFERENCES

Abbey, D. S. and Cowan, P. A.: Incomplete visual feedback and performance on the Toronto Complex Coordinator. *Percept Mot Skills, 11*:43, 1960.

Ammons, R. B.: Effects of knowledge of performance: A survey and tentative theoretical formulation. *J Gen Psychol, 54*:279, 1956.

Baker, C. H. and Young, P.: Feedback during training and retention of motor skills. *Can J Psychol, 14*:257, 1960.

Bell, V. L.: Augmented knowledge of results and its effect upon acquisition and retention of a gross motor skill. *Res Q Am Assoc Health Phys Educ, 39*:25, 1968.

Bilodeau, E. A.: Supplementary feedback and instructions. In Bilodeau, E. A. (Ed.): *Principles of Skill Acquisition*. New York, Academic Press, 1969.

Bilodeau, E. A. and Bilodeau, I. McD.: Variable frequency of knowledge of results and the learning of a simple skill. *J Exp Psychol, 55*:379, 1958.

Bilodeau, E. A., Bilodeau, I. McD., and Schumsky, D. A.: Some effects of introducing and withdrawing knowledge of results early and late in practice. *J Exp Psychol, 58*:142, 1959.

Bilodeau, I. McD.: Information feedback. In Bilodeau, E. A. (Ed.): *Principles of Skill Acquisition*. New York, Academic Press, 1969.

Burkhard, D. G., Patterson, J., and Rapue, R.: Effect of film feedback on learning the motor skills of karate. *Percept Mot Skills, 25*:65, 1967.

Elwell, J. L. and Grindley, G. C.: The effect of knowledge of results on learning and performance. *Br J Psychol, 29*:39, 1938.

Gordon, N. B.: Guidance versus augmented feedback and motor skill. *J Exp Psychol, 77*:24, 1968.

Greenspoon, J. and Foreman, S.: Effect of delay of knowledge of results on learning a motor task. *J Exp Psychol, 51*:226, 1956.

Holding, D. H.: *Principles of Training*. New York, Pergamon Press, 1965.

Karlin, L. and Mortimer, R. G.: Effect of verbal, visual and auditory augmenting cues on learning a complex motor skill. *J Exp Psychol, 65*:75, 1963.

Keele, S. W. and Posner, M. I.: Processing of visual feedback in rapid movements. *J Exp Psychol, 77*:155, 1968.

Lavery, J. J.: The effect of one-trial delay in knowledge of results on the acquisition and retention of a tossing skill. *Am J Psychol, 74*:437, 1964.

Lavery, J. J. and Succon, F. H.: Retention of simple motor skills as a function of the number of trials by which KR is delayed. *Percept Mot Skills, 15*:231, 1962.

Malina, R. M. and Rarick, G. L.: A device for assessing the role of information feedback in speed and accuracy of throwing performance. *Res Q Am Assoc Health Phys Educ, 39*:220, 1968.

Pierson, W. R. and Rasch, P. J.: Effect of knowledge of results on isometric strength scores. *Res Q Am Assoc Health Phys Educ, 35*:313, 1964.

Robb, M.: Feedback and skill learning. *Res Q Am Assoc Health Phys Educ, 39*:175, 1968.

LABORATORY EXPERIMENT

PURPOSE. To study the effects of knowledge of results upon the learning of the balance task.

EQUIPMENT. Stabilometer (see Appendix for illustrations and explanations.)

PROCEDURE. Form two groups, one control and one experimental. No practice trials allowed.

The control group subjects will perform ten thirty-second trials on the stabilometer interspersed with rest periods of thirty seconds. No artificial or augmented knowledge of results will be given as to time-in-balance.*

The experimental group subjects will perform similarly as the control subjects except immediate knowledge of performance score will be given after each of the ten trials.

RESULTS.

1. Record resultant data on master sheet.

---

*This was not a true KR versus non-KR experiment as it was not possible to withhold all KR from the subjects. The control subjects were able to perceive their level of performance through some visual and kinesthetic cues.

2. Plot learning curves for each group, with the mean score of the group for each trial plotted.
3. Determine statistically by means of a t-test if there are differences in learning scores between the two groups using (a) the mean score, and (b) the tenth trial score.

FIELD EXPERIMENT

PURPOSE. To study the effects of knowledge of results upon learning of a novel gross motor task.

EQUIPMENT. Tennis balls and circular wall target.

PROCEDURE. Form two groups, one control and one experimental. Subjects will stand fifteen feet from the target with the side of their non-throwing arm facing the target. The control group subjects will properly position themselves at the throwing line, view the target and then be blindfolded. Thirty behind-the-back tosses at the target with a tennis ball are then performed. No knowledge of performance or score is to be given. The interval time between each trial might be five seconds.

The experimental group subjects will properly position themselves at the throwing line and perform thirty behind-the-back tosses with a tennis ball at the wall target. Subjects will be allowed to view the results of all trials.

RESULTS.
1. Record resultant data on master sheet.
2. Plot learning curves for each group with the mean score of the group of each trial plotted.
3. Determine statistically by means of a t-test if there are differences in the initial scores and the final scores between the groups. Also, compare the mean scores of both groups across all attempts with the t-test.

APPENDIX

PURCHASED EQUIPMENT. One equipment company that produces a stabilometer (Stability Platform Apparatus) is the Marietta Apparatus Company, 118 Maple Street, Marietta, Ohio. Illustration and description of the apparatus is found in Figure 4-7.

CONSTRUCTED EQUIPMENT. A variety of stabilometers may be constructed for this particular experiment.

The stabilometer recommended has a test period timer and a performance timer built into the apparatus. The description and illustrations are as follows:

LABORATORY EXPERIMENT : KR DATA SHEET

Control Group	Trials											
Subjects	1	2	3	4	5	6	7	8	9	10	ΣX	ΣX^2
1												
2												
3												
4												
5												

a) $\bar{X} = \dfrac{\Sigma X}{n} =$

(all trials)

b) $\bar{X} = \dfrac{\Sigma X}{n} =$

(10th trial)

Exp. Group	Trials											
Subjects	1	2	3	4	5	6	7	8	9	10	ΣX	ΣX^2
1												
2												
3												
4												
5												

$\Sigma \Sigma X =$

a) $\bar{X} = \dfrac{\Sigma X}{n} =$

(all trials)

b) $\bar{X} = \dfrac{\Sigma X}{n} =$

(10th trial)

FIELD EXPERIMENT : KR DATA SHEET

CONTROL GROUP

SUBJECTS	1	2	3	4	5	6	7	8	9	10	11	12	13	14	15	16	17	18	19	20	21	22	23	24	25	26	27	28	29	30	ΣX
1																															
2																															
3																															
4																															
5																															

TRIALS

$$\Sigma\Sigma X =$$

a) $\overline{X} = \dfrac{\Sigma X}{n} =$ (all trials)

EXPERIMENT GROUP

SUBJECTS	1	2	3	4	5	6	7	8	9	10	11	12	13	14	15	16	17	18	19	20	21	22	23	24	25	26	27	28	29	30	ΣX
1																															
2																															
3																															
4																															
5																															

TRIALS

$$\Sigma\Sigma X =$$

a) $\overline{X} = \dfrac{\Sigma X}{n} =$ (all trials)

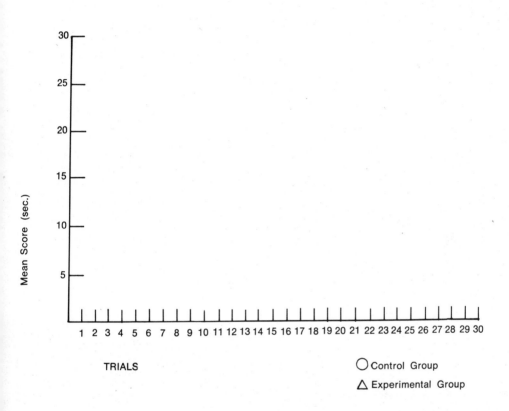

LAB EXPERIMENT : Learning Curves

TRIALS

○ Control Group

△ Experimental Group

FIELD EXPERIMENT : Learning Curves

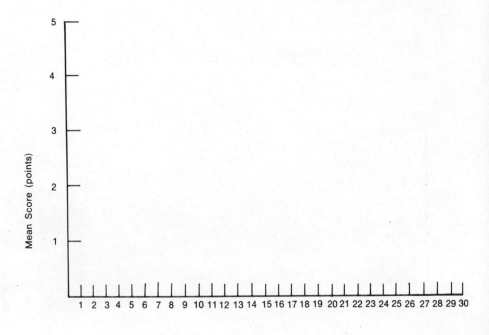

TRIALS

◯ Control Group

△ Exp. Group

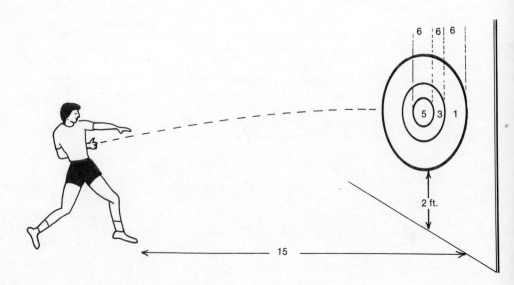

STABILITY PLATFORM APPARATUS

Figure 4-7: This apparatus is used for evaluation of individual ability to maintain bodily balance over a period of time. The subject stands on a free-moving platform, attempting to maintain balance. When he fails to sustain his balance the electrical contact to the timer is broken, thus recording the event. The platform consists of an aluminum deck plate centrally pivoted and suspended from the base by means of ball bearing supports. Rubber bumpers and micro-switches on the underside serve as stops and circuit breakers, and are adjustable in order to lend varying degrees of difficulty to the task. All controls and readout instruments are housed in a separate cabinet and consist of a recycling timer to provide test and rest periods; a digital 1/100th-second timer to provide a readout of in-balance time; a buzzer which may be activated at the examiner's option to indicate when the platform is out of balance; a counter to record the number of test periods; a counter to record the number of times the platform was out of balance; and a light, visible to the subject, to indicate when a test period is in session.

The balance platform of the stabilometer is made of plywood having dimensions of 32 x 22 x 3/4 of an inch. The topside of the plywood platform is covered with a rubber mat to prevent the subject from slipping during testing. The balance platform is supported by 2 x 4 foot beams along its length, notched in the center to allow for passage of the metal axle. The framework of the stabilometer is 36 x 24 x 12 inches in dimension. The side-supporting members have holes drilled eighteen inches from each end and 3½ inches from the floor. These holes allow for the passage of the metal axle upon which rests the balance platform of the stabilometer.

Micro-switches are placed into the side-supporting member. These micro-switches are placed so that an angle of 22 degrees can be transversed without depressing a micro-switch. A wire runs from each microswitch and connects to a .01 second digital timer. The timer is connected to a thirty-second test period timing device. The switch on the timer is left in the *on* position during the entire project because it is activated when the test period timer is turned on. The circuit is closed when the balance platform depresses a micro-switch and in turn turns off the digital timer. When both micro-switches are not depressed, the circuit is completed and the time in balance is recorded.

STABILOMETER WITH TWO MICROSWITCHES

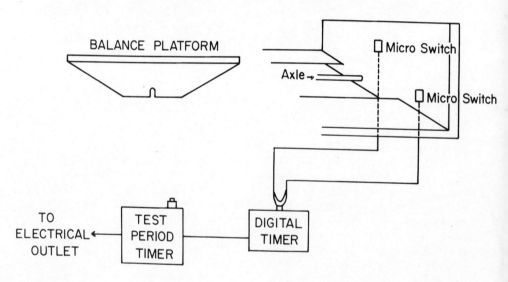

The same type of stabilometer may be built without the test period timer. A stopwatch may be used to record the test period.

The simplest type of stabilometer that may be built would be like a teeter-totter board. The number of contacts that either end of the board would have with the floor may be used as a performance score. Test period time may be recorded with a stopwatch.

PHYSICAL LAYOUT AND WIRING DIAGRAM OF STABILOMETER WITH ONE MICRO-SWITCH

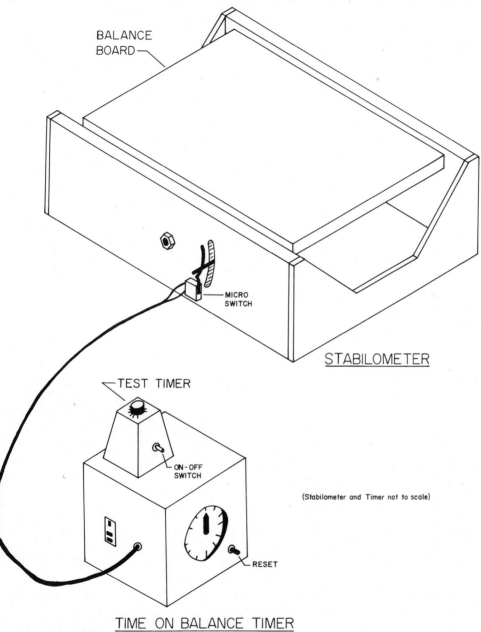

BALANCE BOARD

MICRO SWITCH

STABILOMETER

TEST TIMER

ON - OFF SWITCH

(Stabilometer and Timer not to scale)

RESET

TIME ON BALANCE TIMER

Figure 4-9:

STABILOMETER

TIME ON BALANCE TIMER & TEST TIMER

Wiring Diagram

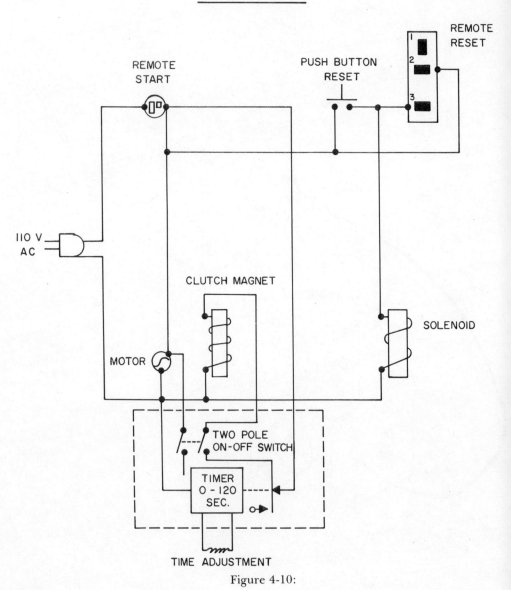

Figure 4-10:

CIRCULAR STABILOMETER

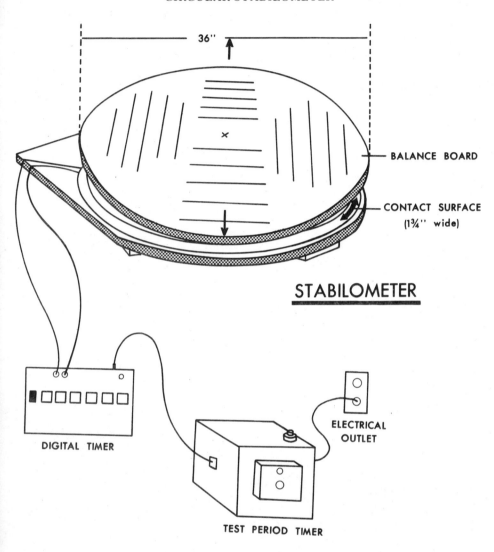

STABILOMETER

Chapter 5

REACTION TIME AND MOVEMENT TIME

INTRODUCTION

Q UICK REACTIONS distinguish the average from the superior performer in many motor skills. Individuals who react quicker and
move faster have an obvious advantage over those who are slower.
Coaches, recognizing the importance of fast reactions and movements in
athletes, devote many hours in drills to develop and maintain them.
Although improvements occur through practice, they are nevertheless
limited by one's neuromuscular structures; that is, all movements are
connected by neural mechanisms as well as being dependent upon muscular mechanisms. An individual may have quick reactions but not move
his body with similar quickness, and vice versa.

There has been some confusion in terminology used in the research
and in everyday language. Such terms as response time, reflex time,
reaction time, and movement time have been used interchangeably although they are not synonymous.

Reaction time (RT) is defined as the elapsed interval of time from the
presentation of a stimulus to the initiation of a response. Woodworth and
Schlosberg (1963) have labelled it as the time required to initiate the overt
response, i.e. the S-R time interval. They have also referred to RT as the
response latency which includes sense organ time, brain time, nerve time,
and muscle time. Botwinick (1966) has dichotomized reaction time into a
premotor component, that is, the period from the presentation of the
stimulus to the appearance of increased muscle motor unit firing (increased action potential), and a motor component. In other words, RT =
PMT + MT. This motor time component represents that period from
the changed action potential to the actual response. His results indicated
that premotor time and reaction time were highly correlated (.92), motor
time was poorly correlated with reaction time (.21), as was the correlation
between premotor and motor time (−.10).

Movement time (MT) has been defined as the time a particular act

83

takes to be completed after it has been initiated. Said another way, it is that period from the beginning of the overt response to the completion of a specified movement.

There are certainly numerous examples of RT and MT in athletics, some of which are (a) in football: defensive halfback reaction drills to the direction of the pass, defensive lineman lateral movement following reaction to the flight of ball; (b) in basketball: defensive reaction and movement to a passed ball; (c) in wrestling: reaction and movement to a particular grip or takedown move; (d) in hockey: the goal keeper's reaction and movement to close-in shots or screened shots.

There is a difference of opinion as to whether RT and MT are related. Henry (1952), Slater-Hammel (1952), Lotter (1960) and others have found that the relationship between speed of reaction and speed of movement does not exist. On the other hand, Pierson (1959), Pierson and Rasch (1961), Kerr (1966) and others have reported positive significant relationships between these two factors. This relationship may possibly depend upon several variables, such as the muscle group used, and limbs involved, and the direction of the movement. Henry (1960) also pointed out that both RT and MT may be related due to a common variable such as the aging process or one's preparatory set, thus resulting in a higher correlation. Generally speaking, most studies have indicated that RT and MT are independent measures.

Studying the relationship among limbs it has been found that leg movements are slower and have longer reaction times than arm movements. Specificity in performance has been found to be greater between both arms or both legs than between the two arms or the two legs. There is also more specificity between diagonally paired arms and legs than between arms and legs on the same side of the body.

Simple reaction time may be measured by purchased or constructed equipment. A cue source and telegraph key merely need be hooked up to chronoscope. The subject is informed to remove his finger as quickly as possible from a depressed switch after hearing the signal or seeing the light signal. Time elapsed from signal to initiation of movement is recorded.

A method of measuring reaction time as well as movement time has been with a relatively simple apparatus consisting of a stimulus (light or a buzzer), a response unit (photo-electric beam), and two chronoscopes. After a preparatory set warning the stimulus and one chronoscope are simultaneously activated. The subject responds to the stimulus by releasing a micro-switch and thrusting his hand through a light beam. When the subject releases the micro-switch the first chronoscope is deactivated and the second chronoscope is activated. The second chronoscope is terminated when the subject interrupts a photo-electric beam placed an appropriate distance in front of him. Reaction time is read from the first chronoscope; that is, the time the stimulus was initiated until the subject reacts to it by releasing the micro-switch. Movement time is read from the second chronoscope; that is, the time from when the subject releases the micro-switch until his hand passes through the photo-electric beam.

In early childhood RT and MT are irregular and do not stabilize until seven or eight years of age. After this time individuals begin to decrease their RT and MT rapidly at first, then steadily, peaking in their late teens or early twenties, with females reaching their peak three or four years before males. After this peaking there is a gradual nonparallel decline. Although an individual is capable of the fastest response around age twenty, he is more consistent in his responses some ten years later. Hodkins (1962) found that RT decreased from six to nineteen years, was stable from nineteen to twenty-six years and increased after age twenty-six.

In all studies reporting a sex variation males are faster both in RT and MT at all ages. Males also maintain their peak longer in MT but females retain a relatively high level longer in RT.

The speed of reaction is affected by the sense organ stimulated. The auditory modality results in the fastest reaction time, followed by sight, pain, taste, smell and touch. The RT to touch, however, differs with the area stimulated since the more sensitive areas as those closer to the brain tend to give quicker responses.

A combination of simultaneous stimuli may stimulate a faster response than any single stimulus. For example:

light	176 mil/secs.
electric shock	143
sound	142
light and shock	142
sound and shock	142
light, shock and sound	127

Closely associated with modality is intensity of the stimulus. The correlation between reaction time and intensity is a curved rather than a linear relationship. Above a certain point additional increases in intensity of stimulus would not prove beneficial.

Individuals will continue to improve for several days or for several hundred trials with the improvement after the first hundred trials being very slight. Older persons may significantly lower their response time with practice.

As a person anticipates the stimulus, general muscular tension occurs throughout the body. Research indicates that muscle tension begins 200-400 milleseconds after the ready signal increasing up until the response. The higher the muscular tension before the response, the quicker the reaction. The peak of one's attention has also been found to decrease if the period between the warning signal and the stimulus is too long, i.e. two to four seconds is optimum for maximum response.

Motivating the individual either by intrinsic or extrinsic rewards may positively affect one's reaction time. Several investigators have used incentives such as money, food, and praise to elicit faster reaction time. This variable would be of great interest to performers in track and in swimming as many times the final outcome of the race is decided in one's start.

A heavier physique, high body temperature, high pulse rate, strenuous exercise, anoxia, large doses of alcohol, and drugs tend to produce slower reaction times. Several types of drugs taken under normal doses, e.g. amphetamines, have been found to quicken reaction times.

Even when all the above experimental factors are held constant, one still cannot predict with any degree of accuracy what an individual's RT will be at a given time because of the one uncontrollable factor, individual differences, as individual RT's have been found to vary from moment to moment and from day to day.

GENERAL RESEARCH FINDINGS

1. Simple RT is correlated lowly with many speed tests.
2. RT is related more highly between the hands than between the feet or between a combination of hands and feet.
3. On the whole, an individual who reacts quickly to one stimulus will react quickly to another.
4. Males are faster than females, with the late teens and early twenties (19-25 years) associated with best performances for both sexes.
5. The weaker the stimulus the slower the RT.
6. The auditory modality elicits the fastest reaction time followed by touch, sight, pain, taste and smell. A combination of stimuli will produce even faster reaction times.
7. Other factors affecting RT and MT are fatigue, drugs, alcohol, prior warning, practice, preparatory set, motivation, plus numerous physiological factors.
8. The majority of research available suggests that reaction time and movement time are not interrelated to any meaningful extent.

REFERENCES

Botwinick, J. and Thompson, C.W.: Premotor and motor components of reaction time. *J Exp Psychol*, 71:9, 1966.

Cattell, J.: The influence of the intensity of the stimulus on the length of the reaction time. *Brain*, 9:512, 1947.

Guilford, J. P.: A system of psychomotor abilities. *Am J Psychol*, 71:164, 1958.

Henry, F. M.: Reaction—movement time correlations. *Percept Mot Skills*, 12:63, 1964.

Henry, F. M.: Independence of reaction and movement times and equivalence of sensory motivators of fast response. *Res Q Am Assoc Health Phys Educ*, 23:43, 1952.

Henry, F. M.: Influence of motor and sensory sets on reaction latency and speed of discrete movements. *Res Q Am Assoc Health Phys Educ*, 31:459, 1960.

Henry, F. M., and Whitley, J. C.: Relationships between individual differences in strength, speed and mass in an arm movement. *Res Q Am Assoc Health Phys Educ*, 31:24, 1960.

Hodgkins, J.:. Reaction time and speed of movement in males and females of various ages. *Res Q Am Assoc Health Phys Educ*, 34:335, 1963.

Howell, M. L.: Influence of emotional tension on speed of reaction time and movement. *Res Q Am Assoc Health Phys Educ*, 21:22, 1953.

Kerr, B. A.: Relationship between speed of reaction and movement in a knee extension movement. *Res Q Am Assoc Health Phys Educ*, 37:55, 1966.

Lotter, W. S. Interrelationships among reaction time and speeds of movement in different limbs. *Res Q Am Assoc Health Phys Educ*, 31:147, 1960.

Mendryk, S.: Reaction time, movement time, and task specificity relationships at ages 12, 22, and 48 years. *Res Q Am Assoc Health Phys Educ*, 31:156, 1960.

Mowbray, G. H.: Choice reaction times for skilled responses. *J Exp Psychol*, 12:193, 1960.

Mowbray, G.H. and Rhoades, M. V.: On the reduction of choice reaction times with practice. *Q J Exp Psychol*, 11:16, 1959.

Noble, C., Baker, B., Blaine, L., and Jones, T.: Age and sex parameters in psychomotor learning. *Percept Mot Skills*, 19:935, 1964.

Owens, J.A.: Effects of variations in hand and foot spacing on movement time and on force of change. *Res Q Am Assoc Health Phys Educ*, 31:66, 1960.

Pierson, W. R.: The relationship of movement time and reaction time from childhood to senility. *Res Q Am Assoc Health Phys Educ*, 30:227, 1959.

Pierson, W. R. and Montoye, H. J.: Movement time, reaction time, and age. *J Gerontol*, 31:418, 1958.

Pierson, W. R. and Rasch, P. J.: Generality of speed factor in simple reaction and movement time. *Percept Mot Skills*, 11:123, 1960.

Pierson, W. R. and Rasch, P. J.: RT—MT correlations and the generality of a speed factor. *Percept Mot Skills*, 12:246, 1961.

Slater-Hammel, A. T.: Reaction time and speed of movement. *Percept Mot Skills, Research Exchange*, 4:109, 1952.

Smith, E. E.: Choice reaction time: An analysis of the major theoretical positions. *Psychol Bull*, 69:77, 1968.

Smith, L. E.: Reaction time and movement time in four large muscle movements. *Res Q Am Assoc Health Phys Educ*, 32:88, 1961.

Tweit, A. H., Gollnick, P. D., and Hearn, G. R.: Effect of training program on total body reaction time of individuals of low fitness. *Res Q Am Assoc Health Phys Educ*, 34:508, 1963.

Weiss, A. D.: The locus of reaction time change with set, motivation, and age. *J Gerontol*, 20:60, 1965.

Woodworth, R. S. and Schlosberg, H.: *Experimental Psychology*. New York, Holt, Rinehart & Winston, 1963.

Youngen, L.: A comparison of reaction and movement times of women athletes and nonathletes. *Res Q Am Assoc Health Phys Educ*, 30:349, 1959.

LABORATORY EXPERIMENT

PURPOSE. To study the relationship between reaction time and movement time.

EQUIPMENT. Dekan Performance Analyzer*, photo-electric cells, stop-clock, interval timer. (See illustration.)

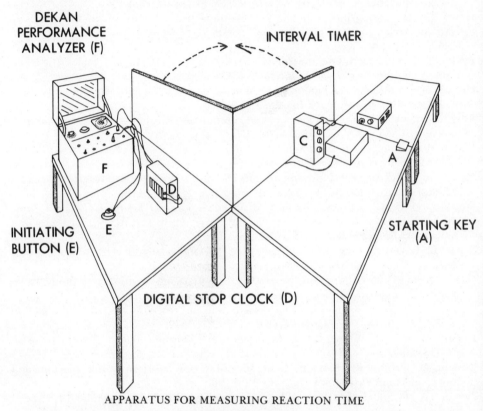

APPARATUS FOR MEASURING REACTION TIME
AND MOVEMENT TIME

DESIGN. Subjects, acting as their own controls, are placed in a task requiring speed of reaction and speed of movement.

PROCEDURE. Each subject begins by depressing a micro-switch and after a preparatory warning signal (electric buzzer) a visual stimulus (light) will be presented. A chronoscope is activated simultaneously with the stimulus light. The subject responds to the stimulus light by thrusting his hand as quickly as possible through the light beam. When the subject releases the micro-switch, the chronoscope stops and a second chronoscope is activated. This second chronoscope is stopped when the subject interrupts the photo-electric beam. Reaction time is read from the first

---

*A description of the Dekan Performance Analyzer is found in the chapter on speed and accuracy.

chronoscope and movement time from the second, both measured to .01 seconds. Ten trials are given, with the mean scores used as the dependent measure.

RESULTS.

1. Record resultant data on master sheet provided.
2. Determine any statistical relationship between reaction time and movement time by means of the Pearson Product Moment correlation technique. Use the mean score of the ten trials as the subject's score.

FIELD EXPERIMENT

PURPOSE. To study the relationship between reaction time and movement time in a gross motor activity.

EQUIPMENT. Dekan Performance Analyzer (measuring at .01 sec.), a termination board, and the use of a swimming pool. A similar experiment may be performed in a gymnasium using sprint starts.

DESIGN. Subjects acting as their own controls. Each subject will perform ten trials after two practice trials. A five-minute rest period is given between test trials.

PROCEDURE. Subjects will stand on the starting blocks or the edge of the pool in the new racer's starting position, that is, with both hands down between the legs pressing backwards on the starting block. On the starting signal each subject will dive forward into the water and swim to one end of the pool and back to the starting point. Reaction time will be measured from the time of the starting signal to the first perceivable movement of the swimmer's hands; the movement time is measured from the termination of reaction to the subject touch on the termination board. The Dekan Performance Analyzer, with appropriate accessories, will be wired to the starting blocks and the termination board. (See Effect of Food Consumption on 200-Yard Freestyle Swim, authored by R. N. Singer and R. E. Neeves, *Research Quarterly*, 39:355-360, 1968, for details of equipment layout and testing procedures.)

RESULTS.

1. Record resultant data on master sheet provided.
2. Determine any statistical relationship between reaction time and movement time by means of the Pearson Product Moment correlation technique. Use the mean score of the ten trials as the subject's score.
3. Compute the reliability for the reaction time scores with the odd-even trial technique. Do the same for the moment time scores.

LABORATORY EXPERIMENT :   RT + MT DATA SHEET

STIMULUS : LIGHT										TRIALS												
SUBJECTS		1		2		3		4		5		6		7		8		9		10		X̄	
		RT	MT	RT	MT	RT	MT	RT	MT	RT	MT	RT	MT	RT	MT	RT	MT	RT	MT	RT	MT	RT	MT
1																							
2																							
3																							
4																							
5																							

FIELD EXPERIMENT :   RT + MT DATA SHEET

											TRIALS												
SUBJECTS		1		2		3		4		5		6		7		8		9		10		X̄	
		RT	MT	RT	MT	RT	MT	RT	MT	RT	MT	RT	MT	RT	MT	RT	MT	RT	MT	RT	MT	RT	MT
1																							
2																							
3																							
4																							
5																							

TABLE EXPERIMENT: SIMPLE REACTION TIME DATA SHEET:

MALES

Subject	Trials																				ΣX	$\bar{X}$
	1	2	3	4	5	6	7	8	9	10	11	12	13	14	15	16	17	18	19	20		
1																						
2																						
3																						
4																						

FEMALES

Subject	Trials																				ΣX	$\bar{X}$
	1	2	3	4	5	6	7	8	9	10	11	12	13	14	15	16	17	18	19	20		
1																						
2																						
3																						
4																						

	MALES		FEMALES	
	$\bar{X}$	X^2	$\bar{X}$	X^2
1				
2				
3				
4				
	$\bar{X}=$	$\Sigma X^2=$	$\bar{X}=$	$\Sigma X^2=$

APPENDIX

Reaction time equipment may be purchased from the Lafayette Instrument Company, P.O. Box 1279, Lafayette, Indiana.

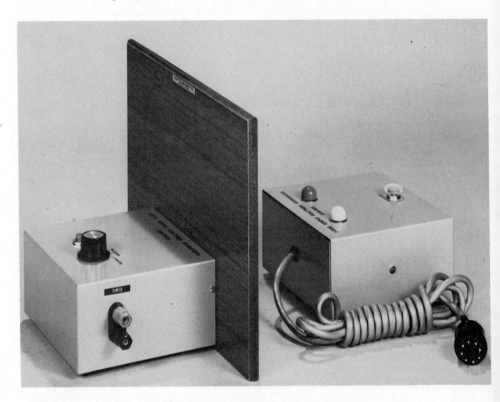

SIMPLE REACTION TIME APPARATUS

Figure 5-5: This new unit, in addition to containing all the features of the earlier 6301 Simple Reaction Time Apparatus, includes the advantage of having the Experimenter Console and the Subject Console separated by fifteen feet of remote control cord. This important feature enables the experimenter and subject to the located in separate rooms or fifteen feet apart, thus eliminating the possibility of any auditory and visual cueing of an upcoming signal. The apparatus will measure reaction time to either red or green lights or a buzzer, and a stop-clock can be connected between the two binding posts to record elapsed reaction time. The stopclock is connected *at the operator's control unit* to prevent the subject from hearing the stimulus sound of the stopclock rather than the stimulus presented. Other advantages of this apparatus include safety features so that no errors can be made, silent switching operation, and response by pressing (not by releasing) of key.

VISUAL CHOICE REACTION TIME APPARATUS

Figure 5-6: This versatile instrument was designed for use with an external clock timer for measuring simple and disjunctive reaction times. The instrument can also be employed to study probability learning, alternation learning, concept formation, and complex information processing. The apparatus consists of two units—an experimenter's control module and a subject's stimulus-display-response module. These modules are isolated by a fifteen foot cable to eliminate the chance of any spurious stimulus cues. The subject module includes four lights, a buzzer, and four response keys. The experimenter selects which stimulus light goes on, and the timer runs until the correct response key is depressed. When the correct response is made, the stimulus light goes off and the timer is stopped. Precise starting of each trial is accomplished with a separate initiate switch on the experimenter control module. Two or more sets of these units may be employed together to simply demonstrate how reaction time increases as a function of the number of stimulus-response alterations is a task. For example, one can plot average reaction time versus the logarithm (base two) of the number of possible stimuli in a series of experiments using two, four, six and eight stimulus lights. A linear function should result for more advanced demonstrations. The unit may be simply modified so that the timer stops whenever any response is made. If the experimenter then keeps track of the percent responses to each stimulus, he may then plot average reaction time versus a measure of the information transmitted by the subject. The resulting linear function is a very dramatic demonstration of a basic characteristic of human performance.

Chapter 6

MASSED AND DISTRIBUTED PRACTICE

INTRODUCTION

Since practice does not necessarily make perfect, it seems obvious that the learning of a task may be facilitated by more favorable conditions during the training period. Arising from earlier attempts to identify these conditions comes the trade-off issue of massed versus distributed practice. Massed practice is usually defined as continuous practice without intermittent pauses. Continuous performance on the pursuit rotor say, for six hundred seconds, or shooting one hundred foul shots in the basket without a rest would be examples of massed practice. Distributed practice may be defined as practice periods divided by designated rest intervals. Five minute rest periods between sixty-second trials on the pursuit rotor, and basketball foul shooting on alternate days with fewer trials, would be examples of distributed practice.

The major question arises as to whether it is better to practice a task with very little interruption for rest or is rest really beneficial to learning and performance? If rest periods are desired, what is the optimal length of the rest interval and the duration of the practice period? The answer is not simple, for factors such as type of task as well as the skill level of the learner must be considered.

The terms *massed* and *distributed* have had different connotations among researchers. In some studies massed practice refers to trials completely uninterrupted by rest. In other studies practice was massed in terms of the number of minutes per day or the number of days per week. In some studies distributed practice was interrupted by seconds, in others by days, and in others by weeks.

In attempting to measure the relative effects of massed and distributed practice on learning and performance, researchers have manipulated the practice variables in numerous ways. Some of the manipulations are: the length (increasing and decreasing) and the frequency of rest periods, imposing and varying the activity during the rest period, massing the number of rest periods or using irregular rest periods, initially massing

94

practice then changing to distributed practice, and employing irregular periods of massed practice.

Most of these studies have been carried out by psychologists employing a variety of learning tasks and apparatus such as pursuit rotors and other various tracking apparatus, mirror tracers, mazes, and nonsense syllable word tests. Very few studies of schedules of practice using gross motor activities have been reported in the literature. Schedules of practice and the effect upon learning and performance are certainly of importance to physical educators and coaches because of the time limitations imposed upon them by schools in which students can be instructed.

The optimum rest period has been investigated for a variety of tasks with the general consensus being that it really depends upon the nature of the task and the length of the practice period. Significant effects have been found for rest periods of several seconds to several days. Even the briefest of rest was beneficial to no rest. Some investigators have reported that optimal improvement is achieved after a full day's rest. Generally, as the task becomes more laborious longer rest periods are necessary for recovery.

The problem remains as to how much rest between practice periods is optimal to still be beneficial to learning and performance. Several studies (Reynolds and Bilodeau, 1952; Lewis and Lowe, 1956) have reported that immediate retention was evident with either distributed or massed practice schedules. Adams and Reynolds (1954) also reported that whether practice had been massed or distributed, no permanent learning effects occurred. There may be a critical point where massed practice inhibits and worsens performance whereas distributed practice appears to be continually beneficial.

Gross motor tasks taught under different practice schedules have produced conflicting results. Niemeyer (1958), studying three sport skills, badminton, volleyball and swimming, reported that initial massing of practice followed by distributed (spaced) practice resulted in the highest performance levels. This finding has been substantiated by other researchers using different motor skills. However, early distributed practice followed later by massed practice trials has also been reported to produce the highest performance levels. In a juggling task Knapp and Dixon (1952) reported that massed practice schedules produced the required learned skill in fewer days but that the distributed schedule was more efficient in respect to actual practice time.

In spite of the seemingly contradictory research evidence, due probably to the nature of the different motor tasks and the combination of various experimental conditions under investigation, the consensus among the researchers and practitioners is that distributed practice schedules are superior to massed practice for the performance of a great majority of motor skills and activities. However, the amount of actual learning may be the same under each condition. Tests of retention often indicate little differences in performance between groups practiced under each condition.

GENERAL RESEARCH FINDINGS

1. Distributed practice schedules yield better immediate performance than massed practice.
2. Distributed practice results in superior immediate retention than massed practice with no difference evident with long-term retention.
3. Wide variations are found as to the optimal rest interval between trials, depending on the intensity and duration of the task employed.

REFERENCES

Adams, J. A. and Reynolds, B.: Effect of shift in distribution of practice conditions following interpolated rest. *J Exp Psychol*, *47*:32, 1954.
Ammons, Robert: Effects of distribution of practice on rotary pursuit hits. *J Exp Psychol*, *41*:17, 1951.
Carron, A.: Performance and learning in a discrete motor task under the massed versus distributed practice. *Res Q Am Assoc Health Phys Educ*, *40*:481, 1969.
Carron, A. V. and Leavitt, J.: Individual differences in two motor learning tasks under massed practice. *Percept Mot Skills*, *27*:499, 1965.
Cook, B. and Hilgard, E.: Distributed practice in motor learning: Progressively increasing and decreasing rests. *J Exp Psychol*, *39*:169, 1949.
Digman, J. M.: Growth of a motor skill as a function of distribution of practice. *J Exp Psychol*, *57*:310, 1959.
Knapp, C. and Dixon, R.: Learning to juggle. I: A study to determine the effect of two different distributions of practice on learning efficiency. *Res Q Am Assoc Health Phys Educ*, *21*:331, 1950.
Lewis, D. and Lowe, W. F.: Retention of skill on the SAM complex coordinator. *Proc Iowa Acad Sci*, *63*:591, 1956.
Mordock, J.: Distribution of practice in paired-associate learning. *Am J Ment Defic*, *73*:399, 1968.
Mohr, D.: The contributions of physical activity to skill learning. *Res Q Am Assoc Health Phys Educ*, *31*:321, 1960.
Niemeyer, R.: Part versus whole methods and massed versus distributed practice in learning of selected large muscle activities. Unpublished doctoral dissertation, University of Southern California, 1958.
Oxendine, J. B.: Effect of progressively changing practice schedules on the learning of a motor skill. *Res Q Am Assoc Health Phys Educ*, *36*:307, 1965.
Reynolds, B. and Bilodeau, I. McD.: Acquisition and retention of three psychomotor tests as a function of distribution of practice during acquisition. *J Exp Psychol*, *44*:19, 1952.

Ryan, E.: Pre-rest and post-rest performance on the stabilometer as a factor of distribution of practice. *Res Q Am Assoc Health Phys Educ*, *36*:197, 1965.

Singer, R. N.: Massed and distributed practice effects on the acquisition and retention of a novel basketball skill. *Res Q Am Assoc Health Phys Educ*, *36*:68, 1965.

Singer, R. N.: *Motor Learning and Human Performance*. New York, Macmillan 1968, p. 190.

Young, O.: Rate of learning in relation of spacing of practice periods in archery and badminton. *Res Q Am Assoc Phys Educ*, *25*:231, 1954.

LABORATORY EXPERIMENT

PURPOSE. To determine the effects of massed and distributed practice upon the learning and performance of a fine motor task.

EQUIPMENT. Pursuit rotor (see Appendix for illustration and explanation of apparatus.)

DESIGN. Two groups randomly assigned, one group practices under massed practice conditions, the other under distributed practice conditions.

PROCEDURE. Without warm-up, on Day I, subjects in the massed practice group will complete the equivalent of twenty thirty-second trials on the pursuit rotor. The rotor will turn at 60 RPM's as the subject is given six hundred seconds of performance without a rest pause. On Day II, five additional trials will be given with fifteen-second rest intervals between trials.

The subjects in the distributed practice group will follow the identical procedure as massed practice subjects on Day I with the exception of the rest period, which will be of fifteen-second duration and administered after each of the twenty trials. On Day II, five additional trials will be given.

The time each subject is on the target disc should be recorded with a timer, preferably at .01 second.

RESULTS.

1. Record the resultant data on the master sheet provided.
2. Test for significant differences between the means of Day I scores, by use of the *t*-statistic.
3. Test for significant differences between the mean scores on Day II.

FIELD EXPERIMENT

PURPOSE. To determine the effects of massed and distributed practice upon learning and performance of a gross motor task.

EQUIPMENT. One bongo-board (a wooden cylinder and board) and a stop-watch (see diagram of task).

DESIGN. Two groups randomly assigned, one group practices under massed practice conditions, the other under distributed practice conditions.

PROCEDURE. Without warm-up on Day I, subjects in the massed practice group will complete the equivalent of fifteen sixty-second trials on the bongo-board: nine hundred seconds (15 minutes) of performance without a rest pause. On Day II, five additional trials will be given with twenty-second rest intervals between trials.

The subjects in the distributed practice group will follow the identical procedure as the massed practice group on Day I with the exception of the rest period which will be of twenty-second duration and administered after each of the fifteen trials. On Day II, five additional trials will be given. The number of times each subject is off-balance, i.e. the side of the board hits the floor, should be recorded.

RESULTS.

1. Record resultant data on the master sheet provided.

2. Test for significant differences between the means of Day I scores, by use of the *t*-statistic.

3. Test for significant differences between the mean scores on Day II.

The bongo-board.

LABORATORY EXPERIMENT: Massed and Distributed Practice Data Sheet

Massed

Subjects	TRIALS DAY I																				ΣX_{1-20}	DAY II					ΣX_{1-5}
	1	2	3	4	5	6	7	8	9	10	11	12	13	14	15	16	17	18	19	20		1	2	3	4	5	
1																											
2																											
3																											
4																											
5																											

$\Sigma\Sigma X =$ $\Sigma\Sigma X =$

Distributed

Subjects	TRIALS DAY I																				ΣX_{1-20}	DAY II					ΣX_{1-5}
	1	2	3	4	5	6	7	8	9	10	11	12	13	14	15	16	17	18	19	20		1	2	3	4	5	
1																											
2																											
3																											
4																											
5																											

$\Sigma\Sigma X =$ $\Sigma\Sigma X =$

FIELD EXPERIMENT Massed and Distributed Practice Data Sheet

Massed

Subjects	TRIALS DAY I															$\Sigma X_{1\text{-}15}$	DAY II					$\Sigma X_{1\text{-}5}$
	1	2	3	4	5	6	7	8	9	10	11	12	13	14	15		1	2	3	4	5	
1																						
2																						
3																						
4																						
5																						
$\Sigma\Sigma X=$																	$\Sigma\Sigma X=$					

Distributed

Subjects	TRIALS DAY I															$\Sigma X_{1\text{-}15}$	DAY II					$\Sigma X_{1\text{-}5}$
	1	2	3	4	5	6	7	8	9	10	11	12	13	14	15		1	2	3	4	5	
1																						
2																						
3																						
4																						
5																						
$\Sigma\Sigma X=$																	$\Sigma\Sigma X=$					

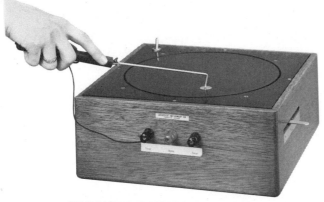

VARIABLE ROTARY PURSUIT

Figure 6-4: This pursuit rotor has become a classic piece of apparatus for the study of perceptual motor skills and for the study of learning. The unit has four speeds for the turntable top of 15, 30, 45, and 60 RPM. However, to replace the standard twenty second ON/20 second OFF testing period, a completely variable solid state percentage timer has been added to enable operator to vary the on and off time.

PHOTO-ELECTRIC ROTARY PURSUIT APPARATUS

Figure 6-5: A photo-electric principle is used to achieve versatile and reliable operation. A sensitivity control allows use of the instrument under virtually any ambient lighting conditions. The target speed is continuously variable from 10 to 100 RPM in *both forward and reverse directions*. This unit is designed to operate:

1. External counters
2. Stopclock—measure time on-time off target
3. Number of target hits.
4. Number of disc revolutions.
5. Provision for external timer to control trial and rest periods.

Variations in disc size and target patterns are limited only by the ingenuity of the experimenter since such changes only require changing the provided glass target patterns or to mask off the pattern desired on a similar size glass.

APPENDIX

PURCHASED EQUIPMENT. Pursuit rotor equipment may be purchased from the Lafayette Instrument Company, P.O. Box 279, 52 By-Pass, Lafayette, Indiana.

EXPLANATION OF APPARATUS. The pursuit rotor consists of a turntable rotating at a designated speed, e.g. 60 RPM. A variable sized metal contact point or target 7.75 cm from the center is set flush into the revolving disc.

The subject holds a stylus probe which is hinged so he can follow the rotating target without being able to press down on it. The time that the stylus is held in contact with the metal target is measured by an electric timer calibrated in .01 seconds. The illustration that follows shows how the pursuit rotor can be used in an isolated testing situation, with the time-on-target timer located outside of the testing booth.

CONSTRUCTED APPARATUS. The following steps should enable one to add the necessary equipment and wiring to a record player to convert it to a pursuit rotor.

Remove the case surrounding the record player and the turntable from the record player itself. Two hot wires leading into the motor should be observable and one wire from each is to be taped off. These two leads should be run into a 12 volt step-down transformer. One of the lead wires from the transformer is attached to the motor casing. If a hole in the casing is drilled and the wire attached to it with a sheet metal screw, make positively sure that neither the drill nor the screw has penetrated the motor's windings or other internal parts. To make the attachment simple, use one of the screws already present in the casing (if any) and attach the wire to it. Take the other wire from the transformer and run it to and through a relay switch and then to the stylus.

Grounding one wire to the casing enables electricity to flow through the casing, through the turntable, and to the contact spot (disc) attached to the top of the turntable. When the stylus comes in contact with the disc on the turntable, the circuit is completed and current flows through it. This flow of current causes the relay switch to close and activate the feedback mechanism.

Now cut a round circle in the rubber facing of the turntable. Do not cut completely through the turntable. The size of the circle is an individual matter and depends on how difficult one wishes to make the task. (Note also that the variable speed of the record player enables one to make the test easier or more difficult.) The circle may be filled with solder, or a coin-sized piece of metal could be soldered in place. Two things to remember are that the disc must have good contact with the metal of the turntable and be kept flush with the surface of the turntable.

Install a connector (screw-on or plug-in socket type) for plugging in a feedback apparatus (timer or counter) to the pursuit rotor. This connector is wired into the relay switch so that when the relay switch is activated, the two wires plugged into it from the feedback mechanism are switched together and form a circuit. Reassemble the phonograph pursuit rotor and test its operation. If it does not operate, check connections against those in the diagram.

To make a stylus is also a simple operation. Obtain a number 20 nail. Attach the lead wire to it securely with solder or tape (be sure the contact is good). Next wrap the nail with adhesive or friction tape leaving the point exposed. This last step makes the stylus easier to handle. The point of the nail may need to be filed so that it is smooth and rounded.

Feedback equipment is more than likely run on 110 volt electricity. Therefore, the wire running from this equipment to the connector on the pursuit rotor carries 110 volts. It would be wise to unplug the feedback apparatus while connecting it to or disconnecting it from the connector on the pursuit rotor. This is especially applicable when the connector consists of screws which are tightened down on the bare leads from the feedback apparatus.

TESTING SITUATION FOR PURSUIT ROTOR

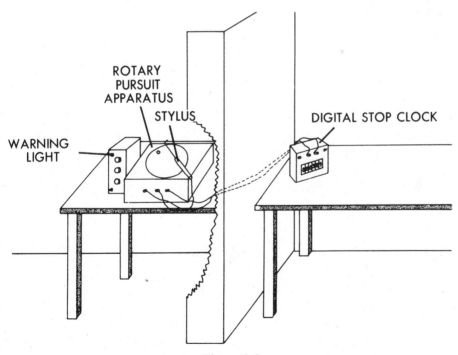

Figure 6-6:

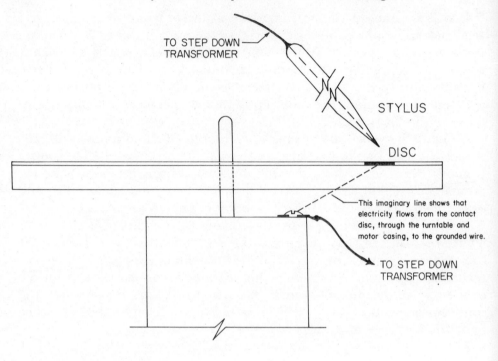

TO STEP DOWN
TRANSFORMER

STYLUS

DISC

This imaginary line shows that
electricity flows from the contact
disc, through the turntable and
motor casing, to the grounded wire.

TO STEP DOWN
TRANSFORMER

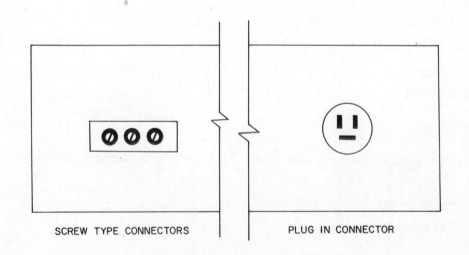

SCREW TYPE CONNECTORS   PLUG IN CONNECTOR

CONNECTORS

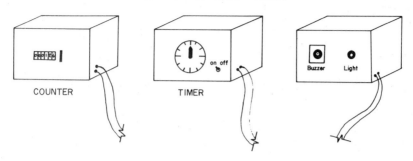

COUNTER   TIMER   Buzzer   Light

ELEMENTARY PURSUIT ROTOR
AND VARIOUS FEEDBACK APPARATUS

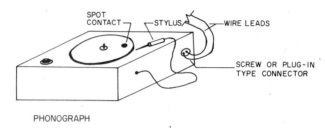

SPOT
CONTACT —   —STYLUS   —WIRE LEADS

SCREW OR PLUG-IN
TYPE CONNECTOR

PHONOGRAPH

ELECTRICAL SCHEMATIC
PURSUIT ROTOR

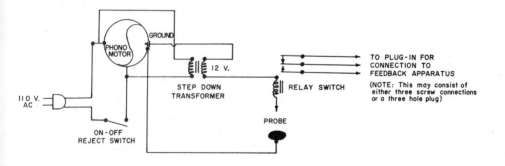

GROUND

PHONO
MOTOR

12 V.

TO PLUG-IN FOR
CONNECTION TO
FEEDBACK APPARATUS

STEP DOWN
TRANSFORMER

RELAY SWITCH

(NOTE: This may consist of
either three screw connections
or a three hole plug)

110 V.
AC

PROBE

ON-OFF
REJECT SWITCH

Chapter 7

TASK GENERALITY VERSUS SPECIFIC-ITY

INTRODUCTION

ONE PROBLEM in motor skill learning that has concerned researchers in psychology and physical education for over a half a century has been whether motor skill is general in nature or task-specific. Generality refers to some common factor or component that may be highly related in a variety of motor skills, whereas specificity implies independence of components in the various skills.

Early researchers, coining such terms as *general motor ability, motor educability,* and *general athletic ability,* believed that such a common underlying motor factor or component existed in all motor activities. It was assumed that if a person could develop a skill with apparent ease and perform well in one task, he would be able to acquire the necessary skills of another motor skill more rapidly and perform at a higher level than one who did not have this basic motor ability. From this assumption attempts were made to predict one's skill level in various athletic activities from scores on a general motor ability test. Several studies produced significant correlation coefficients between different motor skills but of a rather low magnitude which made prediction rather dubious.

More recent researchers, using more refined research methods and statistical techniques, have cast doubt on the validity of generality in the learning and performance of motor skills as earlier indicated.

The foremost proponent of task-specifity in motor learning is Franklin Henry who not only demonstrated support for his proposition through his research but also has offered a theory to explain the specificity nature of tasks. Henry (1960), through his *memory drum theory,* proposed that the higher centers of the brain acted like a modern computer where highly skilled neuromotor patterns were stored until called upon by particular or specific stimuli. These well coordinated movement patterns were the result of practice and experience as well as one's innate ability. If the particular motor pattern was not stored in this motor memory, the new movement task would be uncoordinated and awkwardly performed.

106

The *neurogeometric theory of motion* hypothesized by K. U. Smith (1962) is a further attempt to explain the specificity of skilled movements. Smith theorizes that various neuron systems are differentiated at three levels of the brain and functionally integrate independently the movements of the body and limbs as well as hand-finger manipulation. Refinement of the neurological functioning at these three proposed levels causes the specificity of skilled movement patterns.

Two statistical techniques most employed to determine the commonality of factors are correlational analysis and factor analysis. The correlation technique measures the relationship between two or more variables, with the square of the correlation coefficient indicating the amount of common variance (generality). The remaining variance $(1-r^2)$ is due to the particular task (specificity).

The factor analysis technique is used to identify the underlying basic abilities or factors measured by a large group of tests. Basically, factor analysis utilizes correlation techniques of covariance to interrelate test results in a battery of tests. The variance of the scores for each test can be classified into a variance common to the other tests, a variance specific to the test in question, and a variance caused by error and lack of control. Depending on how much variance each test has in common with others, factor analysis will help one determine which basic factors are measured by the test battery. Fleishman (1956) and Guilford (1958) are two of many researchers who have factor analyzed psychomotor abilities of both fine and gross motor skills, identifying various common factors.

In an attempt to determine whether a general factor underlies motor learning and performance, researchers have studied the various components of gross motor movements, fine manual dexterity skills and motor ability batteries, as well as learning rates. In the area of balance, Bachman (1961) compared subjects' performance on two balance tasks, one a ladder climb, the other a stabilometer, with no significant correlations being obtained. The balance ability required by these two balance tasks was evidently task specific.

Various tests of kinesthesis by Scott (1955) and Wiebe (1954) also indicate a factor specificity as subjects who performed well on one test did not necessarily do so on another test.

In comparing reaction times and movement times Henry's (1961) results produced a relationship so low that the prediction of performance of one to the other was negligible.

Studies involving inter-limb skills whether between arms, legs, or a combination have produced low positive intercorrelations suggesting that individual differences noted in the movements were specific to the limbs used as well as to the task (Singer, 1966; Lotter, 1961).

However, a number of individuals are able to demonstrate a high skill level in a variety of activities, which seems to suggest generality in motor skills. This ability is probably based on the presence of abilities and skills common to certain activities. Another possible explanation is that many independent and specific factors tend to come together to form a distinct movement. Together with past experiences, intensive practice, and a high level of motivation, one is able to perform at a high skill level in a variety of activities.

GENERAL RESEARCH FINDINGS

1. Intercorrelations are low between various motor activities, on the whole, indicating great specificity of motor abilities and skills.
2. Performance from one task to another is independent unless situational cues and movement patterns are directly related.
3. Excellence in one motor ability, sport, or skill provides no assurance of successful accomplishment in others.
4. Inter-limb correlations are very low, indicating that response consistency within an individual is highly specific to a given task.
5. Speed of learning one task is usually not a prediction of how fast a second task will be learned.
6. Low and non significant relationships have usually been obtained when comparing reaction times to speed-of-movement times.

REFERENCES

Bachman, J.: Specificity versus generality in learning and performing two large muscle motor tasks. *Res Q Am Assoc Health Phys Educ, 32*:3, 1961.

Buxton, C. and Humphreys, L.: The effect of practice upon intercorrelations of motor skills. *Science, 81*:441, 1935.

Cratty, B.: *Movement behavior and motor learning.* Philadelphia, Lea & Febiger, 1968, p. 40-51.

Fleishman, E. A.: *The Structure and Measurement of Physical Fitness.* Englewood Cliffs, New Jersey, Prentice-Hall, 1964.

Fleishman, E. A.: Factor analysis of complex psychomotor performance and related skills. *J Appl Psychol, 50*:96, 1956.

Fleishman, E. A. and Ellison, G. A.: A factor analysis of five manipulative tests. *J Appl Psychol, 46*:96, 1962.

Gire, E. and Espenschade, A.: The relationship between measures of motor educability and learning of specific motor skills. *Res Q Am Assoc Health Phys Educ, 13*:43, 1942.

Guilford, J. P.: A system of psychomotor abilities. *Am J Psychol, 71*:164, 1958.

Hempel, W. and Fleishman, E. A.: A factor analysis of physical proficiency and manipulative skill. *J Appl Psychol, 39*:12, 1955.

Henry, F.: Reaction time—movement time correlations. *Percept Mot Skills, 12*:63, 1961.

Henry, F.: Specificity versus generality in learning motor skills. *Proc College Phys Educ Assoc, 61*:126, 1958.

Henry, F. and Rogers, D. E.: Increased response latency for complicated movements and a 'memory drum' theory of neuromotor reaction. *Res Q Am Assoc Health Phys Educ, 31*:448, 1960.

Hoskins, R.: The relationship of measurements of general motor capacity to the learning of specific psycho-motor skills. *Res Q Am Assoc Health Phys Educ, 5*:63, 1934.

Lanier, L.: The intercorrelations of speed of reaction measurements. *J Exp Psychol, 17*:371, 1934.

Lotter, W.: Specificity or generality of speed of systematically related movments. *Res Q Am Assoc Health Phys Educ, 32*:55, 1961.

Lotter, W. S.: Interrelationships among reaction times and speeds of movement in different limbs. *Res Q Am Assoc Health Phys Educ, 31*:147, 1960.

Marteniuk, R.: Generality and specificity of learning and performance on two similar speed tasks. *Res Q Am Assoc Health Phys Educ, 40*:518, 1969.

Mendryk, S.: Reaction time, movement time and task specificity relationships at ages 12, 22, and 48 years. *Res Q Am Assoc Health Phys Educ, 31*:156, 1960.

Oxendine, J.: *Psychology of Motor Learning.* New York, Appleton-Century Crofts, 1968, pp. 278-280.

Pierson, W. and Rasch, P.: Generality of speed factor in simple reaction and movement time. *Percept Mot Skills, 11*:123, 1960.

Scott, M. G.: Measurement of kinesthesis. *Res Q Am Assoc Health Phys Educ, 26*:324, 1955.

Seashore, R.: Individual differences in motor skills. *J Gen Psychol, 3*:38, 1939.

Smith, K. U. and Smith, W. M.: *Perception and Motion.* Philadelphia, W. B. Saunders Co., 1962.

Smith, L.: Influence of neuromotor program alteration on the speed of a standard arm movement. *Percept Mot Skills, 15*:327, 1962.

Singer, R. N.: Inter-limb skill ability in motor skill performance. *Res Q Am Assoc Health Phys Educ, 37*:406, 1966.

Singer, R. N.: *Motor Learning and Human Performance.* New York, Macmillan, 1968, pp. 112-115.

Wiebe, V. R.: A study of tests of kinesthesis. *Res Q Am Assoc Health Phys Educ, 25*:222, 1954.

Williams, L.: Specificity versus generality of motor response. *J Mot Behav, 1*:45, 1969.

LABORATORY EXPERIMENT

PURPOSE. To determine whether motor performance is task-specific or general in nature.

EQUIPMENT. Positioning test board, aftereffect apparatus, and weighted cylinder kit (See Appendix for illustrations and descriptions of the apparatus.)

DESIGN. Subjects will act as their own controls on all three tasks of kinesthetic awareness.

PROCEDURE.

1. Positioning test: Each subject will position himself behind the test board. The subject's preferred arm will point to 0 degrees while his

elbow remains on line but centered on the lower edge of the board. The subject is then blindfolded. The experimenter will move the subject's arm to the desired position and return it to 0 degrees. The subject is then asked to replicate the previous movement. The amount of error (absolute) is recorded. Trials are similarly performed using 35, 70, 110, 135, and 160 degrees. These points are twice randomly presented to the subject.

2. Aftereffect test: While blindfolded, each subject is offered a given point on a standard block and spans its width at that point with his thumb and forefinger. The subject then slides these same two fingers on a variable width block until he feels he has reached a similar width as the standard. Ten trials will be performed using a different standard width each time with the absolute amount of error on the variable scale being recorded.

3. Weight discrimination test: While blindfolded each subject will lift a standard weight (medium of all test weights) and decide whether the comparison weight is heavier or lighter than the standard weight. The ten weights will be twice presented in random order with the total number of correct decisions recorded.

RESULTS.
1. Record the resultant data on the master sheet provided.
2. Calculate the reliability of each test using the test-retest method.
3. Using the mean scores calculate the correlation coefficients between:
   (a) the positioning test and the aftereffects test
   (b) the positioning test and the weight discrimination test
   (c) the aftereffects test and the weight discrimination test.
4. Calculate r^2 to determine generality and $1-r^2$ to determine specificity among the test performances.

FIELD EXPERIMENT

PURPOSE. To determine whether motor learning is general or task specific in nature.

EQUIPMENT. Six softballs and a wall target (See diagram.)

DESIGN. Subjects will act as their own controls on the task of throwing for accuracy.

PROCEDURE. Each subject will perform fifteen overhand throws for accuracy at a wall target using a softball from a distance of thirty-five feet, using the preferred hand. After a five-minute rest, each subject will replicate the task, except using the nonpreferred hand. Half the subjects will be tested in one sequence (preferred—nonpreferred hand) and the other subjects will be tested in the reverse sequence in order to counterbalance practice task order effects.

RESULTS.

1. Record the resultant data on the master sheet provided.
2. Run *t*-tests between the mean score of the initial five trials and the mean score of the last five trials, for each test condition.
3. If the learning effect is significant, a correlation between the learning scores of the preferred hand toss and the nonpreferred hand

LABORATORY EXPERIMENT : Generality Versus Specificity Data Sheet

Subjects	Trials										
Positioning Task	70°	135°	35°	160°	70°	160°	110°	135°	110°	35°	Σ X
1											
2											
3											
4											
5											

$$\Sigma\Sigma X =$$

Subjects	Trials										
After Effect Task	1	2	3	4	5	6	7	8	9	10	Σ X
1											
2											
3											
4											
5											

$$\Sigma\Sigma X =$$

Subjects			Trials																					#Correct
Weight	Disc	Test	1	2	3	4	5	6	7	8	9	10	11	12	13	14	15	16	17	18	19	20	
1																							
2																							
3																							
4																							
5																							

$$\Sigma X =$$

toss should be calculated (the learning score is the mean of the initial five scores minus the mean of the final five scores).

4. Calculate the correlation between the mean scores under each testing condition. Also determine generality (r^2) and specificity ($1-r^2$).

APPENDIX

PURCHASED EQUIPMENT. The kinesthetic figural aftereffect apparatus may be purchased from the Marietta Apparatus Company, 118 Maple Street , Marietta, Ohio.

The weighted cylinders set, consisting of a series of eleven weighted plastic cylinders graduated in 50 gram steps from 100 to 600 grams, may also be purchased from the Marietta Apparatus Company, 118 Maple Street, Marietta, Ohio.

FIELD EXPERIMENT : Generality Versus Specificity Data Sheet

Test I							Trials									ΣX_{1-5}	ΣX_{11-15}	ΣX_{1-15}
Subjects	1	2	3	4	5	6	7	8	9	10	11	12	13	14	15			
1																		
2																		
3																		
4																		
5																		
6																		
7																		
															$\Sigma\Sigma X=$			

Test 2							Trials									ΣX_{1-5}	ΣX_{11-15}	ΣX_{1-15}
Subjects	1	2	3	4	5	6	7	8	9	10	11	12	13	14	15			
1																		
2																		
3																		
4																		
5																		
6																		
7																		
															$\Sigma\Sigma X=$			

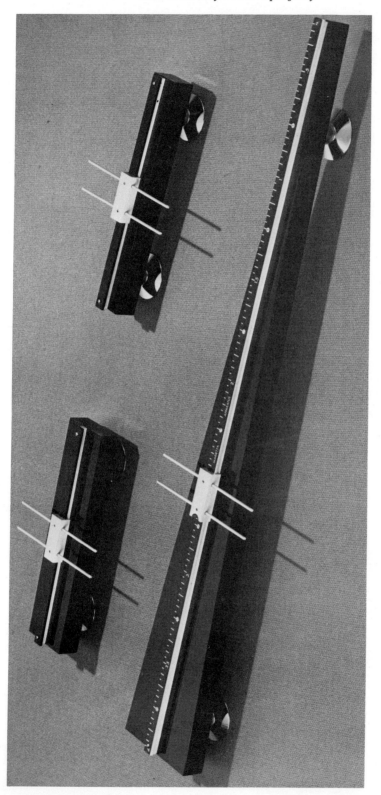

KINESTHETIC FIGURAL AFTEREFFECT APPARATUS

Figure 7-3: This apparatus consists of (a) a variable block, a wedge-shaped piece of hardwood, (b) standard block, parallel-sided, 2.5″ in width, and (c) standard block, parallel-sided, 1.5″ in width.

WEIGHTED CYLINDERS

Figure 7-4: This set, comprised of a series of eleven weighted plastic cylinders graduated in 50 gram steps from 100 to 600 grams, can be used to demonstrate many psychophysical and perceptual phenomena.

Discrimination weights may also be purchased from the Lafayette Instrument Company, P.O. Box 1279, Lafayette, Indiana.

CONSTRUCTED EQUIPMENT. Positioning Test Board: The test board is made of plywood with dimensions 4 feet x 2 1/2 feet x 3/4 inch. A semicircle is lightly traced on the board from one edge to the other. At each degree point along this semicircle, 1-1/2 inch nails are embedded with their heads all approximately one inch above the board. A short six-inch wooden pointer is used to point to the desired degree. (See illustration.)

Aftereffect Apparatus: A number of standard blocks may be made from

WEIGHTS, DISCRIMINATION

Figure 7-5: This set of weights consists of two series. A light series from 75 to 125 grams, and a heavy series from 175 to 225 grams. The two sets have a total of 24 weights. These cartridge type weights come in five gram intervals and are identical in color and size, but are code marked on the bottom. All cartridges are unbreakable vinyl. This series of weights has been designed for rugged and frequent use in any laboratory. Plastic containers have metal sure-sealing tops.

three-fourth inch plywood, parallel-sided, ranging in width from one-half inch to three inches with increments of one-half inch. The variable block is made of one-inch plywood, twenty-four inches long, graduating in width from four inches to 1/4 inch. A twenty-four-inch ruler is attached on top with a sliding block which contains two parallel sticks for calculation of positional error.

Weight Discrimination Test: Identical small glass bottles containing lead shot and packed with cotton. The standard weight bottle weighs 75 grams; the other comparison bottles weigh 60, 65, 70, 80, 85, and 90 grams respectively.

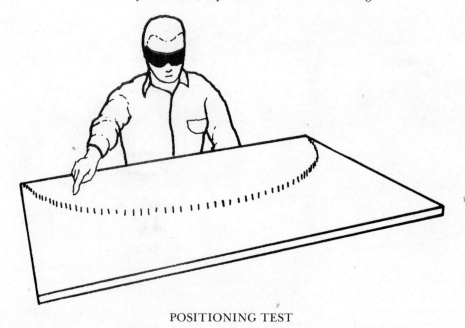

POSITIONING TEST

Figure 7-6: The blindfolded subject attempts to replicate his previous point at a peg.

Chapter 8

MENTAL PRACTICE

INTRODUCTION

A GYMNAST, PREPARING TO PERFORM his routine, stands beside the side horse, closes his eyes, and in his mind's imagination goes through his entire routine. A basketball player is having trouble making foul shots. His coach tells him to sit on the bench and imagine that he is at the foul line and then to imagine that he is shooting ten foul shots. When he completes this procedure, he goes to the foul line and physically attempts ten free throws. A golfer has just hit a beautiful drive. He can't stand on the tee and physically practice the stroke he used, so as he walks down the fairway to his ball, he mentally rehearses the fluid stroke he had on the tee.

Each of these situations are different insofar as their immediate goal is concerned. The gymnast's goal is immediate correct performance. The basketball player's goal is the acquisition or improvement of the skill of foul shooting. The golfer wants to retain the skill he exhibited with his drive so that his next drive will also be a good one. Although the immediate goal may vary, the long range effect of the methods used by these individuals is designed to facilitate learning and performance of a motor skill.

The method used by these individuals is commonly known as mental practice, or the covert rehearsal of a physical skill in the absence of any gross muscular movements. Other terms have been used for mental practice, such as symbolic rehearsal, mental rehearsal, covert rehearsal, introspective rehearsal, imaginary practice, and conceptualization. All these terms, however, refer to one process that most frequently is described in research literature as mental practice.

Investigators in this area of motor learning research have been mainly concerned with mental practice as it relates to three general aspects of learning: (1) initial acquisition of skill, (2) retention of a skill, and (3) improvement of a skill. The results of the research in these areas have generally indicated that mental practice can contribute to the learning and performance of a skill, although contrary findings have been found.

Mental practice as a research topic has usually been studied by the use of experiments having similar designs. The experiments generally consist of three or four groups and involve pretest and posttest situations. Three groups which are almost always used are: (1) no practice (NP) of the task between pretest and posttest; (2) mental practice (MP) only between the tests, and (3) physical practice (PP) only of the task between tests. If a fourth group is used, it is usually a combination mental practice and physical practice (MP-PP) group which practices the task mentally before practicing it physically each practice session.

The methods and procedures used in the experiment depend upon the interest of the experimenter in the three concerns listed above, although the use of the groups will generally be the same. If the experimenter is interested in the initial acquisition of a skill, he must be certain that the task he chooses will be a new one for each of his subjects. If he is concerned with the retention of a skill, the experimenter must establish a criterion score which each subject must attain prior to the mental practice treatment. For testing the improvement of a skill, the experimenter must determine the means of judging how to best indicate amount of improvement. These experiment purpose-specific methodological considerations are but a few of the methodological problems involved in mental practice studies. Some of the general problems involved in mental practice experiments are: (1) instructions to the MP group as to how to mentally practice the task; (2) determining whether or not the subjects actually mentally practiced the task; (3) the amount of practice engaged in during the specified practice time; (4) uncontrolled practice outside the actual practice session; (5) motivation, and (6) the consistent number of practice sessions for every group.

Results of studies concerned with the acquisition of and the improvement in a skill have generally indicated that the performance from the pretest to the posttest (often expressed in percentages) is generally as one might intuitively expect, i.e. that performance is better with PP only than with MP only or NP (e.g. Trussell, 1952; Corbin, 1967). However it has been shown that performance is better with MP only than for NP (e.g. Perry, 1939; Shick, 1970). With the inclusion of the MP-PP combination group, results have indicated that performance is as good as or better than PP (e.g. Stebbins, 1968; Oxendine, 1969).

A question that might come to mind here is, shouldn't performance and the amount of MP that will be beneficial be related to intelligence? Oxendine (1969) considered this question and concluded that IQ scores were not indicative of one's ability to benefit from mental practice.

Results of studies concerning the effect of MP on retention of a motor skill have been inconclusive. Very few studies have been done concerning this aspect of MP, and thus it remains an area with unanswered questions and needed research.

It appears then that the use of mental practice can be an effective means of facilitating the learning of a motor skill. What explanation can account for this phenomenon? Richardson (1967b) presented three explanatory hypotheses: (1) the MP group may be more highly motivated than the NP group since the MP group is involved in the experiment every session while the NP group only attends the first and last session; (2) any person will learn something from his initial physical performance of a skill and the MP group has the opportunity to symbolize elements of the skill and rehearse them, whereas the NP group does not have this opportunity, and (3) "the psychoneuromuscular explanation," which involves the consideration that during the mental practice, the subject, by imagining a movement, produces action currents in the muscle groups used in making the actual movement with feedback information produced, thus allowing the person to make appropriate corrections for the next imagined practice attempt.

Whatever the reason, mental practice does seem to be an aid in the learning and performance of motor tasks. It is definitely better than no practice at all and, if combined properly with physical practice, may be an equally effective means of learning as total physical practice, given the same amount of practice time.

GENERAL RESEARCH FINDINGS

Some of the more conclusive findings in the area of mental practice are:

1. Mental practice positively influences the learning of a motor skill.
2. For the acquisition or learning of a motor skill, performance after physical practice only is generally superior to mental practice only, and performance after mental practice only is generally superior to no practice.
3. Combining mental practice and physical practice trials will result in as good or better improvement of performance as physical practice alone.
4. Efficacy of mental practice does not appear to be related to intelligence.

REFERENCES

Clark, L. V.: Effect of mental practice on the development of a certain motor skill. *Res Q Am Assoc Health Phys Educ, 31*:560, 1960.
Conly, A. G.: A comparative study of the effects of pretest and mental practice on the

ability of athletes and non-athletes to perform a posttest of a motor skill. Unpublished doctoral dissertation, University of New Mexico, 1968.

Corbin, C. B.: Effects of mental practice on the development of a unique motor skill. *Proceedings NCPEAM,* 1965.

Corbin, C. B.: Effects of mental practice on skill development after controlled practice. *Res Q Am Assoc Health Phys Educ, 38*:534, 1967.

Cratty, B. J. and Densmore, A. E.: Activity during rest and learning a gross movement task. *Percept Mot Skills, 17*:250, 1963.

Egstrom, G. H.: Effect of an emphasis on conceptualizing techniques during early learning of a gross motor skill. *Res Q Am Assoc Health Phys Educ, 35*:472, 1964.

Halverson, L. E.: A comparison of three methods of teaching motor skills. Unpublished master's thesis, University of Wisconsin, 1949.

Jones, J. G.: Motor learning without demonstration of physical practice under two conditions of mental practice. *Res Q Am Assoc Health Phys Educ, 36*:270, 1965.

Kelsey, I. B.: Effects of mental practice and physical practice upon muscular endurance. *Res Q Am Assoc Health Phys Educ, 32*:47, 1961.

Leuba, C.; and Dunlap, R.: Conditioning imagery. *J Exp Psychol, 41*:352, 1951.

Morrisett, L. N., Jr.: The role of implicit practice in learning. Unpublished doctoral dissertation, Yale University, 1956.

Oxendine, J. B.: Effect of mental and physical practice on the learning of three motor skills. *Res Q Am Assoc Health Phys Educ, 40*:755, 1969.

Perry, H. M.: The relative efficiency of actual and imaginary practice in five selected tasks. *Arch Psychol, 34*:5, 1939.

Richardson, A.: Has mental practice any relevance to physiotherapy? *Physiotherapy, 50*:148, 1964.

Richardson, A.: Mental practice: A review and discussion. Part I. *Res Q Am Assoc Health Phys Educ, 38*:95, 1967a.

Richardson, A.: Mental practice: A review and discussion. Part II. *Res Q Am Assoc Health Phys Educ, 38*:263, 1967b.

Riley, E. and Start, K. B.: The effect of the spacing of mental and physical practices on the acquisition of a physical skill. *Aust J Phys Educ, 20*:13, 1960.

Rubin-Rabson, G. A.: A comparison of two forms of mental rehearsal and keyboard overlearning. *J Educ Psychol, 32*:593, 1941.

Sackett, R. S.: The influences of symbolic rehearsal upon the retention of a maze habit. *J Gen Psychol, 10*:376, 1934.

Sackett, R. S.: The relationship between amount of symbolic rehearsal and retention of a maze habit. *J Gen Psychol, 13*:113, 1935.

Samuels, T. E.: The effects of mental practice on the acquisition of a perceptual-motor skill. Unpublished doctoral dissertation, Washington State University, 1969.

Shaw, W. A.: The relations of muscular action potentials to imaginal weight lifting. *Arch Psychol, 35*:1, 1940.

Shick, J.: Effects of mental practice on selected volleyball skills for college women. *Res Q Am Assoc Health Phys Educ, 41*:88, 1970.

Short, P. L.: The objective study of mental imagery. *Br J Psychol, 44*:38, 1953.

Singer, R. N. and Witker, J.: Mental rehearsal and point of introduction within the context of overt practice. *Percept Mot Skills, 31*:169, 1970.

Smith, L. E. and Harrison, J. S.: Comparison of the effects of visual, motor, mental and guided practice upon speed and accuracy of performing a simple eye-hand coordination task. *Res Q Am Assoc Health Phys Educ, 33*:299, 1962.

Start, K. B.: Kinesthesia and mental practice. *Res Q Am Assoc Health Phys Educ, 35*:316, 1964.

Start, K. B.: Relationship between intelligence and the effect of mental practice on the performance of a motor skill. *Res Q Am Assoc Health Phys Educ, 30*:644, 1960.

Start, K. B.: The influence of subjectively assessed "games ability" on gain in motor performance after mental practice. *J Gen Psychol, 67*:159, 1962.

Start, K. B. and Richardson, A.: Imagery and mental practice. *Br J Educ Psychol, 34*:280, 1964.

Stebbins, R. J.: A comparison of the effects of physical and mental practice in learning a motor skill. *Res Q Am Assoc Health Phys Educ, 39*:714, 1968.

Steel, W. I.: The effect of mental practice on the acquisition of a motor skill. *J Phys Educ, 44*:101, 1952.

Trussell, E. M.: Mental practice as a factor in the learning of a complex motor skill. Unpublished master's thesis, University of California, 1952.

Twining, W. E.: Mental practice and physical practice in learning a motor skill. *Res Q Am Assoc Health Phys Educ, 20*:432, 1949.

Ulrich, E.: Some experiments on the function of mental training in the acquisition of motor skills. *Ergonomics, 10*:411, 1967.

Vandell, R. A., Davis, R. A., and Clugston, H. A.: The function of mental practice in the acquisition of motor skills. *J Gen Psychol, 29*:243, 1943.

Waterland, J. C.: The effect of mental practice combined with kinesthetic perception when the practice precedes each overt performance of a motor skill. Unpublished master's thesis, University of Wisconsin, 1956.

Wills, B. J.: Mental practice as a factor in the performance of two motor tasks. Unpublished doctoral dissertation, University of Wisconsin, 1956.

Wilson, M. E.: The relative effect of mental practice and physical practice in learning the tennis forehand and backhand drives. Unpublished doctoral dissertation, University of Iowa, 1960.

LABORATORY EXPERIMENT

PURPOSE. To compare the differences in performance gain scores in the acquisition of a simple motor task involving cognitive patterning decisions, under the conditions of no practice (NP), mental practice (MP), physical practice (PP), and a combination of mental practice-physical practice (MP-PP).

EQUIPMENT. Minnesota Dexterity Test (MDT). See the chapter on speed and accuracy for further information concerning this test. Also, a stopwatch or timer.

PROCEDURE. Form four groups of two subjects each. Randomly assign conditions to these groups: No practice (NP); mental practice (MP); physical practice (PP), and mental practice-physical practice (MP-PP).

Give each of the subjects in all groups a pretest, using the following procedures (if only one MDT is available, test only one subject at a time through the entire pretest, practice, posttest sequence):

1. The subject should be seated comfortably at a table. The MDT should be positioned on the table so that the long side of the board faces

the subject. The subject should sit so that his nonpreferred hand will be in direct line with the center of the MDT.

2. Instruct the subject that he is to use his nonpreferred hand and begin to turn the pegs over from the white side up to the black side up in the following sequence:

one peg in row one; three pegs in row two; two pegs in row three; three pegs in row four; two pegs in row three; three pegs in row two; and one peg in row one.

This sequence should allow a stair-step type of pattern and will look like:

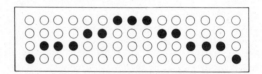

Notice that the pattern is symmetrical and follows a 1-3-2-3-2-3-1 sequence of numbers of pegs turned over. His score will be the amount of time it takes to complete this pattern.

3. Begin the timing with the words "Ready—Go"; record the subject's time on the data sheet provided.

After a subject has been pretested, begin his respective practice sessions. The practice will be as follows:

NP: no practice at all. Give this group a task to do that will insure that it is not mentally practicing the task during its time of no practice. This time period should be for three minutes. At the conclusion of the three minutes, give this group a posttest.

MP: instruct this group to mentally practice the task. The subjects should think of the pattern used and its method for turning over the pegs. Each subject should mentally rehearse ten trials, after which time will follow the posttest.

PP: Instruct this group to begin a series of ten practice trials. Time each trial but give no knowledge of results. At the conclusion of the ten trials, administer the posttest.

MP-PP: This group will practice the task mentally for one trial then physically for one trial and so on for ten trials. At the conclusion of the ten trials, administer the posttest.

The time between trials should be only the amount of time needed by the experimenter to turn the pegs back to the white side up position. Each subject is to continue the task for each trial until the pattern is correct. If he completes the task but the pattern is incorrect, the experimenter should say, "Wrong, the pattern is 1-3-2-3-2-3-1." Allow the clock to run during this time and for his correction.

Do not permit members of other groups to observe the testing or permit subjects that have been tested to communicate with those waiting to be tested. Do not explain the procedure to any subject until he arrives for the pretest.

RESULTS. Record the times for each subject for the pretest and the posttest.

Calculate a gain score for each subject and, using a *t*-test for correlated measures, determine if any significant improvement from the pretest to the posttest occurred for the groups. Thus, four *t*-tests should be calculated.

Using the gain score as the dependent measure, determine if the groups improved similarly by means of a one-way ANOVA. If a significant *F* is found, determine where the differences are by using the Newman-Keuls test or any other multiple comparison test. These statistical procedures are explained in Chapter 1.

FIELD EXPERIMENT

PURPOSE. To compare the difference in gain in the acquisition of a motor skill, the basketball bounce pass, under the conditions of no practice (NP), mental practice (MP), and physical practice (PP).

EQUIPMENT. Regulation basketball, wall marking material (chalk or tape)

PROCEDURE. For this experiment assign subjects to groups by equating them according to test scores. This is done by first pretesting all subjects on the task and to then equally divide them into the three groups.

The pretest, and the subsequent practice and posttest, will consist of using the non-preferred hand; the subject will bounce a basketball to a target on a wall fifteen feet in front of him.

The target should be drawn as three concentric squares, with twelve inches between squares. The outer square should be sixty inches square (5' x 5'):

Score values for the target are: center square—3 pts; second square—2 pts.; outside square—1 pt. A ball hitting a line should count for the higher value. Draw or mark a restraining line five feet long, fifteen feet from the target and parallel to it.

For the pretest and the posttest, the subject will bounce the basketball with his nonpreferred hand to the target. No practice trials should be given. The subject's score will be his total points for the ten trials.

For the practice sessions, the following procedures will be used:

NP: no practice between pre and posttests; engage these subjects in other activity during the practice time to prevent any rehearsal of

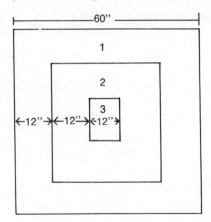

any kind. The practice session time can be estimated to be approximately five or six minutes.

MP: mental practice only between the pre and posttests. These subjects are to mentally practice attempting to hit the center of the target with the basketball. They should imagine that they are performing this task for three series of ten trials each with a one-minute rest between each series of trials.

PP: physical practice only between the pre and posttests. Each subject in this group receives three series of ten trials each, with a one-minute rest between each series of trials. Record the total points for each series.

The posttest should be conducted as soon as the practice sessions are completed. This test should be conducted exactly as the pretest. Record all data on the data sheet provided.

RESULTS. Compare pre and posttest scores for each group by means of a gain score analysis, a correlated *t*-test. This test will indicate if the group in fact performed better on the posttest than on the pretest.

Since the groups were assumed to be equal at the beginning of the experiment, an analysis of the posttest scores will indicate if there are real differences between the groups after the various practice conditions. A one-way ANOVA should be used here. If a significant F is obtained, a multiple comparison test, such as the Newman-Keuls, should be used to determine where the differences are.

Since this experiment suggests only two subjects per group, consider using nonparametric tests for these analyses. A Wilcoxon matched-pairs signed-ranks test may be used to determine if the posttest—pretest scores are different. The matched-pair here is the pretest and posttest for each subject. Thus rank each subject according to difference between the two tests. To test for posttest differences, a Kruskal-Wallis one-way analysis of variance may be used. Both of these tests may be found in: Siegel, S.: *Nonparametric Statistics for the Behavioral Sciences.* New York, McGraw-Hill, 1956.

A bar-graph of the gain or improvement scores may also be used to pictorially represent the differences between the groups' improvement scores. The horizontal axis of the graph should be the three groups; the vertical axis should be the gain scores.

LABORATORY EXPERIMENT : MENTAL PRACTICE DATA SHEET

GROUP	S	PRETEST	POSTTEST	GAIN (G)	G^2
NP	1				
	2				
				$\Sigma G=$ $\frac{\Sigma G}{N=}$ $\bar{G}=$	$\Sigma G^2=$ $\quad t=$
MP	1				
	2				
				$\Sigma G=$ $\frac{\Sigma G}{N=}$ $\bar{G}=$	$\Sigma G^2=$ $\quad t=$
PP	1				
	2				
				$\Sigma G=$ $\frac{\Sigma G}{N=}$ $\bar{G}=$	$\Sigma G^2=$ $\quad t=$
MP-PP	1				
	2				
				$\Sigma G=$ $\frac{\Sigma G}{N=}$ $\bar{G}=$	$\Sigma G^2=$ $\quad t=$

ANOVA TABLE :

source	df	SS	MS	F
Treatment				
Subjects x Treatment				
Total				

FIELD EXPERIMENT : MENTAL PRACTICE DATA SHEET

GROUP	S	PRETEST	POSTTEST	GAIN (G)	G^2
NP	1				
	2				
				$\Sigma G=$ $\frac{\Sigma G}{N=}$ $\bar{G}=$	$\Sigma G^2=$ $\underline{t}=$
MP	1				
	2				
				$\Sigma G=$ $\frac{\Sigma G}{N=}$ $\bar{G}=$	$\Sigma G^2=$ $\underline{t}=$
PP	1				
	2				
				$\Sigma G=$ $\frac{\Sigma G}{N=}$ $\bar{G}=$	$\Sigma G^2=$ $\underline{t}=$
MP-PP	1				
	2				
				$\Sigma G=$ $\frac{\Sigma G}{N=}$ $\bar{G}=$	$\Sigma G^2=$ $\underline{t}=$

ANOVA TABLE :

source	df	SS	MS	F
Treatment				
Subjects x Treatment				
Total				

Chapter 9

WHOLE AND PART PRACTICE METHODS

INTRODUCTION

A PRIMARY CONCERN IN the teaching of motor skills is the learner's ability to initially comprehend the task at hand. Pursuit rotor tracking is a skill which is somewhat difficult to master but certainly not difficult to comprehend. The object of the task is to maintain a stylus in contact with a rotating target, nothing more. On the other hand, the skill of bowling requires a considerably greater cognitive involvement on the part of the learner. The object is simple: knock down the pins with a ball. However, successful bowling combines a number of sub-skills necessary for execution. The holding of the ball, approach, arm swing, and release are vital *parts* of bowling. It is rare for the naive learner to initially comprehend the parts or sub-skills of bowling sufficiently to perform adequately. The learner cannot process and subsequently perform all of the parts of the skill when first confronted with them.

The speed and effectiveness with which motor skills are acquired depend upon the nature of the task and the optimum method of practice. Practice on the whole task is suitable for many simple activities, with practice on the parts suggested for more difficult tasks. Often there is no suggested ideal method of practice and the student's preferred learning style might be the determining factor.

Since 1900 the whole-part problem has been rather extensively investigated although much of the work has been in the cognitive areas of memorizing prose, poetry, or nonsense syllable learning. The majority of the research concerning motor skills has taken place in the laboratory setting with very few sports skills having been investigated.

Some clarification of the interpretation of whole and part methods of instruction is in order. The whole skill can refer to the tennis serve or the sport of tennis. However, execution of the total serve usually represents the whole method of practice. If emphasis is placed on the troublesome parts of the serve following whole practice, a whole-part sequence is the result.

Should the tennis serve be taught by the pure part method, then the order of practice would go somewhat like this: (a) toss the ball to the proper height, (b) move racket upward and cock behind the body with the elbow upward, (c) extend the arm fully, and (d) follow through with the racket as if to make contact with the ball. Each of these sub-skills would be mastered before any attempt to integrate them into the whole skill.

The progressive part method allows one to learn (a), learn (b), combine (a) and (b), learn (c), combine (a), (b), and (c) until the whole skill is learned. Still another alternative is the simplified whole method which is practice of all but one or two of the pure parts of the whole skill. For an adequate understanding of the whole-part problem consideration must be given to the particular type of the whole and part practice regimen.

Naylor and Briggs (1963) have made an effort to formulate a workable model or structure by which the proper method of skill presentation can be predicted on the basis of the nature of the skill. Naylor and Briggs found the efficiency of either method related to an interaction of the complexity of a task and its component organization. This *model*, although based essentially on a non-motor task, can be quite effectively applied to motor tasks.

Task complexity is defined as the demands which are placed on the learner's information processing and/or memory storage capacity by each of the various dimensions of the task. The complexity of bowling then may be appraised by identifying the dimensions, e.g. approach, arm swing, release, and assigning a value of complexity to each dimension. In dealing with sport skills it is oftentimes difficult to differentiate between skills on the basis of complexity. Firstly, the dimensions must be isolated, being rather arbitrary in skills of a continuous nature. Secondly, demand charcteristics of the dimensions must be generalized to account for vast individual differences in the learner's previous experiences, intelligence, level of motivation, and body strength.

The organization of a task is determined by the ease with which the task dimensions fit together. Organization is assessed by examining the interrelationships existing among the task dimensions and arbitrarily assigning a value corresponding to the demands placed on the learner to put the dimensions together fluidly. Having isolated the dimensions of bowling, one must determine the demands placed on the learner to incorporate and display proper form characteristic of a skilled bowler.

To facilitate the application of the complexity-organization model a continuum of dimension complexity may be formed moving from skills of low complexity to those of high complexity. The same procedure may be followed for the factor of task organization. The predictive value of the model can be expressed in these two ways: (1) For skills of high organization and low complexity, the whole method should be more efficient than the part method, and (2) For skills of low organization and high complexity, better results should be obtained through use of the part method.

The following illustration will help summarize the task complexity and organization interrelationships.

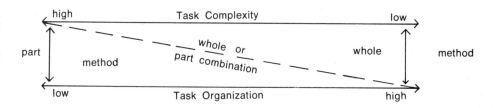

Results of studies by Naylor and Briggs (1963) and Briggs and Naylor (1962) support the model directly. An analysis of task components in a number of other studies also support the predictive validity of the model, e.g. Barton (1921); Beeby (1930); Briggs and Brodgen (1954); Crafts (1932); Cross (1937); Niemeyer (1958); Seagoe (1936); and Sharpe (1957).

GENERAL RESEARCH FINDINGS

1. In general, for skills of low organization and high complexity, better results will be obtained through the use of the part method.
2. In general, for skills of high organization and low complexity, better results will be obtained through the use of the whole method.
3. Mature learners of above average intelligence profit more from a whole method of presentation than young and dull learners.
4. Should the disparity of the parts of a skill lose their relationships with the whole skill, motivation will suffer due to boredom and lack of direction.
5. Part practice should not be used until the learner understands the entire pattern and can fill in mentally the other parts of the act he is practicing.

REFERENCES

Barton, J. W.: Smaller versus larger units in learning the maze. *J Exp Psychol, 4*:414, 1921.
Beeby, C. E.: An experimental investigation into the simultaneous constituents in an act of skill. *Br J Psychol, 20*:336, 1930.

Bilodeau, E. A.: Variations in knowledge of component performance and its effects upon part-part and part-whole relations. *J Exp Psychol, 50*:215, 1955.

Bilodeau, E. A. and Bilodeau, I.: The contribution of component activities to the total psychomotor task. *J Exp Psychol, 47*:37, 1954.

Briggs, G. F. and Brodgen, W. J.: The effects of component practice on performance of a lever-positioning skill. *J Exp Psychol, 48*:375, 1954.

Briggs, G. E. and Naylor, J. C.: The relative efficiency of several training methods as a function of transfer task complexity. *J Exp Psychol, 64*:505, 1962.

Briggs, G. E. and Waters, C. K.: Training and transfer as a function of component interaction. *J Exp Psychol, 56*:492, 1958.

Brown, R. W.: A comparison of the whole, part, and combination methods of learning piano music. *J Exp Psychol, 11*:235, 1928.

Crafts, L. W.: Whole and part methods with visual and spatial material. *Am J Psychol, 44*:526, 1932.

Crafts, L. W. and Allen, R. N.: A comparison of two methods of learning an act requiring the simultaneous use of two hands. *Psychol Bull, 31*:625, 1934.

Cross, T. J.: A comparison of the whole method, the minor game method, and the whole part method of teaching basketball to ninth grade boys. *Res Q Am Assoc Health Phys Educ, 8*:49, 1937.

Davies, D. B.: A comparative study of the whole and part methods of teaching handball to beginning students. Unpublished doctoral dissertation, University of Oregon, Eugene, 1971.

Davis, A. J. and Meenes, M.: Factors determining the relative efficiency of the whole-part method of learning. *J Exp Psychol, 15*:716, 1932.

Fleishman, E. A. and Fruchter, B.: Component and total task relations at different stages of learning a complex tracking task. *Percept Mot Skills, 20*:1305, 1965.

Freedle, R. O., Zauala, A., and Fleishman, E. A.: Studies of component-total task relations: Order of component-total task practice and total task predictability. *Hum Factors, 10*:283, 1968.

Goggin, J. and Postman, L.: Whole versus part learning of serial lists as a function of meaningfulness and intralist similarity. *J Exp Psychol, 68*:140, 1964.

Holt, A., Thorpe, I. A., and Holt, L.: Two methods of teaching beginning swimming. *Res Q Am Assoc Health Phys Educ, 41*:371, 1970.

Knapp, C. G. and Dixon, W. R.: Learning to Juggle: II a study of whole and part methods. *Res Q Am Assoc Health Phys Educ, 23*:398, 1952.

Lawther, J. D. and Cooper, J. N.: Methods and principles of teaching physical education. *College Phys Educ Assoc Proc, 58*:25, 1955.

Luh, C. M.: Combination and division of a motor skill. *Chung Hwa Educational Review, 23*:233, 1935.

McGeoch, G. O.: The IQ as factor in the whole-part problem. *J Exp Psychol, 24*:333, 1931.

McGeoch, G. O.: Whole-part problem. *Psychol Bull, 28*:713, 1931.

McGuigan, F. J.: Variations of whole-part methods of learning. *J Educ Psychol, 51*:213, 1960.

McGuigan, F. J. and MacCaslin, E. F.: Whole and part methods of learning a perceptual motor skill. *Am J Psychol, 68*:658, 1955.

Mathis, M. D.: Whole-part versus the part-whole method in teaching the golf swing. Unpublished masters thesis, Florida State University, Tallahassee, 1959.

Naylor, J. C. and Briggs, G. E.: Effects of task complexity and task organization on the relative efficiency of part and whole training methods. *J Exp Psychol, 65*:217, 1963.

Nelson, N. H.: The effect of non-instruction on the learning of badminton skills. Paper presented at AAHPER National Convention, Boston, 1969.

Niemeyer, R. K.: Part versus whole methods and massed versus distributed practice in the learning of selected large muscle activities. *College Phys Educ Assoc Proc, 62*:122, 1958. (badminton & volleyball)

O'Donnell, D. J.: The relative effectiveness of three methods of teaching beginning tennis to college women. Unpublished doctoral dissertation, Indiana University, Bloomington, 1955.

Pechstein, L. A.: Whole vs. part methods in motor learning, a comparative study. *Psychol Monogr, 23*, No. 99, 1917.

Purdy, B. J. and Stallard, M. L.: Effect of two learning methods and two grips on the acquisition of power and accuracy in the golf swing of college women. *Res Q Am Assoc Health Phys Educ, 38*:480, 1967.

Ritche, C.: The part versus the whole method in motor learning as a function of prior familarization with the skill. *Dissertation Abstracts, 28* (6-A), 2145, 1967 (batting)

Seagoe, M. V.: Qualitative wholes: A re-evaluation of the whole-part problem. *J Educ Psychol, 27*:537, 1936.

Sharpe, C. H.: A comparative study of the whole versus the part method in teaching the breast stroke. Unpublished masters thesis, Florida State University, Tallahassee, 1957.

Shay, C. T.: The progressive part vs. the whole method of learning motor skills. *Res Q Am Assoc Health Phys Educ, 5*:62, 1934.

Toole, T.: The effect of three teaching methods in golf on achievement of learners with differential skill in related task. Paper presented at AAHPER National Convention, Seattle, 1970.

Wickstrom, R.: Comparative study of methodologies for teaching gymnastics and tumbling stunts. *Res Q Am Assoc Health Phys Educ, 29*:109, 1958.

LABORATORY EXPERIMENT

PURPOSE. To determine whether the whole or the part method is the most effective way of learning a novel typing skill.

EQUIPMENT. Two identical manual typewriters, a metronome, and sufficient typing paper and a table wide enough to accommodate the two machines side by side (Fig. 9-3).

PROCEDURE.

1. Determine the total number of subjects to be used and form two groups. Attempt to balance the groups according to previous typewriting experience. Assign one group the part method and the other group the whole method of practice.

2. The part group will practice with the left hand by placing the four fingers over the Ⓜ ⊙ ⊙ Ⓩ keys of the left typewriter. The little finger on the Ⓜ , ring finger on the ⊙ etc. With the metronome set at 60 BPM the subject will repeatedly depress the keys in the following sequence with the left hand:

   Ⓜ , Ⓩ , ⊙ , ⊙ . The margins of the typewriter should be set so that the subject can type the sequence twenty times before the carriage must be returned. All responses should be recorded on typing paper.

The warning bell should sound on the eighteenth trial with the experimenter (fellow subject) moving the carriage rapidly back to the starting position. Allow each subject one hundred 4-letter sequences (4 carriage returns) with the left hand.

The subject will then place his right hand over the Ⓩ , Ⓧ , Ⓒ , Ⓥ keys of the second typewriter located to the right of the first one; the index finger on the Ⓩ key, the middle finger on the Ⓧ key, etc.

With the metronome set at 60 BPM the subject will repeatedly type the following sequence with the right hand: z, v, x, c. The remaining procedures for subjects in the part group are identical to the previously outlined task for the left hand.

3. The method of practice for the whole group is simply the combined use of both hands as outlined separately above. The experimenter should return both carriages simultaneously, the action being initiated by the carriage which is first to sound the warning bell. This can be effectively accomplished by standing behind the machines and reaching over the carriages. The carriages should be returned four times yielding one hundred sequences.

4. The criterion measure of the effectiveness of each practice method shall be determined by an additional one hundred sequences using the whole technique.

5. Subjects should be urged to keep a rhythm and strike a key(s) with each beat of the metronome. It may be desirable to use portions of the keyboard other than those indicated, particularly if a better typed copy will result due to malfunctioning keys. Labels may be cut and pasted on the keys directly above those used in the task. This would provide an additional visual cue. Numbers may be used to indicate the proper sequence of key depression, e.g. 1, 4, 2, 3.

RESULTS.

1. The total number of errors made (both hands combined) for the one hundred criterion measure sequences will be analyzed by a *t*-test.

2. To determine the number of errors, first take the data recorded by the left hand. Count the number of times the letter *m* appears on the five lines of typed material. The total number of times the *m* appears represents the total number of trials for the left hand. Beginning with each *m* typed, record one error for each misplaced symbol following until the next *m* is reached; begin counting errors for the next trial summing the errors for the left hand. Follow the same procedure for the right hand. Here is an example of a left hand sequence. The errors are circled.

m , . / m , . / m ⊚⊚ / ⊚ m⬭ . ⊚ m , . / m , ⊚ / ⊚⊚ m , . / m ⊚⊚ / m ⊚⊚ / m , . / = 12 errors.

By using the first required symbol in the sequence as the beginning point for the determination of errors, some variation in the total number of trials will result across subjects.

Express the error score for each subject as the sum of the errors made for both hands. Enter it on the data sheet provided in the appropriate space. The mean number of errors for subjects in the part group will be compared statistically to the mean number of errors in the whole group.

FIELD EXPERIMENT

PURPOSE. To determine whether a whole method or a part method of practice is the most effective in the learning of a novel gross motor skill.

EQUIPMENT. A bicycle with twenty inch tires and standard touring handlebars, four pylons, and stopwatch.

PROCEDURE.
1. Sufficient space must be provided (inside or out) to allow the design of a simple slalom course. Four movable pylons should be placed

on the same linear plane twenty feet apart with as much space as possible provided at the end of the course for a turn. The course layout and direction of travel are as follows:

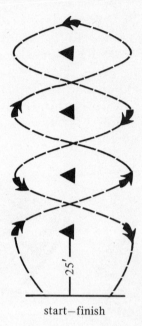

start—finish

2. The task requires the subject to traverse the course with the right hand on the left handlebar grip and the left hand on the right handlebar grip (cross-armed). The available subjects should be divided into groups, part method and whole method. Males and females should be equally represented in each group.
3. Each subject in the part group will be given a five-minute interval of time to practice the task with only the right hand placed on the left grip. Following a two-minute rest he will practice with the left hand on the right grip for five minutes. In either case the free hand may be used in any desired way to facilitate performance.
4. Members of the whole group will be given two five-minute practice sessions of the complete cross-armed task. A two-minute interval between sessions should be provided.
5. Criterion performance shall consist of three complete circuits of the course with the hands in the crossed position. Performance shall be assessed by recording the number of errors made during the three circuits. Record one error each time the subject (a) moves his hand(s) to a position other than the proper cross-armed grip; (b) touches the floor with one or both feet, or (c) falls or misses a pylon (see score sheet). Each fall or failure to negotiate a pylon will be multiplied by a constant of five to yield an error score.

RESULTS.

1. Using the error data sheet provided place a hash mark in the appropriate place for each error made during the performance of each subject. With five points assigned each fall or missed pylon and

LABORATORY EXPERIMENT: WHOLE AND PART PRACTICE DATA SHEET

Part Practice Group				Whole Practice Group		
Subject #	Number of Errors (X)	X^2		Subject #	Number of Errors (X)	X^2
1				1		
2				2		
3				3		
4				4		
5				5		
6				6		
$N =$	$\bar{X} = \frac{\Sigma X}{N} =$ $(\Sigma X)^2 =$	$\Sigma X^2 =$		$N =$	$\bar{X} = \frac{\Sigma X}{N} =$ $(\Sigma X)^2 =$	$\Sigma X^2 =$

one point for all other errors, add the total number of error points for each subject and record.

2. Transfer the total error score to the field experiment data analysis sheet.

3. Compute the group means and analyze for real differences by using a *t*-test.

FIELD EXPERIMENT : WHOLE AND PART PRACTICE DATA SHEET

Part Practice	Improper Hands	Feet Touch Ground	Falls ; missed pylons (x5)	Total Score*
S₁				
S₂				
S₃				
S₄				
S₅				
S₆				
Whole Practice				
S₁				
S₂				
S₃				
S₄				
S₅				
S₆				

*Transfer to data analysis sheet

FIELD EXPERIMENT: WHOLE AND PART PRACTICE DATA ANALYSIS SHEET

Part Practice Group				Whole Practice Group		
Subject #	Number of Errors (X)	X^2		Subject #	Number of Errors (X)	X^2
1				1		
2				2		
3				3		
4				4		
5				5		
6				6		
$N =$	$\bar{X} = \dfrac{\Sigma X}{N} =$ $(\Sigma X)^2 =$	$\Sigma X^2 =$		$N =$	$\bar{X} = \dfrac{\Sigma X}{N} =$ $(\Sigma X)^2 =$	$\Sigma X^2 =$

Chapter 10

SPEED AND ACCURACY

INTRODUCTION

SKILL HAS BEEN DESCRIBED as being composed of speed, accuracy, form (efficiency), and adaptability (Johnson, 1961). Attention will be focused upon the first two components in this section. There has been considerable discussion on the relative importance of speed and accuracy, leaving the teacher of motor skills several important questions for consideration. In the initial learning phase, should the emphasis be placed upon speed, upon accuracy, or equally upon both speed and accuracy? Would this emphasis change as learning progresses? Is it possible to separate speed and accuracy from other fundamentals as the skill is being taught or learned?

Speed may be mathematically defined as equal to linear distance divided by the time required to traverse that distance. In this definition speed is a scalar quantity having magnitude but no definite direction. For the purpose of this discussion, a more general definition will apply, namely, that speed is the rate at which a particular motor task is performed.

Accuracy may be described in an operational fashion as either the terminal position of an object on a target or the deviation of a response from a designated end point for any particular task. Hartmann's (1928) definition tends to summarize the operational definitions when he states that "accuracy is that characteristic of measurable behaviour which is indicated by relative freedom from errors—an error being considered as a deviation from an objectively correct standard."

Writings in the early part of this century suggested that in skill learning where speed and accuracy were required, one should retard the speed in the early stages until 100 percent accuracy is attained. Then speed could be gradually increased while maintaining accuracy. This idea assumes that it is easier to speed up accurate responses than to correct inaccurate ones. Errors were felt to be primarily due to the speed factor. These early writings with their emphasis upon accuracy have greatly influenced teaching methodology in most sport skills with the traditional teaching method stressing an initial emphasis upon accuracy followed by a gradual increase in speed.

Kinesiologists have reported that slow movements are different *in form* from the same movements produced rapidly. If one attempts to learn a particular movement slowly in order to gain accuracy, the correct movement that is finally required would not be learned easily. Timing, coordination, force, and joint angles, to name a few, would all change in the transformation of a slow movement to a fast movement. Correct movements must then be emphasized from the beginning with actual required speed and thus the factor of speed becomes more important.

Researchers in the 1930's and 1940's commonly compared two groups in performance on such tasks as typewriting, sorting cards, tracing, and complex reaction time. One group practiced under the speed-set, the other under the accuracy-set. During the initial training periods the speed group gained in speed but lost in accuracy while the accuracy group gained in accuracy but lost in speed. When the emphasis was later reversed, each group tended to lose on the original factor while gaining in the newly emphasized factor. It appeared, however, that the speed group lost less and regained more quickly their speed developed during the initial training period than did the accuracy group with their initial factor. Toward the end of these experiments the difference between the groups diminished to the point where their speed and accuracy were almost equal.

Later researchers employed three experimental groups, a speed-set group, an accuracy-set group, and group that was advised to perform equally in speed and accuracy. Speed that developed under initial emphasis of speed readily transferred into performance where both speed and accuracy were considered important. Accuracy gained at low rates of speed was lost almost immediately when the rate of performance was increased. In situations where an equal amount of speed and accuracy was desirable in the final performance, the group that practiced under this condition performed best. From all indications, these three experimental groups were also approaching equal levels of speed and accuracy at the end of these experiments. A logical conclusion might be that the three groups were in the process of adjusting their speed to a comparable level of accuracy. Fitts and Posner (1967) suggest that humans have this ability to trade off speed for accuracy and that in everyday tasks such as talking, writing, and the like, we perform at a speed that will be efficient and/or effective despite some error.

Later research has shifted away from the speed-accuracy confrontation *per se* and is now revealing the various factors that affect speed and accuracy in performance. One such study, in which the different information feedback conditions upon speed and accuracy were examined, indicated that accuracy appeared to be more affected by withholding accuracy information than speed was affected by withholding speed information feedback. Both speed and accuracy were found to improve under practice conditions in which the respective type of feedback was provided, with the accuracy improvements being more variable (Malina, 1969).

One particular component of skill is often emphasized in many sports. Examples would be speed in track and in swimming, form in diving and in gymnastics, as well as accuracy in archery and in riflery. The coach or physical education teacher must decide whether the most important criterion for success is speed, accuracy, or a combination of both. Should the fencer initially emphasize speed, accuracy, or both equally? Should the beginning golfer practice the swing in slow motion or at a fast speed? Should the ice hockey player practice shooting at the net from a relatively stationary position or while moving at high speed? Research has indicated that when a person practices at high speed and then attempts to incorporate accuracy, the basic movement need not be changed. However, the individual who stresses accuracy at a slow speed finds that when he attempts to carry out the same movement at a fast speed, the whole movement pattern has changed along with body control. In ballistic skills where accumulation of momentum is required for successful performance, it would obviously be detrimental to place early emphasis upon accuracy.

GENERAL RESEARCH FINDINGS

Some of the more conclusive findings in the area of speed and accuracy are as follows:

1. Speed and accuracy are really a function of the task being performed and the decision of which one to emphasize in practice depends upon the criterion task. Emphasis should relate to final expectations.
2. Neither speed nor accuracy movements may be considered general factors but rather tend to be task specific.
3. When speed is the predominant factor in the performance of the skill, early emphasis upon speed is best. When accuracy is the criterion performance, early emphasis upon accuracy is best.
4. If during learning the attention is directed solely to accuracy, the speed will gradually improve. If attention is directly solely to speed, the accuracy tends to diminish.

REFERENCES

Alderman, R. B.: Influence of local fatigue on speed and accuracy in motor learning. *Res Q Am Assoc Health Phys Educ, 36*:131, 1965.

Drinkwater, B. E. and Fling, M. M.: Response speed and accuracy during anticipatory stress. *J Motor Behav, 1*:220, 1968.

Drinkwater, B. L.: Speed and accuracy in decision responses of men and women pilots. *Ergonomics, 11*:61, 1968.

Drowatzky, J. N.: Evaluation of mirror tracing performance measures as indicators of learning. *Res Q Am Assoc Health Phys Educ, 40*:228, 1969.

Fitts, P. M.: Cognitive aspects of information processing: III set for speed vs. accuracy. *J Exp Psychol, 71*:849, 1966.

Fulton, R.: Speed and accuracy in learning a ballistic movement. *Res Q Am Assoc Health Phys Educ, 13*:30, 1942.

Fulton, R. E.: Speed and accuracy in learning movements. *Arch Psychol, 41*:1, 1945.

Garrett, H. E.: A study of the relation of accuracy and speed. *Arch Psychol, 8*:1, 1922.

Hansen, C. F.: Serial action as a basic measure of motor capacity. *Psychol Monogr, 31*:320, 1922.

Hartmann, G. W.: Precision and accuracy. *Arch Psychol, 100*:1, 1928, p. 8.

Malina, R. M.: Effects of varied information feedback practice conditions on throwing speed and accuracy. *Res Q Am Assoc Health Phys Educ, 40*:134, 1969.

Meyers, G. C.: Speed versus accuracy in the development of industrial skills. *J Personnel Research, 4*:20, 1925.

Singer, R. N.: Speed and accuracy of movements as related to fencing success. *Res Q Am Assoc Health Phys Educ, 39*:1080, 1968.

Skubic, V. and Hodgkins, J.: Effect of warm-up activities on speed, strength and accuracy. *Res Q Am Assoc Health Phys Educ, 28*:147, 1957.

Smith, L. E. and Harrison, J. S.: Comparison of the effects of visual, motor, mental and guided practice upon speed and accuracy of performing a simple eye-hand coordination task. *Res Q Am Assoc Health Phys Educ, 33*:299, 1962.

Solley, W. H.: Speed, accuracy or speed and accuracy as an initial directive in motor learning. *Motor Skills Research Exchange, 3*:47, 1951.

Solley, W. H.: The effects of verbal instruction of speed and accuracy upon learning of a motor skill. *Res Q Am Assoc Health Phys Educ, 23*:231, 1952.

Straub, W. F.: Effect of overload training procedures upon velocity and accuracy of the overarm throw. *Res Q Am Assoc Health Phys Educ, 39*:370, 1968.

Sturt, M.: A comparison of speed and accuracy in the learning process. *Br J Psychol, 12*:289, 1921.

West, L. J.: Verbally induced sets toward speed and accuracy in elementary typewriting. *Natl Business Educ Q, 21*:45, 1953.

LABORATORY EXPERIMENT

PURPOSE. To study the effects of instructional emphasis on speed and accuracy upon the level of performance of a skill.

EQUIPMENT. Electronic apparatus designed to measure response time and accuracy of the thrust movement with a fencing foil. (See Appendix for construction and description of apparatus.)

DESIGN. Three groups of subjects randomly assigned. On Day I, one group will practice stressing speed (speed group), another accuracy (accuracy group), and the third group stressing both speed and accuracy (speed and accuracy group). On Day II all three groups will be tested for speed and accuracy.

PROCEDURE. On Day I, subjects in each group will take the on-guard ready position, facing the target with the lead foot depressing the foot pedal. Each subject determines his appropriate lunging distance from the target.

When initiating the lunge toward the target in response to the light stimulus, the subject's foot leaves the foot pedal and the Dekan Timer circuit is broken. When the subject touches the target with the foil and knocks it over, the micro-switch breaks the circuit, stopping the chronometer. This chronometer reading indicates the total time it took to complete the movement, which is referred to as response time. Lunging accuracy is determined by the target circle touched by the foil arriving at a score on a nine, seven, five, three, one point basis. After two trials to familiarize oneself with the testing equipment, each subject will perform twenty lunges (trials) with the results being recorded. Rest periods of fifteen seconds will be given between trials. Subjects should not be informed of their reaction and response times.

On the second day each subject in each group will perform twenty more lunges. The speed group subjects will be instructed to consciously and overtly emphasize speed in lunging toward the target. Subjects in the accuracy group will be instructed to consciously and overtly emphasize

Lunging test for accuracy and/or speed.

accuracy in lunging toward the target. Subjects in the speed and accuracy group will be instructed to consciously and overtly emphasize a simultaneous combination of speed and accuracy.

RESULTS.

1. Record resultant data for each lunge on the master sheet provided.
2. Plot the learning curves for Day II for each group.
3. Test the mean of the differences among the groups for speed, accuracy, and speed-accuracy on each of the two days by use of analysis of variance (repeated measures). The speed score will be determined by the response score, the accuracy score by the number of points attained on the target, and the speed and accuracy score by the product of the response time and total points (speed − accuracy = response time × total points).

FIELD EXPERIMENT

PURPOSE. To demonstrate the effects of instructional emphasis on speed and accuracy upon the level of preformance of motor skill.

EQUIPMENT. Automobile tire, stopwatch, and several dozen tennis balls. (See p. 148 for task.)

DESIGN. Three groups of subjects formed as in the laboratory experiment.

PROCEDURE. On Day I each subject will be given five trials in throwing tennis balls through an automobile tire with rest periods of twenty seconds between each trial. Each ball tossed through the tire will be one point. The distance of each toss will be twenty-five feet under the following conditions: (a) the speed group will be instructed to throw as many balls as quickly as possible in thirty seconds through the tire; (b) the accuracy group will be instructed to throw balls as accurately as possible through the tire in thirty seconds, and (c) the speed-accuracy group will toss as many balls as possible in thirty seconds through the tire emphasizing both speed and accuracy. On Day II each subject in each group will perform five additional trials.

RESULTS.

1. Record the resultant data on data sheets provided.
2. Test the mean of the differences for speed, accuracy, and speed-accuracy on each of the two days using analysis of variance techniques. The speed score will be measured by the number of balls thrown in thirty seconds, the accuracy score by the number of balls passing through the tire, and the speed-accuracy score by the product of the number of balls tossed and the number passing through the tire in thirty seconds.

LABORATORY EXPERIMENT: Speed and accuracy data sheet

Speed	Trials														Day II						ΣX
Subject	1	2	3	4	5	6	7	8	9	10	11	12	13	14	15	16	17	18	19	20	
1																					
2																					
3																					
4																					
5																					

$\Sigma\Sigma X=$

Accuracy	Trials														Day II						ΣX
Subject	1	2	3	4	5	6	7	8	9	10	11	12	13	14	15	16	17	18	19	20	
1																					
2																					
3																					
4																					
5																					

$\Sigma\Sigma X=$

Speed-Accuracy	Trials														Day II						ΣX
Subject	1	2	3	4	5	6	7	8	9	10	11	12	13	14	15	16	17	18	19	20	
1																					
2																					
3																					
4																					
5																					

$\Sigma\Sigma X=$

LABORATORY EXPERIMENT: Speed and accuracy data sheet

Speed Subject	Trials Day I																				Σ X
	1	2	3	4	5	6	7	8	9	10	11	12	13	14	15	16	17	18	19	20	
1																					
2																					
3																					
4																					
5																					

Σ Σ X =

Accuracy Subject	Trials Day I																				Σ X
	1	2	3	4	5	6	7	8	9	10	11	12	13	14	15	16	17	18	19	20	
1																					
2																					
3																					
4																					
5																					

Σ Σ X =

Speed-Accuracy Subject	Trials Day I																				Σ X
	1	2	3	4	5	6	7	8	9	10	11	12	13	14	15	16	17	18	19	20	
1																					
2																					
3																					
4																					
5																					

Σ Σ X =

FIELD EXPERIMENT : Speed and accuracy data sheet

Speed Group	Trials Day I						Trials Day II					
Subjects	1	2	3	4	5	Σ X	1	2	3	4	5	Σ X
1												
2												
3												
4												
5												
					$\Sigma\Sigma$X=						$\Sigma\Sigma$X=	

Accuracy Group	Trials Day I						Trials Day II					
Subjects	1	2	3	4	5	Σ X	1	2	3	4	5	X
1												
2												
3												
4												
5												
					$\Sigma\Sigma$X=						$\Sigma\Sigma$X=	

Speed-Accuracy	Trials Day I						Trials Day II					
Subjects	1	2	3	4	5	Σ X	1	2	3	4	5	Σ X
1												
2												
3												
4												
5												
					$\Sigma\Sigma$X=						$\Sigma\Sigma$X=	

LABORATORY EXPERIMENT : Learning Curves

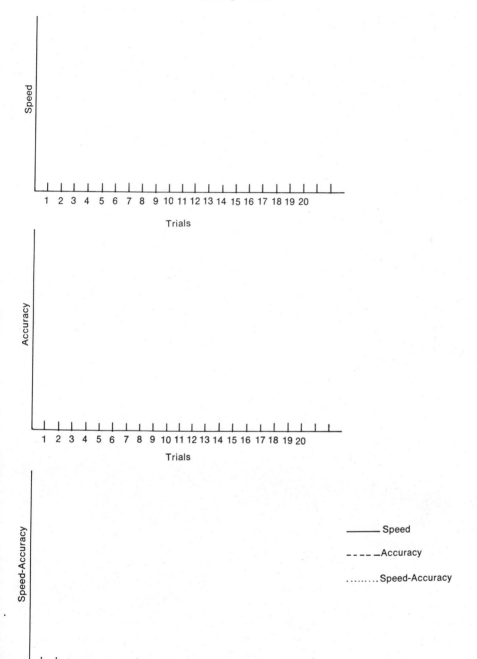

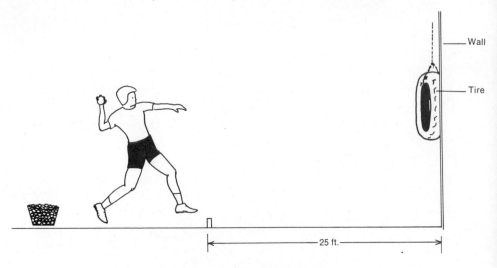

Tennis ball tossed for speed and/or accuracy.

APPENDIX

PURCHASED EQUIPMENT. The Minnesota Dexterity Test may be used as a speed-accuracy test, and it may be purchased from the Lafayette Instrument Company, P. O. Box 1279, Lafayette, Indiana.

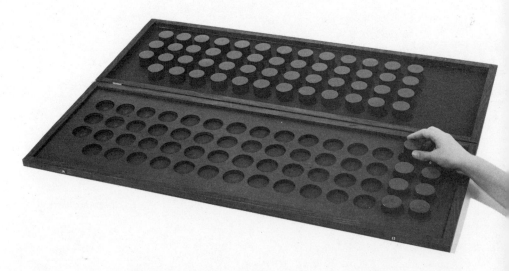

MINNESOTA MANUAL DEXTERITY TEST

Figure 10-7: This widely used test is designed for school, business and industry. The test measures the subjects' speed with how fast he can move 60 identical wooden cylinders from a basic position to a pre-cut masonite board with holes. Performance is based only on gross movement of hands and arms.

CONSTRUCTED EQUIPMENT. The fencing speed-accuracy apparatus is described and illustrated as follows: The target part of the apparatus consists of a 2-foot square of quarter inch plywood, connected by two straps hinged to a wooden base of two by fours. Concentric circles in similar fashion to an archery target are drawn on the plywood. A micro-switch is placed at the bottom of the actual target so that when the target is upright the microswitch is depressed thus maintaining the circuit in a closed position. A pilot light, located in the center of the target area, is used as the light stimulus.

Two timing devices are used in conjunction with the target, an electric chronometer powered by a direct current supply unit, and a Dekan Timer Performance Analyzer, both calibrated to .01 seconds and capable of measuring up to sixty seconds. A foot pedal and the light stimulus on the target are connected to the Dekan Timer; the micro-switch is connected to the chronometer and the power unit.

In order to activate the apparatus two switches must be turned on by an assistant at exactly the same time: one on the Dekan timer that presents the light stimulus and also starts the timer, and one on the power supply unit, that starts the chronometer.

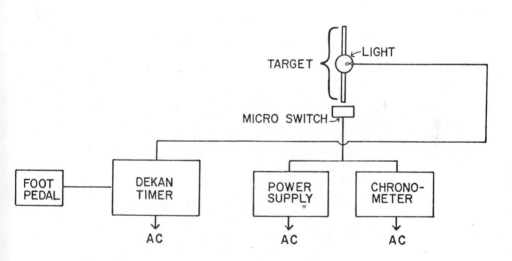

PURCHASED EQUIPMENT. A millisecond digital timer is one of a number offered by Lafayette Instrument Co., P. O. Box 1279, Lafayette, Indiana.

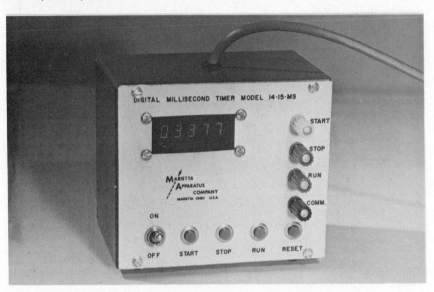

The Dekan Performance Analyzer is manufactured by Dekan Timing Devices, P. O. Box 712, Glen Ellyn, Illinois.

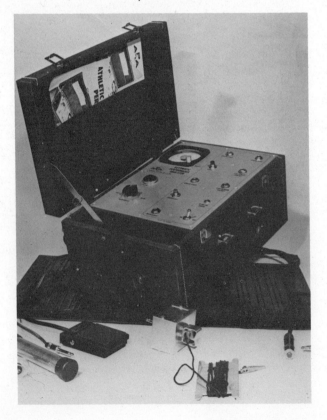

Timers may be purchased from the Hunter Manufacturing Co., Iowa City, Iowa.

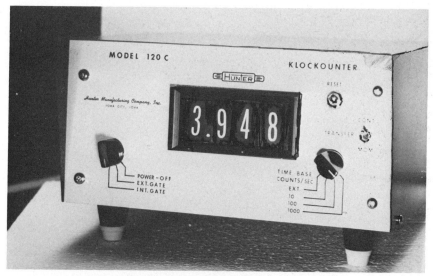

Hunter Model 120C Klockounter

Figure 10-11A:

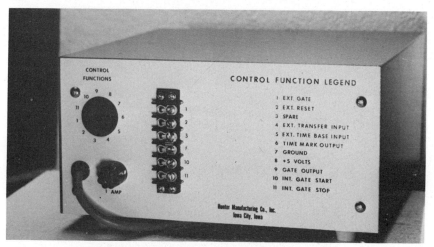

Hunter Model 120C Klockounter (Rear Panel)

Figure 10-11B: The Hunter Model 120C Klockounter is a completely self-contained, precision solid state instrument capable of performing two basic functions: (1) in the Time Interval Measurement mode the Model 120C Klockounter is a precision clock, and, (2) the timing may be started and stopped by means of a contact closure during the timing interval.

In the Event Counter model, the counting circuit responds to electrical pulses applied to the input connector. The accumulating count may be directly observed, or if desired, the display circuits will hold the count for recording while a new count is being entered in the storage circuits.

The Hunter Model 120A Klockounter

Figure 10-12: This is a precision-action instrument which will time or count a variety of electrical impulses. When used as a timing device or *clock* the Klockounter displays measured time intervals in either 0.1, 0.01, or 0.001 second increments. The total elapsed time measured ranges from 9.999 seconds to 999.9 seconds, depending upon the setting of a range selector switch. When used as an events *counter*, the Klockounter counts up to 9,999 events at a maximum counting rate of 2,000 counts per second.

Chapter 11

MOTIVATION

INTRODUCTION

IT IS A WIDELY accepted principle that motivation is one of the most important variables that contributes to the learning process. The optimal level of motivation is not only essential for learning but is also a determinant of performance, influencing one's attitude, preparatory set, and general state of readiness.

Motivation has been broadly defined as the urge to push toward a specific goal, a general level of arousal to action. The activity level, alertness, fatigue, and other factors besides learning determine human output at any moment, and needs are created within the individual which force him to seek particular goals to satisfy those needs. A *motive* is often referred to as a specific condition (particular needs or drives) that directs or channels behavior toward goals. The resultant behavior in attaining the desired goal will in turn reduce or remove the particular drive or need.

Two general approaches have been taken with regard to the study of motivation, one functional in character, the other theoretical. The functional approach considers that motives energize (motivate) behavior, arouse activity, or provide the energy of movement, as well as interacting with innate or learned habits to produce overt behavior. The theoretical approach hypothesizes that the motivational function arises from or is related to a specified class of internal (intrinsic) or external (extrinsic) conditions. Intrinsic motivation implies self-actualization and ego involvement; that is, a person does something for its own sake.

An extrinsic motivated person does something only for glory, recognition, or material gain and is therefore fulfilling a *need-deficiency*. Individuals often demonstrate the drive or need for security, mastery, recognition, love, or belonging. This latter approach of need has been incorporated into numerous learning theories that cannot be expounded here except by identification: (a) the instinctual; (b) need-primary, i.e. the drives of hunger, thirst, elimination and sexual gratification; (c) the multi-factor theory, i.e. physiological, psychological and social needs, and

153

(d) the capacity-primary theory, i.e. the basic need to interact with one's environment.

Although there is an optimal level of arousal within which most efficient motor performance may occur, the Yerkes-Dodson law formulated in 1908 suggests that complex tasks are performed best when one's arousal or drive level is relatively low, but optimum proficiency in simple tasks is attained when the arousal is high. Intense arousal can interfere with learning and have a marked disruptive effect on the performance of more complex tasks. The optimal level of arousal would seem to fluctuate due to a number of factors such as individual differences, the nature of the task, and prior experience or skill level. The *inverted U hypothesis* which is yet another explanation for this phenomenon proposes that the quality of performance increases as anxiety increases up to a certain point, after which additional increases in anxiety results in increasingly inferior performance.

Boredom as elicited from inactivity or by a monotonous repetitive task may induce fatigue which in turn negatively affects performance. Evidence indicates that more stimulating and complex activity together with sufficient rest periods will negate the detrimental effects of fatigue upon performance.

One of the most common techniques for inducing learning and performance has been the use of rewards and punishments. Rewards may take various forms. They may be materialistic, symbolic, or psychological (intrinsic), with the latter form being considered the more desirable by educators. Punishment can be an effective means of directing behavior, but caution must be exerted against possible side effects, such as anxiety, fear, and confusion which could have a detrimental effect on subsequent learning and performance.

Much of the incentive that motivates one's activities comes as a result of one's own movement. Information gained as a result of a response, known as feedback, can serve as motivation to continue the task. Intrinsic feedback (a natural consequence of the movement itself) and augmented feedback (extrinsic to the individual) are two types of feedback regularly employed in learning research, and both can increase motivational levels.

The presence of an audience or spectators has been found to affect performance levels. Whether the effects are negative or positive depends primarily upon one's skill level and stage of learning. One common finding has been that audiences have a detrimental effect upon the performance of the less proficient performers while the more skillful tend to improve or are not affected.

Involved in group interaction are a number of variables such as the size of the group, sex makeup, age, intelligence level, and the like. Research studies suggest that there is an optimum group size depending upon the task and the type of skill involved.

Although competition is a powerful incentive and motivational technique and has generally been demonstrated to positively affect performance, its function depends primarily upon the personality of the individual as well as the nature of the task. It has also been found that individuals who have a high need for achievement and who are highly anxious compared to low anxious individuals, perform poorly under competitive stress.

GENERAL RESEARCH FINDINGS

1. A high level of motivation is advantageous for performance in gross motor tasks involving speed, strength, endurance, and for the learning of simple motor tasks.
2. A high level of motivation interferes with performance involving fine motor steadiness, precision, concentration and the learning of complex motor tasks.
3. Reinforcement as a form of reward increases the probability of the desired act to occur.
4. As the intensity of motivation increases, there is also a general increase in tension, both muscular and emotional.
5. The greater the level of skill, the higher the arousal can be without causing disruption in performance.

REFERENCES

Bayton, J. A. and Conley, H. W.: Duration of success background and the effect of failure upon performance. *J Genet Psychol, 56*:179, 1957.

Bruning, J. L., Sommen, D. K. and Jones, B. R.: The motivational effects of cooperation and competition in the means—independent situation. *J Soc Psychol, 68*:269, 1966.

Burton, E. C.: State and trait anxiety achievement motivating and skill attainment in college women. *Res Q Am Assoc Health Phys Educ, 42*:139, 1971.

Burwitz, L. and Newell, K. M.: The effects of the mere presence of coactors on learning a motor skill. *J Motor Behav, 4*:71, 1972.

Caskey, S. R.: Effects of motivation on standing broad jump performance of children. *Res Q Am Assoc Health Phys Educ, 39*:54, 1968.

Cox, F. N.: Some effects of test anxiety and presence or absence of other persons on boys' performance on a repetitive motor task. *J Exp Child Psychol, 3*:100, 1966.

Friedlander, F.: Motivations to work and organizational performance. *J Appl Psychol, 50*:143, 1966.

Hammond, L. J. and Goldman, M.: Competition and noncompetition and its relationship to individual and group productivity. *Sociometry, 24*:46, 1961.

Hill, K. T. and Sevenson, H. W.: The effects of social reinforcement vs. nonreinforcement and sex of E on the performance of adolescent girls. *J Pers, 33*:30, 1965.

Latane, B. and Arrowood, J.: Emotional arousal and task performance. *J Appl Psychol,* 47:324, 1963.

Martens, R.: Effects of an audience on learning and performance of a complex motor skill. *J Pers Soc Psychol, 12*:252, 1969.

Martens, R. and Landers, D. M.: Effect of anxiety, competition, and failure on performance of a complex task. *J Motor Behav, 1*:1, 1969.

Roberts, G. C.: Effect of achievement, motivation and social environment on performance of a motor task. *J Motor Behav, 4*:37, 1972.

Rushell, B. S. and Pettinger, J.: An evaluation of the effects of various reinforcers used as motivators in swimming. *Res Q Am Assoc Health Phys Educ, 40*:540, 1969.

Samorajczyk, J. F.: Children's responsiveness to motivational suggestions during school entry. *Res Q Am Assoc Health Phys Educ, 40*:546, 1969.

Singer, R. N.: Effect of an audience on performance of a motor task. *J Motor Behav, 2*:88, 1969.

Singer, R. N.: Effect of spectators on athletes and non-athletes performing a gross motor task. *Res Q Am Assoc Health Phys Educ, 36*:473, 1965.

Strong, C. H.: Motivation related to performance of physical fitness tests. *Res Q Am Assoc Health Phys Educ, 34*:497, 1963.

Voor, J. H., Lloyd, A. J. and Cole, R. C.: The influence of competition on the efficiency of an isometric contraction. *J Motor Behav, 1*:210, 1969.

LABORATORY EXPERIMENT

PURPOSE. To determine the effect of an incentive upon the performance of a motor task.

EQUIPMENT. Tapping board with two stainless steel plates attached to an electric counter and a stopwatch. (See Appendix for illustration.)

DESIGN. Two randomly assigned groups of subjects, one control, the other experimental. Their task is simply to alternate their tapping on two steel plates with their dominant hand as quickly as possible with a stylus.

PROCEDURE. Each subject in the control group will be given ten thirty-second trials of tapping with between-trial rest periods of forty-five seconds.

Each subject in the experimental group will experience a similar number and type of trial as in the control group. However, experimental group subjects will be informed that the best performer in terms of numbers of successful taps in a trial as well as the best performance throughout all ten trials will each receive a one dollar bill.

RESULTS.
1. Record the resultant data on the master sheet provided.
2. Plot learning curves for both groups.
3. Compare mean differences in performance between the two groups with the use of the *t*-test.

FIELD EXPERIMENT

PURPOSE. To determine the effects of verbal motivation on the performance of a gross motor task.

EQUIPMENT. A running area of eighty yards and a stopwatch.

DESIGN. Two randomly assigned groups, one control, the other experimental. No knowledge of results will be given after each trial.

PROCEDURE. Each subject in the control group will perform five sixty-yard dashes with between trial rest periods of five minutes.

Each subject in the experimental group will experience a similar number and type of trials as in the control group. However, the experimental group subjects, after their three trials and during the rest period, will be informed that the mean dash time of the control group was superior to theirs and they are now strongly encouraged to do better. Two additional trials will now follow separated by five-minute rest periods each. The design is as follows:

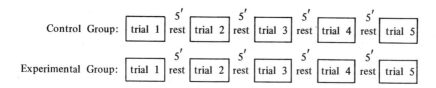

RESULTS.
1. Record resultant data on the master sheet provided.
2. Plot the performance curves for each group.
3. Compare the mean differences in performance between the two groups for trials one, two, and three with the use of the *t*-test. No differences should exist. Run another *t*-test, comparing both groups on the means of trials four and five.

APPENDIX

PURCHASED EQUIPMENT. A tapping board and stylus may be purchased from the Lafayette Instrument Company, P.O. Box 1279, 52 By-Pass, Lafayette, Indiana.

CONSTRUCTED EQUIPMENT. A board of any size could be used, upon which two steel plates would be attached at the ends. When wired properly, and with the use of a counter, each tap on a plate would be counted.

LABORATORY   EXPERIMENT : Motivation Data Sheet

Control Group	Trials										
Subjects	1	2	3	4	5	6	7	8	9	10	ΣX
1											
2											
3											
4											
5											

$\Sigma\Sigma X =$

Experimental Group	Trials										
Subjects	1	2	3	4	5	6	7	8	9	10	ΣX
1											
2											
3											
4											
5											

$\Sigma\Sigma X =$

FIELD EXPERIMENT : Motivation Data Sheet

Control Group	Trials					
Subjects	1	2	3	4	5	$\Sigma X_{4,9}$
1						
2						
3						
4						
5						
				$\Sigma \Sigma X_{4,9} =$		

Experimental group	Trials					
Subjects	1	2	3	4	5	$\Sigma X_{4,9}$
1						
2						
3						
4						
5						
				$\Sigma \Sigma X_{4,9} =$		

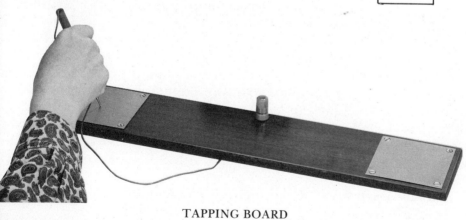

TAPPING BOARD

Figure 11-4: Stainless steel plates located at each end of board will complete a circuit when stylus contacts one or the other. Designed for versatility and durability.

Chapter 12

INTER-TASK TRANSFER

INTRODUCTION

ONE OF THE MOST important considerations in the area of learning has been the transfer of training. Transfer of training refers to the fact that the learning or training that has taken place in one task carries over, or transfers to a second task. If the learning of one task aids in the learning of a second task, it is an example of positive transfer, but if the learning of the first task hinders the learning of the second task, negative transfer has occurred.

Numerous theories have been formulated to explain transfer of skill but space allows only a short description of several of the more popular theories.

The famous psychologist, Thorndike, proposed in 1913 the "identical elements theory" in which he held that only those elements, skills, knowledges, techniques, and the like which are identical or common to the two tasks are transferable. This S-R theory implies that unless there are identical *stimulus elements* in the two situations and unless these were perceived by the learner, transfer would not occur. However, research on learning sets suggests that factors other than identical stimulus elements may affect transfer, such as the learner acquiring some general principle and responding to this principle rather than to the specific stimuli in a particular situation.

The "transposition theory" proposed by the Gestaltists suggests that transfer occurs when a pattern of dynamic relationships are discovered to exist in two learning situations with transposition occurring when practice in one task is found to facilitate the learning of another. This also suggests that basic understandings in previous task experiences would enable one to transfer experiences to a broader spectrum of situations in difference to the limitations associated with S-R connotations (Cratty, 1964).

Several basic transfer designs have been employed to study the variables which operate in transfer:

DESIGN I

Group A	Learn Task 1	Learn Task 2

Group B	Rest	Learn Task 2

This model is designed to determine the amount of proactive transfer, that is, the effect (positive or negative) learning Task 1 has on the learning of Task 2.

DESIGN II

Group A	Learn Task A	Learn Task B	Test on Task A
Group B	Learn Task A	Rest	Test on Task A

This model is designed to determine the amount of retroactive transfer, the effect that learning a second task has on the retention of the initial task.

DESIGN III

Group A	Learn Task 1	Learn Task 2(a)
Group B	Learn Task 1	Learn Task 2(b)

This model is designed to determine if, following the learning of Task 1, it is easier to learn Task 2 (a) than it is to learn Task 2 (b). Task 2 (a) and 2 (b) would be equivalent in difficulty.

Two other designs, although not frequently used, are:

DESIGN IV

Group A	Learn Task 1	Learn Task 2
Group B	Learn Task 2	Learn Task 1

This model is designed to determine the transfer effects on learning a task by one method on the learning of the same task by a second method, e.g. examining the transfer of form discrimination from one sensory modality to another.

DESIGN V

Group A	Learn Task 1	Learn Task 2
Group B	Learn Task 1	Learn Task 2

In this design the investigator is not interested in examining the influence of a task variable, but, rather, is concerned with the contribution of the temporal interval interpolated between the learning of the first and second task. Both groups learn the same tasks but the difference lies in the amount of time interpolated between Task 1 and Task 2.

In measuring transfer, most investigators favor raw scores which would be obtained by using a rate of response measure such as seconds or errors. The direction and amount of transfer is obtained by subtracting the smaller score made by one group on Task 2 from the larger score of the other group on the same task. A percentage of transfer score may be obtained by dividing the control group's score into the difference and multiplying by one hundred. Thus the formula:

$$\text{Experimental Score} - \text{Control Score}$$
$$\text{or}$$
$$\text{Percentage of transfer} = \frac{\text{Control Score} - \text{Experimental Score}}{\text{Control Score}} \times 100$$

The limitation with this type of measurement is that it prevents one from making comparisons of the amount of transfer obtained in one task with that of another.

Analysis of variance techniques may be applied to the first three designs to determine significant differences that may exist between the groups on the designated tasks. A simple *t*-test may also be used for the final two tasks.

Another way to examine transfer measurement is to compare the amount of transfer that has taken place with the maximum amount of improvement which can take place. The percentage of transfer score may then be obtained by dividing the sum of the experimental and control groups' scores on the final task into the difference between the two groups and multiplying by one hundred.

$$\text{Percentage of transfer} = \frac{\text{Experimental Score} - \text{Control Score}}{\text{Experimental Score} + \text{Control Score}} \times 100$$

Although empirical support is readily available for either direction of transfer, i.e. from a difficult or complex task to an easy or simple task or vice versa, the evidence is conflicting as to which situation might result in most effective transfer. Gains in learning (efficiency) appear to be increased if the transition from the easy to the difficult task involves intermediate steps of difficulty rather than being abrupt. Transfer would obviously be greatly enhanced if the complex task included all the elements of the easier task.

Transfer of verbal material has been reported to increase with additional practice on the initial task, and it is assumed to also exist in learning motor skills.

Another variable closely associated to the degree of initial learning has been the phenomenon of *warm-up,* i.e. that part of an increase in efficiency during the first minutes of a work period which is lost by a moderate rest period. Several studies in motor learning have confirmed the positive effects of warm-up in transfer of learning, but what the significant variables are that contribute to its presence are still under investigation.

The amount of transfer is generally affected by the similarity of the task initially learned to the second task in which the occurrence of transfer is observed. The more dissimilar the responses required for a similar stimulus, the more negative the transfer. Positive transfer occurs in reverse manner. This can be observed in the illustration from Robinson.

Stimulus similarity implies that the more similarity there is in the tasks, the greater the transfer of response, when the same response is needed for the two tasks.

When materials or tasks undertaken are alike, improvements result

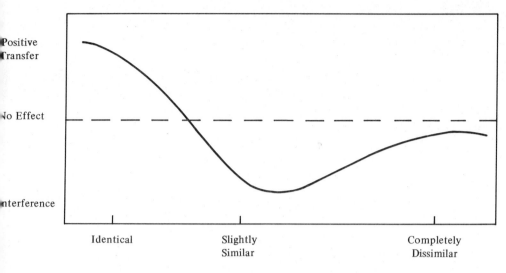

SIMILARITY BETWEEN TWO TASKS

Figure 12-1: When the two tasks are highly similar, transfer is at a highest level (positive). As the task similarity approaches minimum, transfer (negative) is greatest. When the two tasks are completely dissimilar, little or no effect transfer results. (Adapted from Robinson, E. S.: The 'similarity' factor in retroaction, *Am J Psychol, 39*:299, 1927.)

merely from learning how to learn them. Subjects become test-wise. This problem may be controlled, however, through proper experimental design.

Other factors, such as motivation, part versus whole methods of training, massed versus distributed practice, shape and speed of target, as well as weight and velocity, have been demonstrated to affect transfer.

GENERAL RESEARCH FINDINGS

1. If the new skill presents stimuli that are similar or identical to those in a previous learning situation, and the stimuli demands similar or identical responses, high positive transfer usually results.
2. If the new situation presents stimuli that are similar or identical to those in a previous learning situation but demands dissimilar or incompatible responses, initial negative transfer results.
3. If the new skill involves stimuli dissimilar to the old but requires similar responses, slight positive transfer occurs.
4. When a second task is quite dissimilar to the original task, little or no transfer usually results.

5. Transfer is influenced by such factors as the amount of practice on the prior task, motivation to transfer skill, method of training, task difficulty, and similarity of tasks.
6. Positive transfer increases with increasing initial mastery of the original task.

REFERENCES

Barch, A. M. and Lewis, D.: The effect of task difficulty and amount of practice on proactive transfer. *J Exp Psychol, 48*:134, 1954.

Briggs, G. E. and Naylor, J.: The relative efficiency of several training methods as a function of transfer to task complexity. *J Exp Psychol, 64*:505, 1962.

Cratty, B. J.: *Movement Behavior and Motor Learning.* Philadelphia, Lea & Febiger, 1964, p. 270.

Cratty, B. J.: Transfer of small-pattern practice to large-pattern learning. *Res Q Am Assoc Health Phys Educ, 33*:523, 1962.

Goldstein, D. A. and Newton, M. M.: Transfer of training as a function of task difficulty in a complex control situation. *J Exp Psychol, 63*:370, 1962.

Johnston, W. A.: Transfer of team skills as a function of type of training. *J Appl Psychol, 50*:102, 1966.

Kerr, B. A.: Weight and velocity influences on kinesthetic learning and transfer of learning. *J Motor Behav, 3*:195, 1970.

Laszlo, J. I. and Pritchard, D. A.: Transfer variables in tracking skills. *J Motor Behav, 1*:317, 1969.

Nelson, D. O.: Studies of transfer of learning in gross motor skills. *Res Q Am Assoc Health Phys Educ, 28*:364, 1957.

Noble, C. E.: The learning of psychomotor skills. *Annu Rev Psychol, 19*:203, 1968.

Rivenes, R. S.: Multiple-task transfer effects in perceptual motor learning. *Res Q Am Assoc Health Phys Educ, 38*:485, 1967.

Scannell, R. J.: Transfer of accuracy training when difficulty is controlled by varying target size. *Res Q Am Assoc Health Phys Educ, 39*:341, 1968.

Singer, R. N.: Transfer effect and ultimate success in archery due to degree of difficulty of the initial learning. *Res Q Am Assoc Health Phys Educ, 37*:532, 1966.

Welch, M.: Specificity of heavy work fatigue: Absence of transfer from heavy leg work to coordination tasks using the arms. *Res Q Am Assoc Health Phys Educ, 40*:402, 1969.

LABORATORY EXPERIMENT

PURPOSE. To determine the effects of inter-task transfer on the learning of a motor task.

EQUIPMENT. Stabilometer* and a bongo-board **.

---

*Stabilometers are explained in the chapter on Knowledge of Results (Feedback).

**A bongo board is an apparatus consisting of a flat board (10″ x 24″ x3/4″) placed over a wooden cylinder (10″ x 3″).

DESIGN. Randomly assign subjects to two groups, one designated experimental, the other control. Although randomization assumes equality of initial performance, an alternate design would be to pretest on the final criterion task to be learned. Therefore, provide both groups with two trials on the stabilometer.

PROCEDURE. Each subject in the control group will perform ten thirty-second trials on the stabilometer interspersed with thirty-second rest periods. No warm-up will be given. (See Design I described under "Transfer Designs and Measurement.")

Each subject in the experimental group will first perform ten thirty-second trials on the bongo-board with thirty-second rest periods between trials. Record the number of touches the board makes with the floor each trial in order to observe if the subjects are improving with practice. After a ten-minute rest period, subjects will then perform ten thirty-second trials on the stabilometer interspersed with thirty-second rest periods. The design is as follows:

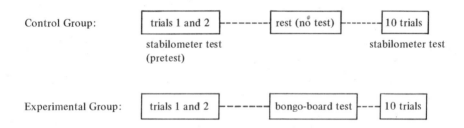

RESULTS.

1. Record stabilometer data on the master sheets provided.
2. Determine transfer by use of the following formula:

$$\frac{10 \text{ trials}}{10} - \frac{\text{pre-trials (1 and 2)}}{2} = d_1 \text{ (for control group)}$$

$$\frac{10 \text{ trials}}{10} - \frac{\text{pre-trials (1 and 2)}}{2} = d_2 \text{ (for experimental group)}$$

Test for significant differences between d_1 and d_2.

3. Test for significant differences between the mean scores (ten trials) for the two groups on the stabilometer using the t-test statistic.

FIELD EXPERIMENT

PURPOSE. To determine the effects of inter-task transfer on the learning of a motor skill.

EQUIPMENT. Five footballs, five volleyballs, and the availability of using football goal posts. Goal posts could also be taped on gym wall.*

DESIGN. Subjects are randomly assigned to two groups, control or experimental. Each subject will attempt to drop-kick (kicking the ball after only one bounce) the ball over the cross-bar and between the uprights of a football goal-post from a distance of ten yards. (See illustration.) No warm-up trials allowed.

PROCEDURE. Using a football each subject in the control group will attempt twenty drop-kicks *over* the cross-bar with thirty-second rest periods between kicks (trials).

Using a volleyball each subject in the experimental group will first attempt twenty drop-kicks over the cross-bar with thirty-second rest periods between trials. After a ten-minute rest period, subjects will attempt twenty additional drop-kicks using a football with twenty-second rest periods between trials.

RESULTS.

1. Record resultant data on master sheets provided.
2. Test for significant differences between the mean scores of the two groups on the football drop-kicks using the chi square statistic.

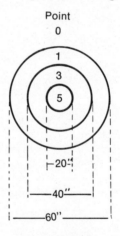

Point
0

WALL TARGET

---

*If a more qualitative scoring system is desired, a target may be employed instead of goal posts. This target could look like this:

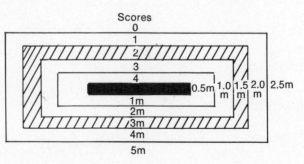

Scores

LABORATORY EXPERIMENT : transfer data sheet

Control Group stabilometer		PRE							Trials						
Subjects		1	2	1	2	3	4	5	6	7	8	9	10	Σ X
1														
2														
3														
4														
5														
Σ Σ X=													Σ Σ X=	

Experimental Group Bongo Board		PRE							Trials						
Subjects		1	2	1	2	3	4	5	6	7	8	9	10	Σ X
1														
2														
3														
4														
5														
Σ Σ X=													Σ Σ X=	

Experimental group Stabilometer		PRE							Trials						
Subjects		1	2	1	2	3	4	5	6	7	8	9	10	Σ X
1														
2														
3														
4														
5														
Σ Σ X =													Σ Σ X=	

FIELD EXPERIMENT : transfer data sheet

Control Group Football		Trials																				
Subjects		1	2	3	4	5	6	7	8	9	10	11	12	13	14	15	16	17	18	19	20	Σ X
1																						
2																						
3																						
4																						
5																						

$\Sigma \Sigma$ X=

Experimental group Volleyball		Trials																				
Subjects		1	2	3	4	5	6	7	8	9	10	11	12	13	14	15	16	17	18	19	20	Σ X
1																						
2																						
3																						
4																						
5																						

$\Sigma \Sigma$ X=

Experimental Group Football		Trials																				
Subjects		1	2	3	4	5	6	7	8	9	10	11	12	13	14	15	16	17	18	19	20	Σ X
1																						
2																						
3																						
4																						
5																						

$\Sigma \Sigma$ X=

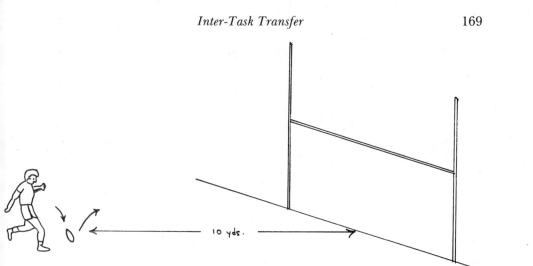

DROP-KICK OR BALL OVER CROSS-BAR

Fig. 12-7:

Chapter 13

SIMPLE REACTION TIME

INTRODUCTION

IN THE 1972 OLYMPIC GAMES in Munich, an American swimmer lost the gold medal by a few thousandths of a second. This is just one example of many in which medals or games have been won or lost by a seemingly insignificant amount of time. When the athlete attempts to determine what he could have done to better that time, invariably he must consider the factor of reaction time.

Reaction time (RT) or response latency, is best defined as the time between the onset of a stimulus to the initiation of a response. It is the time required to initiate an overt response. Woodworth and Schlosberg (1963) state that it is the S-R time interval. The individual cannot begin to move the instant he observes the stimulus. Various physiological processes are involved from the time the stimulus is observed until the response is begun. The sense organ must be aroused, the nerves must conduct the impulse to the brain and then from the brain to the muscles, and the muscles must contract before an overt response can be effected. These processes involve time, thus the occurrence of the S-R time interval or RT.

Experiments involving RT have been of several different kinds. When the subject must initiate a response to a single stimulus, it is called simple RT. The subject knows in advance what stimulus will come and what response is required. Another kind of RT experiment involves alternatives where there are different stimuli calling for different responses. This type experiment involves choice RT; the subject must make the proper response to the corresponding stimulus. For example, there are three stimulus lights, each a different color. Each light has associated with it a response key. The subject must depress or release the proper response key according to the stimulus light that flashes. A third type of RT experiment is the associative RT experiment. This procedure involves words and the amount of time required to associate a word with its correct associate. Other variations of RT experiments have been used but these three types will suffice as examples of what is involved when one speaks of RT. The concern of this chapter will be only with simple RT.

RT is relatively easy to measure. As a result, it has been a popular topic for experimentation. In a review of simple RT studies only, Teichner (1954) referred to 163 studies. Kamlet and Boisvert (1969) compiled a bibliography of 540 abstracted references dealing with RT in selected human information-processing tasks. Symington (1971) added 351 references to the Kamlet and Boisvert bibliography. These are by no means exhaustive but serve to indicate the extensiveness of the research dealing with RT.

From this extensive research, it is possible to consider the relation of various factors or conditions to RT. These factors include variables such as the type of stimulus, the intensity and duration of the stimulus, the response required, the nature of the subject, and performance factors. RT has been shown to vary, i.e. be faster or slower, by including in the experiment variations of any of these factors.

Time of reaction has generally been found to depend on the sense organ that is stimulated. Woodworth and Schlosberg (1963) stated that it has been almost universally found that RT is slowest to a visual stimulus as compared to tactile and auditory stimuli. Conflicting evidence has been reported concerning the order of latency for tactile and auditory stimuli.

The strength or intensity of the stimulus is another factor which can affect RT. Generally it has been found that the RT is long when the stimulus is weak and becomes shorter as the stimulus increases to medium and high intensities (Woodworth and Schlosberg, 1963). Teichner (1954) stated, however, that this relationship between the RT and stimulus intensity is a nonlinear one, that above a certain point this relation does not continue to increase but stabilizes. This would indicate that beyond that point, additional increases in intensity of the stimulus would not be beneficial.

Another factor which appears to affect RT is the subject's readiness to respond to the stimulus. Teichner (1954) reported that investigations have shown that the use of a *ready* signal prior to the onset of the stimulus yields faster RT's than the omission of such a signal. Most RT experiments therefore involve the use of the ready signal. The period of time between this ready signal and the onset of the stimulus has been termed the foreperiod. It is during this time that the subject prepares or readies himself to respond to the coming stimulus. Woodworth and Schlosberg (1963) state that if the foreperiod is too short, the subject will not have time to get ready, but if it is too long, his readiness may fade away. It has generally been agreed that the optimal foreperiod is between 1.0 and 4.0 seconds. Thus, in order to utilize the optimal foreperiod and to prevent the subject from attempting to synchronize his response with the stimulus, randomizing the length of the foreperiod from 1.0 to 4.0

...s has generally been adopted as a proper procedure for RT ...iments.

...actice is another consideration in RT experiments. The average ...ject continues to improve for several hundred trials spaced over several days. However, the largest improvement, and the only improvement which can really affect the results of an RT experiment, occurs in the first few trials. Norrie (1967) indicated this effect showing that practice does not affect the amount of true score variance except for the first few trials. The reason for this early practice effect on such a simple task has not been adequately explained. But, since there is an effect, the experimenter may want to permit a few trials of practice at the beginning of any RT experiment if he wishes to determine a more reliable and valid estimate of RT.

The age of the subject is also a variable which affects RT. Goodenough (1935) indicated that RT improves rather steadily until about age fifteen. Pierson and Montoye (1958) tested over four hundred subjects ranging in age from eight to eighty-three years. The fastest RT's were recorded for persons in their early twenties. Hodgkins (1963) tested 930 people from ages six to eighty-four and found similar results, with speed of response increasing steadily to approximately age nineteen and then decreasing. For the experimenter, these findings indicate a need to be aware of the age of the subjects being used in the experiment since RT has been shown to be related to age. In general, it appears that RT improves steadily until about the late teens or early twenties and then steadily declines. Sex of the subject is also related to RT. Males generally demonstrate faster RT's than females.

Other factors which appear to be related to RT include the body limb involved, reaction to the cessation or onset of a stimulus, the duration of the stimulus, and the effect of strenuous exercise. Further investigations of these considerations are needed before definite conclusions can be made concerning their relation to simple RT.

Thus RT experiments can be seen to be not as easy or uncomplicated as one might suspect when one considers the many variables related to and affecting performance. The experimenter must consider many factors before proceeding with his experiment. Pilot studies should be used to answer such problems as how much practice should be given each subject, how many trials each subject should receive, and which trials should be used in the analysis of data.

GENERAL RESEARCH FINDINGS

Some of the more conclusive findings in the study of simple RT are:
(1) Visual stimuli usually produce slower RT's than auditory or tactile

stimuli. No definite conclusion can be made concerning the order of auditory and tactile stimuli, but evidence usually favors the latter.

2. RT is a function of age, with RT's improving until the late teens or early twenties and then steadily slowing down.
3. RT for men is generally faster than for women.
4. The foreperiod, the time between the ready signal and the onset of the stimulus, should be randomly varied from 1.0 to 4.0 seconds, for best performance.
5. RT improves as the intensity of the stimulus increases until a certain point where the RT's stabilize and do not continue to improve.

REFERENCES

Aiken, L. R.: Reaction time and the expectancy hypothesis. *Percept Mot Skills, 19*:655, 1964.

Atwell, W. O. and Elbel, E. R.: Reaction time of male high school students in 14-17 year age groups. *Res Q Am Assoc Health Phys Educ, 19*:22, 1948.

Beise, D. and Peaseley, V.: The relation of reaction time, speed and agility of big muscle groups to certain sport skills. *Res Q Am Assoc Health Phys Educ, 8*:133, 1937.

Borghi, J. H.: Distribution of human reaction time. *Percept Mot Skills, 21*:212, 1965.

Carlton, R. M., Zimmerli, W., Farr, S. D., and Bashnagel, N. A.: Effect of strenuous physical activity upon reaction time. *Res Q Am Assoc Health Phys Educ, 40*:332, 1969.

Cattell, J. M.: The influence of the intensity of the stimulus on the length of reaction time. *Brain, 9*:512, reprinted 1947.

Drazin, D. H.: Effects of foreperiod, foreperiod variability, and probability of stimulus occurrence on simple reaction time. *J Exp Psychol, 62*:43, 1961.

Elbel, E. R.: A study of response time before and after strenuous exercise. *Res Q Am Assoc Health Phys Educ, 11*:86, 1940.

Elliot, R.: Simple visual and simple auditory reaction time: A comparison. *Psychonomic Sci, 19*:335, 1968.

Foley, P. J.: The foreperiod and simple reaction time. *Can J Psychol, 13*:20, 1959.

Forbes, G.: The effect of certain variables on visual and auditory reaction time. *J Exp Psychol, 35*:153, 1945.

Goldstone, S.: Reaction time to the onset and termination of lights and sounds. *Percept Mot Skills, 27*:1023, 1968.

Goodenough, F. L.: The development of the reactive process from early childhood to maturity. *J Exp Psychol, 25*:431, 1935.

Henry, F. M.: Force-time characteristics of the sprint start. *Res Q Am Assoc Health Phys Educ, 23*:301, 1952.

Hodgkins, J.: Reaction time and speed of movement in males and females of various ages. *Res Q Am Assoc Health Phys Educ, 34*:335, 1963.

Johnson, H. M.: Reaction time measurements. *Psychol Bull, 20*:562, 1923.

Kamlet, A. S. and Boisvert, L. J.: Reaction time: A bibliography with abstracts. Aberdeen Proving Grounds, Md., U. S. Army Human Engineering Laboratories, 1969.

Kaswan, J. and Young, S.: Effect of luminance exposure duration and task complexity on reaction time. *J Exp Psychol, 69*:393, 1965.

Kornblum, S. and Koster, W. G.: The effect of signal intensity and training on simple reaction time. *Acta Psychol, 27*:71, 1967.

Kroll, W.: Quality of simple reaction time and the psychological refractory period. *Res Q Am Assoc Health Phys Educ*, *40*:105, 1969.

Lanier, L. H.: The interrelations of speed and reaction experiments. *J Exp Psychol*, *17*:371, 1934.

Liu, I. and Kuo, S.: Initial improvement in simple reaction time. *J Exp Psychol*, *78*:593, 1968.

Locke, E. A.: Effects of knowledge of results, feedback in relation to standards, goals on reaction time performance. *Am J Psychol*, *81*:566, 1968.

May, M. J.: Sensitive reaction time switches. *Percept Mot Skills*, *18*:360, 1964.

Medeiros, R. R., White, R. K., and Ayoub, M. M.: The effect of light and sound variables on reaction time. *J Engineering Psychol*, *4*:9, 1965.

Nakamura, H.: An experimental study of reaction time of the start in running a race. *Res Q Am Assoc Health Phys Educ*, *5*:33, 1934 supplement.

Olsen, E. A.: Relationship between psychological capacities and success in college athletics. *Res Q Am Assoc Health Phys Educ*, *27*:79, 1956.

Pease, V. P.: The intensity-time relation of a stimulus in simple visual reaction time. *Psychol Record*, *14*:157, 1964.

Pierson, W. R.: Comparison of fencers and nonfencers by psychomotor, space perception, and anthropometric measures. *Res Q Am Assoc Health Phys Educ*, *27*:90, 1956.

Pierson, W. R. and Montoye, H. J.: Movement time, reaction time, and age. *J Gerontol*, *13*:418, 1958.

Pierson, H. R. and Rasch, P. J.: Determination of a representative score for a simple reaction and movement time. *Percept Mot Skills*, *9*:107, 1959.

Poulton, E. C.: Perceptual anticipation and reaction time. *Q J Exp Psychol*, *2*:99, 1950.

Raab, D. H.; and Fehrer, E.: The effect of stimulus duration and luminance on visual reaction time. *J Exp Psychol*, *64*:326,1962.

Rains, J. D.: Reaction time to onset and cessation of a visual stimulus. *Psychol Record*, *11*:265, 1961.

Rangazas, E. P.: A comparative analysis of selected college athletes and non-athletes on several hand-foot reaction time measures. Unpublished doctoral dissertation. Indiana University, 1957.

Singer, R. N. and Weiss, S. A: Effects of weight reduction on selected anthropometric, physical, and performance measures of wrestlers. *Res Q Am Assoc Health Phys Educ*, *39*:361, 1968.

Symington, L. G.: Reaction time: A bibliography with abstracts. Supplement I. Aberdeen Proving Ground, MD., U. S. Army Human Engineering Laboratories, 1971.

Teichner, W. H.: Recent studies of simple reaction time. *Psychol Bull*, *51*:128, 1954.

Telford, C. W.: The refractory phase of voluntary and associative responses. *J Exp Psychol*, *14*:1, 1931.

Tuttle, W. W., Morehouse, L. E., and Armbruster, D.: Two studies in swimming starts. *Res Q Am Assoc Health Phys Educ*, *10*:89, 1939.

Wilkinson, J. J.: A study of reaction-time measures to a kinesthetic and visual stimulus for selected groups of athletes and non-athletes. *Proceedings NCPEAM*, 1959.

Woodworth, R. S. and Schlosberg, H.: *Experimental Psychology* (revised). New York, Holt, Rinehart and Winston, 1963.

LABORATORY EXPERIMENT

PURPOSE. To compare RT to a visual stimulus with an auditory stimulus.

EQUIPMENT. Simple reaction time apparatus and timer*

PROCEDURE. Each subject will be tested twice in this experiment, once reacting to the visual stimulus (a light) and once to the auditory stimulus (a buzzer). All subjects should be given five practice trials and twenty test trials for each of these tests.

Divide a group of four subjects into two groups each. One group will be tested first with the visual stimulus, the other group with the auditory stimulus first. This procedure will balance for order effects in the experiment. Thus all visual and auditory stimulus data may be statistically treated without concern for bias due to order-of-tests effect. Test all subjects on their first test before administering their second test.

The RT testing equipment should be set-up on a table, preferably with an opaque screen between the subject and experimenter. The digital timer and control for the RT apparatus should be in front of the experimenter. The subject's response box, light, and key should be on the opposite side of the screen in front of the subject. A chair should be provided for the subject.

The following procedures should be followed for every subject on each test:

1. Ask the subject to be seated and to arrange his chair so that he is comfortable with his preferred arm and hand resting on the table.
2. Explain to the subject that he is to rest his finger on the button of the response box in front of him and that he is to depress that button *as fast as possible* as soon as he sees the light in front of him go on or hears the buzzer, depending on the test being administered to the subject.
3. Give the subject a verbal "ready" as a warning signal. This signal should precede the onset of the stimulus by a random one to four seconds for every trial.
4. Allow the subject five practice trials to insure he knows what to do. Twenty test trials should then follow immediately.
5. Record the times from the timer on the data sheet provided.
6. If you notice that on a certain trial the subject obviously anticipated the stimulus, discard that trial and replace it with another. If the subject continually does this, you should not use his data.

RESULTS.

Record the times for each subject for the visual stimulus and auditory stimulus.

For purposes of statistical calculation, do not use the decimals. Without the decimals, the times become milliseconds rather than thousandths of a second (e.g. .212 becomes 212 ms). Determine a RT score for each subject on both tests by calculating the mean of the twenty trials. Thus

*Reaction time apparatus is explained in the chapter entitled, "Reaction-Time—Movement Time."

each subject will have one score for visual stimulus and one score for auditory stimulus. Next, calculate the mean and standard deviation for each test and then proceed with a *t*-test for related measures. A significant *t* will indicate that RT with one stimulus (the one with a faster mean RT) is better than with the other stimulus.

FIELD EXPERIMENT

PURPOSE. To compare the difference between male and female RT on a sprinter's start in track.

EQUIPMENT. Automatic Performance Analyzer (Dekan Timing Devices, Model 631) and Special Start Switch (an accessory included with the Automatic Performance Analyzer). Further information concerning this equipment is found in the chapter on speed and accuracy. Whistle.

PROCEDURE. Secure the Special Start Switch (the foot pedal) in such a way that it will not slip when the subject responds to the starting signal. Set up the Performance Analyzer so that the experimenter will be behind and to the side of the subject.

Divide the class into two groups of four males and four females. Each subject of each group should receive five practice trials followed by twenty test trials. The following procedures should be followed for each subject:

1. Instruct the subject to take a sprinter's start in such a way that his right foot is on the foot pedal switch. A demonstration by the experimenter of the proper position is suggested.
2. Explain that the procedure for each trial will be first a verbal "Take your mark" and then a blast on the whistle. When he hears the whistle, he is, as fast as possible, to move a few yards straight ahead. Randomly vary the amount of time between the verbal warning and the whistle blast between one and four seconds.
3. Give the subject five practice trials to insure that he understands the directions.
4. Record the times for each trial to the nearest .01 of a second on the data sheet provided.

RESULTS.

For purposes of statistical calculation, do not use the decimal for the recorded times. Determine an RT score for each subject by calculating the mean time for the twenty test trials. Record these scores on the data sheet provided. Next, calculate the mean and standard deviation for the males and for the females. To determine if a real difference does exist between these means, use an independent *t*-test. A significant *t* indicates that one group is faster than the other.

LABORATORY EXPERIMENT : SIMPLE REACTION TIME DATA SHEET

	Test 1 Visual Stim.	Test 2 Auditory Stim.		Test 1 Auditory Stim.	Test 2 Visual Stim.
S_1			S_3		
Trial 1	_____	_____	Trial 1	_____	_____
2	_____	_____	2	_____	_____
3	_____	_____	3	_____	_____
4	_____	_____	4	_____	_____
5	_____	_____	5	_____	_____
6	_____	_____	6	_____	_____
7	_____	_____	7	_____	_____
8	_____	_____	8	_____	_____
9	_____	_____	9	_____	_____
10	_____	_____	10	_____	_____
11	_____	_____	11	_____	_____
12	_____	_____	12	_____	_____
13	_____	_____	13	_____	_____
14	_____	_____	14	_____	_____
15	_____	_____	15	_____	_____
16	_____	_____	16	_____	_____
17	_____	_____	17	_____	_____
18	_____	_____	18	_____	_____
19	_____	_____	19	_____	_____
20	_____	_____	20	_____	_____
	$\Sigma X=$_____	$\Sigma Y=$_____		$\Sigma Y=$_____	$\Sigma X=$_____
	$\overline{X}=$_____	$\overline{Y}=$_____		$\overline{Y}=$_____	$\overline{X}=$_____

	Test 1 Visual Stim.	Test 2 Auditory Stim.		Test 1 Auditory Stim.	Test 2 Visual Stim.
S_2			S_4		
Trial 1	_____	_____	Trial 1	_____	_____
2	_____	_____	2	_____	_____
3	_____	_____	3	_____	_____
4	_____	_____	4	_____	_____
5	_____	_____	5	_____	_____
6	_____	_____	6	_____	_____
7	_____	_____	7	_____	_____
8	_____	_____	8	_____	_____
9	_____	_____	9	_____	_____
10	_____	_____	10	_____	_____
11	_____	_____	11	_____	_____
12	_____	_____	12	_____	_____
13	_____	_____	13	_____	_____
14	_____	_____	14	_____	_____
15	_____	_____	15	_____	_____
16	_____	_____	16	_____	_____
17	_____	_____	17	_____	_____
18	_____	_____	18	_____	_____
19	_____	_____	19	_____	_____
20	_____	_____	20	_____	_____
	$\Sigma X=$_____	$\Sigma Y=$_____		$\Sigma Y=$_____	$\Sigma X=$_____
	$\overline{X}=$_____	$\overline{Y}=$_____		$\overline{Y}=$_____	$\overline{X}=$_____

LABORATORY EXPERIMENT : SIMPLE REACTION TIME DATA SHEET

Mean RT for each subject :

	Visual Stimulus (X)	Auditory Stimulus (Y)	D	D^2
S1				
2				
3				
4				
$\Sigma X=$	$\Sigma Y=$	$\Sigma D=$	$\Sigma D^2=$
$\bar{X}=$	$\bar{Y}=$		

D = Difference score between X and Y pair.

FIELD EXPERIMENT : SIMPLE REACTION TIME DATA SHEET :

MALES

Subject	Trials																			
	1	2	3	4	5	6	7	8	9	10	11	12	13	14	15	16	17	18	19	20
1																				
2																				
3																				
4																				

FEMALES

Subject	Trials																			
	1	2	3	4	5	6	7	8	9	10	11	12	13	14	15	16	17	18	19	20
1																				
2																				
3																				
4																				

	MALES			FEMALES	
	$\bar{X}$	X^2		$\bar{X}$	X^2
1			1		
2			2		
3			3		
4			4		
	$\bar{X}=$	$\Sigma X^2=$		$\bar{X}=$	$\Sigma X^2=$

Chapter 14

STRESS

INTRODUCTION

STRESS MAY GENERALLY be defined as occurring when a particular situation threatens a person in his attainment of some goal, causing a temporary physiological and psychological imbalance. This imbalance, Selye (1956) theorizes, is a disruption in the homeostasis of the organism, and by various internal chemical reactions the body attempts to regain normal equilibrium. The stimuli that cause this condition are called stressors, and may arise from various physiological, psychological, social, or environmental origins, or even a combination of them. Whatever the basis, stress is unavoidable, as any situation or event places the individual under it to some degree.

Due to the individual differences inherent and developed in man, stress does not affect everyone in the same manner or to the same extent. A particular stressful event such as the presence of an audience may be beneficial to the performance of some, have negligible effects for others, and yet be disruptive to others. Generally, the human organism does have a wide tolerance to stress, but when the stresses go beyond man's limits of tolerance, changes in performance result. Too much stress by overstimulation with such variables as noise, temperature, illumination, humidity, and the like, or too little stress or stimulation (sensory deprivation), result in disruptive effects upon performance levels. Optimal performance usually occurs when stimulation falls between such extremes. However, research has indicated that the nature of the task, the proficiency level of the performer as well as his personality, are important variables of consideration when predicting output under stress-induced conditions.

The measurement of stress in humans has been rather indirect, being confined mainly to the evaluation of various physiological parameters. The biological functions utilized for measurement have usually been cardiovascular and respiratory rates, body temperature, blood pressure, and palmar skin conductance. Other measurements have included the measurement of changes in eosinophil count, keterosteroids in the urine, and the production of antidiuretic hormones secreted in the thalamus.

Changes in muscular tension have also been recorded as measures of stress. Another technique employed has been the polling of the subject directly in regard to the effect of a stressor upon his present feelings or upon future performance. In most motor tasks stress has been measured by its disruptive effect upon the performance level of the individual. Learning curves demonstrate this phenomenon graphically.

Experimentally produced stress is of two main types: (1) stress induced through failure, and (2) stress induced by the nature of the task itself, by conditions surrounding the task, and by pretest conditions.

Stress induced through failure may be accomplished by presenting the subjects with an unsolvable task, by interrupting before the subjects can complete a task, and by introducing false norms that are above the levels of performance for the individual. Stress induced by the task itself may be accomplished by strong extraneous sensory input (noise, light), verbal disparagement, too many things for the subject to accomplish in a particular time interval, or insufficient time allotted to complete the task.

Individuals, as it has been stated before, differ to a great extent in their reactions to a particular stressor. Some people can achieve at a much higher level under certain apparent stressful conditions whereas others tend to suffer severe decremental effects in performance. The main cause may be motivational in nature as low anxious subjects tend to improve in performance in complex tasks under stressful conditions. More highly anxious individuals seem to be hampered by high levels of motivation and stress when under similar conditions.

Prior experience and skill level are two variables that tend to allow one to resist the disruptive effects of stress. Exhibition or pre-season games afford the athlete not only the opportunity to practice his skills under game-like situations but they also allow him to adapt to some of the stress encountered by playing in front of spectators and by the very nature of the competitive event itself. The more skillful the performer, whether an athlete or a musician, the less disruptive will be the effects of the stressor upon his performance.

GENERAL RESEARCH FINDINGS

Some of the more conclusive findings in the area of stress are as follows:

1. A more complex skill is more hampered by stressors than is a simple task. Performance in simple tasks may actually be facilitated. Studies in which anxiety levels of subjects are compared demonstrate that highly anxious individuals perform better at simple tasks under stress whereas low anxious individuals are more effective at complex tasks.

2. Stress introduced early in learning causes some decrement whereas introduction late in learning has been found to produce a slight facilitation in performance.
3. The higher the level of proficiency in a particular skill, the less effect stress will have upon performance.

REFERENCES

Berkun, M. M., Biaklek, H. M., Kern, R. P., and Yagi, K.: Psychological stress in man. *Psychol Monogr*, 76:1, 1962.

Carron, A. V.: Motor performance under stress. *Res Q Am Assoc Health Phys Educ*, 39:463, 1968.

Carron, A. V. and Morford, W. R.: Anxiety, stress and motor learning. *Percept Mot Skills*, 27:507, 1968.

Castaneda, A.: Effects of stress on complex learning and performance. *J Exp Psychol*, 52:9, 1956.

Castaneda, A. and Lipsitt, L. P.: Relation of stress and differential position habits to performance in motor learning. *J Exp Psychol* 57:25, 1959.

Castaneda, A., and Palermo, D. S.: Psychomotor performance as a function of amount of training and stress. *J Exp Psychol*, 50:175, 1955.

Deese, J.: Skilled performance and conditions of stress. In Glaser, R. (Ed.): *Training Research and Education*. Pittsburgh, University of Pittsburgh Press, 1962.

Jacobs, I. A. and Kowalski, C.: A method for inducing stress in a laboratory setting. *Int J Soc Psychiatry*, 12:273, 1966.

Kemp, G. L. and Ellestad, M. H.: The current application of maximal treadmill stress testing. *Calif Med*, Nov., 1967, p. 406.

Lazarus, R. S., Deese, J., and Osler, S. F.: The effects of psychological stress upon performance. *Psychol Bull*, 49:293, 1952.

Lazarus, R. S., Speisman, J. C., Mordkoff, A. M., and Davidson, L. A.: A laboratory study of psychological stress produced by a motion picture film. *Psychol Mongr*, 76: 1962.

Ryan, E. D.: Motor performance under stress as a function of the amount of practice. *Percept Mot Skills*, 13:103, 1961.

Ryan, E. D.: Effects of stress on motor performance and learning. *Res Q Am Assoc Health Phys Educ*, 33:111, 1962.

Ryan, E. D.: Relationship between motor performance and arousal. *Res Q Am Assoc Health Phys Educ*, 33:279, 1962.

Selye, H.: *The Stress of Life*. New York, McGraw Hill, 1956.

Willis, M. P.: Stress effects on skill. *J Exp Psychol*, 74:460, 1967.

Ulrich, C.: Stress and sport. In Johnson, W. R. (Ed.): *Science and Medicine of Exercise and Sports*. New York, Harper and Row, 1960.

LABORATORY EXPERIMENT

PURPOSE. To study the effects of stress upon the learning of a motor task.

EQUIPMENT. Star-tracer and a shock source with two electrodes.

DESIGN. Two groups, matched according to initial skill on task or on a random basis.

PROCEDURE. Each subject, using the dominant hand, will perform ten trials on the star-tracer. One electrode is attached to the top and one to the bottom of the forearm of the non-dominant hand during stress testing trials. The subjects will not be able to directly view their hand or star pattern but will observe them directly via the mirror. The groups will be tested as follows:

Group A
        Stress Condition   Nonstress Condition

          | trials 1 – 5 | | trials 6 – 10 |

Group B
        Nonstress Condition   Stress Condition

          | trials 1 – 5 | | trials 6 – 10 |

The object of the task is to trace one complete star pattern with the electrically attached stylus as quickly as possible making the fewest number of touches (errors) to the sides of the pattern. The examiner will record the length of time required to complete the task with a .1 sec. stopwatch plus the number of touches (errors) of the stylus against the boundaries of the pattern. During the shock trials the subjects will be shocked every five seconds for a five second duration. The shock intensity will be constant for each shock and for each subject until the trial is completed. The average pain threshold for the subjects might be determined in a pilot test. Lower starting shock intensities may be required for female subjects. Rest intervals of thirty seconds will be given between trials.*

RESULTS.

1. Record resultant data on the master sheet provided.
2. Plot learning curves for each subject.
3. Calculate a score for each individual determined by the following formula:

$$\frac{(errors) + (time\ in\ secs.)}{2}$$

---

*It is probably desirable to measure a physiological index of stress effect (for example, heart rate). In this way, the effect of the shock source, as monitored throughout the shock trials, can be determined physiologically as well as in star tracing performance.

4. Calculate trial 5 — trial 1 for each group as well as trial 10 — trial 6 for each group. Determine the statistical difference between the two groups on the trial difference scores in both cases with the use of *t*-tests.

FIELD EXPERIMENT

PURPOSE. To study the effects of stress upon the performance of a gross motor task.

EQUIPMENT. Basketball court and basketballs.

DESIGN. One group acting as their own controls.

PROCEDURE. Without prior warm-up each subject will stand alone at the foul-line and perform twenty consecutive trials, attempting to bounce the basketball off the floor on one bounce into an official basketball basket. Ten second rest periods should be given between each block of trials (five trials in a block). Stress in the form of noise and distraction produced by the remainder of the subjects will be presented to each individual subject during the stress trials. Score five points for each successful basket; three points for hitting the rim; one point for hitting the backboard (Fig. 14-2). The design is as follows:

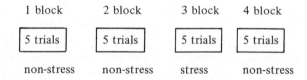

RESULTS.

1. Record resultant data on sheet provided.
2. Plot performance curves for each subject.
3. Use test-retest method of determining reliability of performance. (Correlate mean scores for each subject for block 1 and block 2.)
4. Determine statistical difference between blocks 1 and 4 with *t*-test to test for the learning effect. Use *t*-tests for blocks 2 and 3 and 3 and 4 to examine the effects of stress on performance.

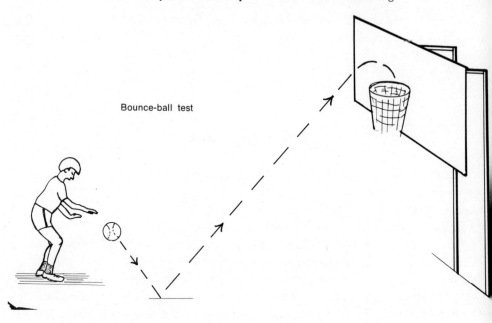

Bounce-ball test

APPENDIX

PURCHASED EQUIPMENT. The BRS-Foringer Company, A Division of TECH SERV., INC., 5451 Holland Drive, Beltsville, Maryland, 20705 manufactures one type of Mirror Tracer. The Lafayette Instrument Company, P. O. Box 1279, 52 By-Pass, Lafayette, Indiana, offers another type of Mirror Tracer.

One unit is automatic in the recording of the errors while tracing while the other model is non-automatic. The Marietta Apparatus Company, 118 Maple Street, Marietta, Ohio, produces yet another Mirror Tracing model. This unit is automatic in that the errors are recorded on a counter. This company also offers a Two-Arm Tracing Apparatus that may be used in tasks requiring the use of both arms.

The Lafayette Instrument Company, P. O. Box 1279, 52 By-Pass, Lafayette, Indiana, offers several models of shock sources.

CONSTRUCTED EQUIPMENT. Mirror Tracer: The construction of a Mirror Tracer is a relatively easy task. The platform is made of plywood with dimensions thirteen by thirteen by one inch. The surface is sanded allowing for a smooth trace of the pattern. Two posts, nine inches long, are attached at one end on either side of the platform to hold the shield in place. This shield, thirteen by nine by one-half inches is adjustable in

GROUP A   LABORATORY EXPERIMENT : STRESS DATA SHEET

Subjects \ Trials	1	2	3	4	5	6	7	8	9	10	1 - 5	6 - 10
1												
2												
3												
4												
5												

$\bar{X} =$

FIELD EXPERIMENT : STRESS DATA SHEET

Subjects \ Trials	BLOCK 1					BLOCK 2					BLOCK 3					BLOCK 4					BLOCKS			
	1	2	3	4	5	6	7	8	9	10	11	12	13	14	15	16	17	18	19	20	1 $\bar{X}$	2 $\bar{X}$	3 $\bar{X}$	4 $\bar{X}$
1																								
2																								
3																								
4																								
5																								
6																								
7																								
8																								

$\bar{X} =$

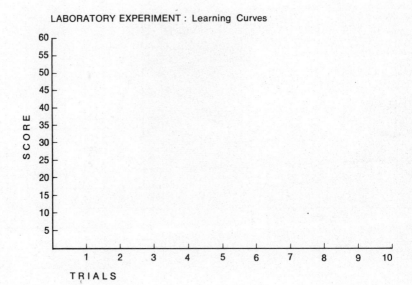

LABORATORY EXPERIMENT : Learning Curves

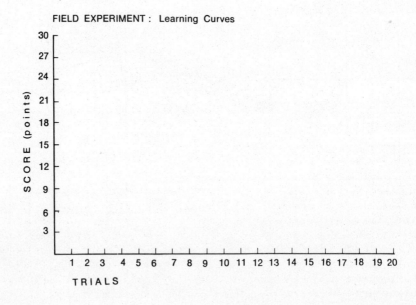

FIELD EXPERIMENT : Learning Curves

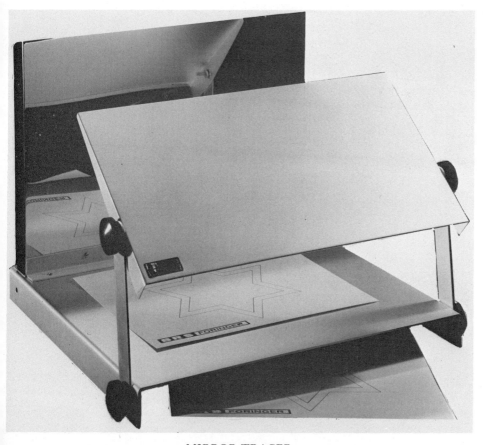

MIRROR TRACER

Figure 14-6: The Mirror Tracer is an instrument manufactured by BRS-Foringer. It is designed to demonstrate the results of a conflict in sensory information. The sensory information given when using the Mirror Tracer is both visual and kinesthetic. In this experiment, the subject must trace around a printed form while looking at the form and his hand in a mirror. The subject is prevented from directly seeing the form or his hand by the adjustable shield. Thus, in effect, his eyes, seeing an inverted image, "say" he should move his hand up, for example. But when his hand moves up, it is the wrong direction. The subject must learn to translate his visual information (called "feedback" or "cues") to correspond with his kinesthetic feedback. Or the subject must learn to pay no attention to what his hand says is "right" and act only on his visual feedback.

AUTOMATIC SCORING MIRROR TRACER

Figure 14-7: Incorporated in this new Auto Tally Mirror Tracer are many outstanding features. The unit is durable, portable and extremely trouble-free.

It will automatically record every error as the subject moves off the insulated star pattern onto the conductive aluminum base. The insulated star is flush with the plate so that no sensory cues are given. A light will flash when the subject skews from the star pattern onto the conductive plate. Two outputs are provided so a stop clock can be connected to record total error time.

MIRROR TRACING APPARATUS WITH ELECTRICAL READOUT

Figure 14-8: This apparatus consists of a metal star pattern with a metal bottom plate arranged so that the subject can trace the pattern with a stylus by watching in the mirror but is shielded from direct vision of the pattern.

Readout is accomplished by means of a counter which registers the number of errors as the subject touches the pattern edges. A light is provided to show when the stylus is in contact with the base plate of the pattern. The counter switch has a momentary position for intermittent timing of the counter switch and a lock position for continuous operation. Reset is accomplished by means of a reset wheel on the right of the counter.

TWO-ARM TRACING APPARATUS

Figure 14-9: This tracing apparatus proposes a motor learning task which makes use of both arms. The subject moves the tracing point forward or back by bringing his arms closer together or further apart, respectively. For sideward motion of the point, subject must move both arms in the desired direction while maintaining equal spacing between them. Simple tasks might include writing initials, name, or following a pattern.

order to prevent the subject from directly viewing his hand as he traces the pattern. At the opposite end of the platform, a mirror is attached to a nine by four and one-half by one-half inch piece of plywood on a three inch stand. The mirror is placed at such an angle as to allow the subject to view by reflection his hand and the pattern to be traced. A pencil is used to trace the pattern. Two sample patterns used in star tracers are presented on the following page. The solid-line star pattern requires that the subject trace inside the boundaries with a pencil. Count one error each time the boundary lines are touched. The star pattern designed with a series of circles requires that the subject connect each circle as progression is made around the star pattern. Count one error for each circle left unconnected.

Shock Source: The shocker may be constructed from equipment that is easily found in most laboratories. The description and illustration is as follows:

A shocker can be used to test the effects of anxiety on motor performance. It produces a mild electrical shock which introduces an anxiety-producing stimulus in the test subject. The subject's performance may then be compared to a previous test without shock. The shocker consists of a normally-off push-button switch, a variable transformer, a step-up transformer, and two 100,000 ohm resistors. (See schematic diagram.) These components are housed in a sheet metal box which is mounted on a plywood base. A rectangular hole has been cut in the base to provide a handhold for portability.

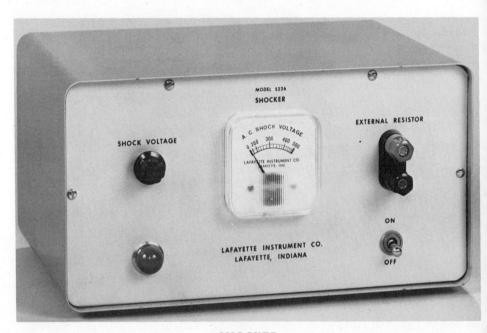

SHOCKER

Figure 14-10: This is an excellent economical AC shocker capable of constant voltage or constant current output. The voltage range or current range is continuously variable from subliminal to electro-convulsive. Voltage is monitored by a meter on the front panel. Voltage is variable from 0 to 500 volts. Maximum current is 40 milliamps.

A special plug-in resistor of 500,000 ohms converts the shocker from constant voltage to constant current, with a range of 0 to 1 milliamp (the most popular and useful range).

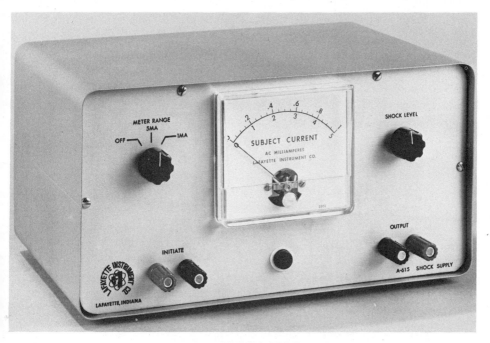

MASTER SHOCKER

Figure 14-11: The Master Shocker is a constant current generator with more flexibility of use than found in most shockers. The maximum voltage produced by this shocker is 2500 volts AC. The current range is from 0 to 5 milliamps and is continuously monitored on a front panel meter. This range includes all current values used in 95 percent of animal studies reported in recent literature. Most of the studies that used currents exceeding 5 milliamps were employing electro-convulsive shock. Any current from 0 to 5 milliamps can be selected with the continuously variable shock voltage control.

A special and important feature of this shocker is a set of decade switches which allows the Behavioral Scientist to select values of internal current limiting the resistor from 500 thousand to 4 million ohms in 10,000 ohm steps. A large value limiting the resistor maintains the shock current at a constant level independent of the animal resistance. The many values of internal limiting resistance that are available in this shocker allow the researcher to replicate a very broad range of shock conditions.

The shocker may be turned ON and OFF manually or by remote control with a simple switch closure.

The primary of the variable transformer is connected to the 117 volt, 60 H Z power line whenever the push-button switch is depressed. Zero to 117 volts AC from the secondary of the variable transformer are sent to the primary of the step-up transformer. Each side of the secondary of this transformer is connected to the output through a 100,000 ohm resistor. This provides an output isolated from both ground and the power line for safety of the subject.

It has been determined that electrical shock must be applied as a

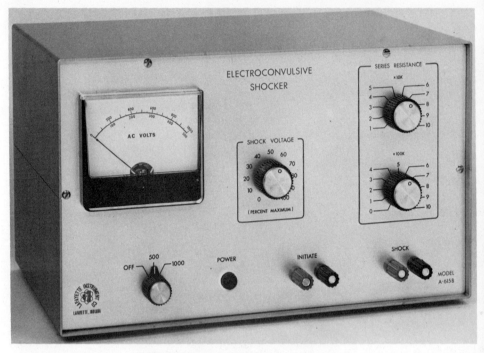

SHOCKER, ELECTRO-CONVULSIVE

Figure 14-12: This shocker is a constant current generator especially designed for use in the electro-convulsive shock range. The maximum voltage produced by this shocker is 700 volts AC. The current range is from 0 to 90 milliamperes. This range includes all current values used in 98 percent of electro-convulsive shock studies found in recent literature. Any current from 0 to 90 milliamps can be selected with the continuously variable dial.

A special and important feature of this shocker is a set of decade switches which allows the Behavioral Scientist to select any value internal limiting the resistor up to 4 megohm in 10,000 ohm steps. The use of the internal limiting resistor puts a resistor in series with the subject, thus creating a constant current at a given voltage. The many values of internal limiting resistance that can be produced with this shocker allow the researcher to replicate a very broad range of shock conditions.

The shocker may be turned ON and OFF manually or by remote control with a simple switch closure.

controlled voltage is used. Besides introducing unknown factors into the data, an uncontrolled current may cause abnormal discomfort or injury to the subject if certain limits are exceeded. A controlled voltage (1-600 vac) appears at the secondary of the step-up transformer. If this voltage is applied to the subject through a resistor having a value much larger than the subject's skin resistance, the current which will flow through the subject is calculated as:

$$\text{Current} = \frac{\text{Voltage}}{\text{resistance of resistor} + \text{Subject's skin resistance}}$$

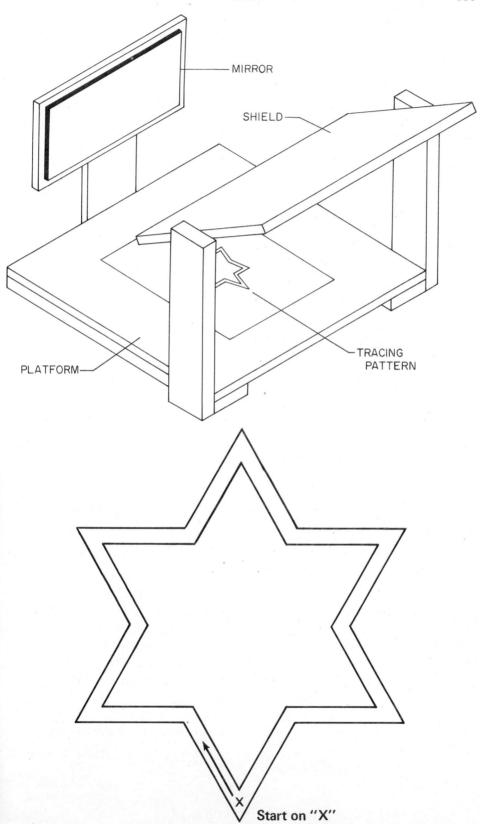

MIRROR

SHIELD

PLATFORM

TRACING PATTERN

X

Start on "X"

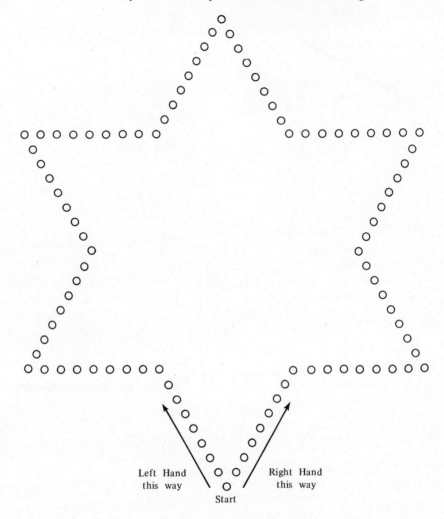

This current is relatively independent of the subject's skin resistance. For example, if the skin resistance does not exceed 10 percent of the value of the resistor, current will be held constant to within about 10 percent. It is imperative that both electrodes be attached to the same limb so that shock current cannot pass through the heart. For this reason two flat surface electrodes should be covered with electrode paste and held firmly in place on the subject's arm by a surgical rubber belt. The paste greatly lowers the skin resistance resulting in better control of current and an avoidance of a pin-pricking sensation caused by arcing between the electrode and dry skin.

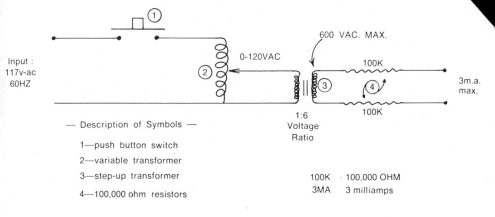

— Description of Symbols —

1—push button switch

2—variable transformer

3—step-up transformer

4—100,000 ohm resistors

100K - 100,000 OHM
3MA   3 milliamps

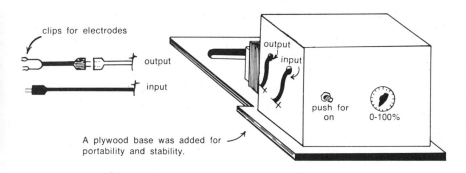

clips for electrodes

output

input

A plywood base was added for portability and stability.

push for on

0-100%

Table 24
CURRENT THROUGH THE ELECTRODES AT VARIOUS
SETTINGS ON THE VARIABLE TRANSFORMER
(As Measured through a 1000 OHM Resistor)

Percentage	Maximum	Actual*	Resistance**
10 %	.5 MA	.2 MA	301,500 OHM
15 %	.6	.4	
20 %	.8	.55	91,364
25 %	1.0	.7	
30 %	1.2	.85	82,765
35 %	1.3	.9	
40 %	1.4	1.1	54,818
45 %	1.5	1.2	
50 %	1.7	1.4	43,071
55 %	1.9	1.6	
60 %	2.1	1.8	35,166
65 %	2.3	2.0	
70 %	2.5	2.2	28,764
75 %	2.6	2.3	
80 %	2.8	2.5	25,320
85 %	2.95	2.65	
90 %	3.1	2.8	22,607
95 %	3.2	2.9	
100 %	3.3	3.0	21,100

MA = Milliamps

* Saline jelly used for making positive contact.

** The higher the current, the lower the R

——————— Chapter 15 ———————

SOCIAL FACILITATION: INDIVIDUAL VERSUS COACTING PERFORMANCE

INTRODUCTION

MOTOR SKILL PERFORMANCE has been shown to be influenced by the social context in which it occurs. Social facilitation deals with the consequences upon an individual's behavior resulting from the presence of others during his performance. Zajonc (1965) classifies social facilitation research into two experimental paradigms: audience effects and coaction effects. The audience paradigm, although not the major concern of this chapter, has recently received a good deal of attention by physical educators. In the laboratory setting the mere presence of passive spectators has been shown to have an influence on performance when compared to normal solitary conditions of practice (Martens, 1969). Should performance be enhanced by spectator presence, the practice of sport skills would best take place in a real or pseudo-real situation rather than the typical practice environment. After all, one's ability to shoot free throws is measured during the game and not during an isolated practice session in a corner of the gymnasium.

The experimental paradigm of coaction involves the simultaneous working of two or more individuals on the same tasks. The effect each individual exerts on the other members performing, although subtle in many cases, can lead to the enhancement or deterioration of a particular individual's achievement. Imagine four bowlers standing side by side on adjacent lanes preparing to roll their first balls. The mere presence of the other bowlers may have an effect on the ultimate performance of any one of the bowlers and this effect is termed coaction.

There are several variables which must be controlled in order to accurately contrast isolated performance and coactive performance. If the external rewards of task completion (it appears that task completion itself is internally reinforcing) are to be distributed equally among members of a coacting group, we assume a cooperative effort between members of the group. Should all or additional reward go to the individual(s) best performing in the coactive situation thus excluding some individuals from recognition, competition is the underlying performance drive. The effects of cooperation and competition on motor performance must be controlled before the true coactive influences on performance can be compared to individual performance (Carment, 1970a).

The effects of coaction appear to be dependent upon the subject's awareness that he can be evaluated in some way. When several performers were working together on a novel task with opaque screens preventing any visual contact, Martens and Landers (1972) found little difference between the coactive situation and an alone condition. The absence of the experimenter during testing was found to produce lower rates of motor responding as well as eliminate previously found differences between a coactive group and individual performance (Carment and Latchford, 1970). It appears that the mere physical presence of others is not always a necessary or sufficient condition for producing coaction effects upon performance (Cottrell, 1968).

In order to better predict the direction of effect that coaction or audience presence has on the performance of motor skills, a generalized theory of social facilitation proposed by Zajonc (1965) may be applied. The underlying assumption of the theory is that the mere presence of others increases the general arousal level (drive) of the individual, thereby increasing his response rate. For an individual there exists a large number of possible motor responses from which he must choose the appropriate ones to satisfy the demands of a task. The nearly infinite number of possible responses may be termed the response repertoire. Skilled performance requires only a select few of the responses in the repertoire. An unskilled learner would normally emit incorrect responses, thus, the arousing effect of the presence of others would increase the rate of incorrect responses causing abnormally poor performance. Conversely, the skilled performer emitting primarily correct response would find his performance facilitated by the presence of others.

GENERAL RESEARCH FINDINGS

1. The presence of others enhances the emission of dominant responses by increasing an individual's general drive or level of arousal.
2. Coaction, as well as the presence of an audience, enhances skilled performance and impairs initial learning.
3. In general, the effects of coaction on learning (initial stages) are negative. However, benefits may be obtained if others in the coact-

ing group provide the individual with clues about what is the correct and what is an incorrect response.

4. The presence of others is a learned source of arousal contingent upon the amount and kind of the individual's previous social experiences; the mere physical presence of others (unable to observe or evaluate performance) is not sufficient to produce coacting effects.

5. Females appear to be more sensitive than males to coaction effects on motor performance.

REFERENCES

Beasley, J.: Comparison of the peformance of individuals and three-member groups in a maze learning situation. *Percept Mot Skills, 8*:291, 1958.

Burwitz, L. and Newell, K. M.: The effects of the mere presence of coactors on learning a motor skill. *J Motor Behav, 4*:99, 1972.

Carment, D. W.: Rate of simple motor responding as a function of coaction, competition, and sex of the participants. *Psychonomic Science, 19*:342, 1970a.

Carment, D. W.: Rate of simple motor responding as a function of differential outcomes and the actual and implied presence of a coactor. *Psychonomic Science, 20*:115, 1970b.

Carment, D. W. and Latchford, M.: Rate of simple motor responding as a function of coaction, sex of the participants, and the presence or absence of the experimenter. *Psychonomic Science, 20*:253, 1970.

Cottrell, N. B.: Performance in the presence of other human beings; Mere presence, audience, and affiliation effects. In Simmel, E. C., Hoppe, R. A., and Milton, G. A. (Eds.): *Social Facilitation and Imitative Behavior*. Boston, Allyn and Bacon, 1968.

Landers, D. M. and Martens, R.: Interpersonal attraction and task difficulty effects on the motor performance of coacting groups. Paper presented at AAHPER National Convention, Houston, 1972.

McDavid, J. W., and Harari, H.: *Social Psychology: Individuals, Groups, Societies*. New York, Harper & Row, 1968.

Martens, R: Effect of an audience on learning and performance of a complex motor skill. *J Pers Soc Psychol, 12*:252, 1969.

Martens, R., and Landers, D. M.: Evaluation potential as a determinant of coaction effects. *J Exp Soc Psychol, 8*:347, 1972.

Singer, R. N.: Effect of spectators on athletes and non-athletes performing a gross motor task. *Res Q Am Assoc Health Phys Educ, 36*:473, 1965.

Singer, R. N.: Social facilitation. In Morgan, W. P. (Ed.): *Ergogenic Aids and Muscular Performance*. New York, Academic Press, 1972.

Triplett, N.: The dynamogenic factors in pacemaking and competition. *Am J Psychol, 9*:507, 1897.

Zajonc, R. B.: Social facilitation. *Science, 149*:269, 1965.

Zajonc, R. B.: *Social Psychology: An Experimental Approach*. Belmont, California, Wadsworth, 1966.

LABORATORY EXPERIMENT

PURPOSE. To compare individual versus coacting performance on a speed-of-movement task.

EQUIPMENT. Two identical tapping boards,* two styli, and two counters wired to a single interval timer. A partition should be constructed so the experimenter, timer, and counters are not in view of the subjects.

PROCEDURE. It is important that subjects be naive to the nature of the experiment. Randomly divide eight subjects into four pairs and randomly designate two pairs to receive the individual treatment first with the remaining two pairs to receive the coacting treatment first. All pairs will receive both treatments in the balanced order.

In the individual treatment, each subject will perform the task by alternately tapping the steel plates as rapidly as possible with the stylus in the preferred hand. Give each subject ten trials of twenty seconds duration followed by twenty seconds rest. The experimenter must remain isolated from the subject and no knowledge of results are to be given. The number of successful contacts is to be recorded for each trial and the counter reset. The experimenter should give an audible signal denoting the start of each trial and then immediately activate the interval timer.

In the coacting treatment, subjects will perform in pairs in such a way that they are facing each other. Follow the same practice/rest schedule as in the individual condition. The experimenter should emphasize to the pair that competition is not intended.

RESULTS.

Record the number of taps for each subject for each trial under the two conditions. Compute the means for the individual and the coacting practice situations, and run a *t*-test for correlated means.

FIELD EXPERIMENT

PURPOSE. To examine the effects of individual versus coacting performance in the skill of archery.*

EQUIPMENT. An intact archery class having already received basic instruction in technique should be used. Sufficient tackle of similar quality for all students in the class and a facility for shooting which allows at least four students to stand abreast are necessary. Target faces should be thirty-six inches in diameter.

PROCEDURE. Randomly divide the class in half (Group I and Group II) and balance for sex if the class is co-ed. During a regular class meeting

---

*A tapping board is described in the chapter on motivation.

*Any substitute activity class can be used in similar fashion.

the subjects in Group I are to be scheduled to return on an individual basis at a designated time before the next regular class period. Individually, each subject will shoot one warm-up end (six arrows) and then six ends for score at twenty yards distance from the target. Group I should skip the next regular class meeting. When Group II reports to the

LABORATORY EXPERIMENT : INDIVIDUAL vs COACTING PERFORMANCE DATA SHEET

Subject #	Individual Practice Trials										Total Taps
	1	2	3	4	5	6	7	8	9	10	
1											
2											
3											
4											
5											
6											
7											
8											
9											
10											
N=										$\Sigma X=$ $\overline{X}=$	

Subject #	Coaction Practice Trials										Total Taps
	1	2	3	4	5	6	7	8	9	10	
1											
2											
3											
4											
5											
6											
7											
8											
9											
10											
N=										$\Sigma X=$ $\overline{X}=$	

regular class period, have them shoot four abreast, one warm-up end and six scored ends. Score all ends on a scale of gold—9, red—7, blue—5, etc.

RESULTS.

1. Record the resultant data on the master sheet provided.
2. Statistically compare the Group I and the Group II scores using a *t*-test for independent means.

FIELD EXPERIMENT : INDIVIDUAL vs COACTING PERFORMANCE DATA SHEET

Chapter 16

EFFECTS OF SUPPLEMENTARY CUES

INTRODUCTION

THE STUDENT IS FACED WITH many situational cues in the skill learning situation from which he must selectively attend for effective performance. The visual sense provides information about the immediate environment and can provide knowledge of the results of performance. The proprioceptive senses are vital in providing the proper amounts of muscular contraction, relaxation, and a feel for the skill. The auditory sense modality helps one to perceive a starting signal or to recognize a verbal prompt from a teammate. Those cues which the learner perceives will best promote the acquisition of the skill when there is a modification of cue attention as practice ensues. It is impossible, indeed, undesirable, to attend to every cue in a normal environmental situation.

There is evidence to suggest that visual cues are the most relevant early in learning and in latter learning proprioceptive cues become more important (Fleishman and Rich, 1963).

The beginning archer is oftentimes overly concerned with the tactile stimulation of the bow string on the fingers, the physical position of the bow arm (so the arm won't get hit by the bow string), and the visual image of the gold portion of the target. Cues failing to gain recognition are body posture, foot position, loosing techniques, and draw arm mechanics. For the novice archer it is difficult to determine which cues are most important. Each cue should be considered but since all the cues cannot be processed simultaneously, a cue time sharing system is necessary. Of major importance, then, is the duration of the particular cue image in the processing system of the archer. It is possible to place external emphasis on the less recognized cues and to de-emphasize the more obvious ones in order to facilitate the learning of a skill. Again, the most relevant cues depend upon the stage of skill development.

The probable effect of over-attending to a specific cue is the ignoring or minimizing of another equally appropriate or even more important cue. Thus, the archer may repeatedly fail to assume a perpendicular position to the restraining line due to too much concern for the people around him or the number of feet the arrow must travel to hit the target.

Learning will be impeded. The learning process can be enhanced when a knowledgeable observer provides supplementary cues or reminders to the learner. This is the typical function of a coach or teacher. Greater efficiency will result by increasing the emphasis on specific cues throughout practice.

There are many examples of cue emphasis and supplementation techniques. Verbal cues are most commonly used in physical education. The student is verbally informed of errors in his technique and informed of ways to reduce these errors. "Keep your head down" and "keep your eye on the ball" are simple examples in learning golf. Visual cues as distinguished from visual aids (loop films, video tape replay) are also used in enhancing the learning of skills. Blinders are placed on race horses to reduce their peripheral vision thus helping them to attend to the track ahead and not the horses around them. The spots found on a bowling lane aid in the determination of an aiming point allowing more accurate placement of the ball (Summers, 1957). Nearer and clearer visual cues in general are more beneficial to learning than vague and general ones (Singer, 1968). Those persons who cannot clearly see the bowling pins will find spots on the alley a particularly valuable visual cue.

Cue supplementation can take the form of a loud sound issued during actual performance. To make a distinction between an audio cue and a verbal cue an assumption is made that the audio cue is not a coherent linguistic statement. During the execution of a gymnastics routine concurrent verbal statements are somewhat meaningless to the performer intently concentrating on more necessary cues. The use of a brief loud single word (e.g. now, go) is regarded as an audio cue. The sound *per se* is the cue, not the meaning of the word. Of course a grunt or whistle can serve as an audio cue. The particular cadence used by the quarterback serves as a cue for the offensive lineman. A loud noise can also aid the diver in determining when he should open his tuck and enter the water.

Tactile cues are used to facilitate performance. Physical assistance during the actual practice of a skill (spotting) is the most common example. Manual assistance can take the form of guiding the involved body part through the skill, generating correct proprioceptive feedback and eliminating much trial and error. Cratty (1967) concludes that manual guidance is more effective during the early stages of learning and when imposed during this period quicker learning occurs.

The introduction of supplementary tactile cues and the effect on the reduction of unwanted ones may serve to promote skill acquisition. For example, the thickness of the finger tab or absence of one could serve to better make the learner conscious of the loosing technique in archery. Merriman (1972) investigated the effects of reducing the obnoxious irritants inherent in learning to swim. Although no differences were found under traditional teaching techniques and techniques using goggles, nose clips, and ear plugs, the reduction of unwanted tactile stimulation could prove effective in other skill situations. Powell (1969) found that an electric shock cue administered during the execution of a gymnastic skill facilitated learning, the effect being attributed to helping the learner acquire the necessary timing of the response. Within the realm of skilled movement a gentle touch, a slap, or a similar cue could be of value in promoting skill learning.

GENERAL RESEARCH FINDINGS

1. With respect to visual cues, clear and precise cue presentations are more easily attended to than vague and general ones. Specifically, when visual cues are used to facilitate aiming, cues nearer the performer are preferred to those further away.
2. Consideration must be given to the stage of practice in which supplementary cues are used. In general, cues are most effective in initial skill acquisition and become less effective and perhaps even unnecessary as continual performance aids during later practice.
3. The novelty of supplementary cues oftentimes provides incentive to the learner helping him to maintain a high level of interest and motivation during extended practice.
4. Tactile and audio cues can have an additional facilitory effect on movements which involve an element of timing.

REFERENCES

Anderson, T.: A study of the use of visual aids in basket shooting. *Res Q Am Assoc Health Phys Educ*, *13*:532, 1942.

Battig, W. F.: The effect of kinesthetic, verbal, and visual cues on the acquisition of a lever-positioning skill. *J Exp Psychol, 47*:371, 1954.

Chui, E. F.: A study of Golf-O-Tron utilization as a teaching aid in relation to improvement and transfer. *Res Q Am Assoc Health Phys Educ, 36*:147, 1965.

Church, K. R.: The effect of different teaching methods and spot of aim technique on bowling achievement of college men. Unpublished doctoral dissertation, Indiana University, Bloomington, 1963.

Cox, G. A.: The effectiveness of instruction using a visual electronic unit in the development of beginning bowling skill of college women. Unpublished masters thesis, University of Washington, Seattle, 1963.

Cratty, B. J.: *Movement Behavior and Motor Learning.* Philadelphia, Lea & Febiger, 1967.

Dailey, L., Wessel, J. A., and Nelson, R. C.: Effectiveness of a mechanical aid for university bowling instruction. *Res Q Am Assoc Health Phys Educ, 34*:136, 1963.

Fleishman, E. A. and Rich, S.: Role of kinesthetic and spatial visual abilities in perceptual motor learning. *J Exp Psychol, 66*:6, 1963.

Geollner, W. A.: Comparison of the effectiveness of three methods of teaching beginning bowling. *Res Q Am Assoc Health Phys Educ*, *28*:386, 1956.

Karlin, L. and Mortimer, R. G.: Effects of visual and verbal cues on learning a motor skill. *J Exp Psychol*, *64*:608, 1962.

Layton, T. W.: The effect of a basketball training glove on shooting accuracy. Unpublished masters thesis, Mankato State College, Mankato, Minnesota, 1971.

McCatty, C. A. M.: Effects of the use of a floatation device in teaching nonswimmers. *Res Q Am Assoc Health Phys Educ*, *39*:621, 1968.

Mathews, D. K. and McDaniel, J.: Effectiveness of using Golf Lite in learning the golf swing. *Res Q Am Assoc Health Phys Educ*, *33*:488, 1962.

Merriman, J. W.: The effect of augmented vision and the elimination of obnoxious irritants on learning to swim. Paper presented, AAPHER National Convention, Houston, 1972.

Nichols, B. A.: A comparison of two methods of developing the overhand throw for distance in four, five, six, and seven year old children. Unpublished doctoral dissertation, University of Iowa, Iowa City, 1971.

Powell, F. M.: The effects of electrical stimulation on the performance of a selected gymnastic skill, an exploratory study. Unpublished masters thesis, University of North Carolina, Chapel Hill, 1969.

Singer, R. N.: *Motor Learning and Human Performance*. New York, Macmillan, 1968.

Summers, D.: Effect of variations of delivery and aim on bowling achievement of college women. *Res Q Am Assoc Health Phys Educ*, *28*:77, 1957.

LABORATORY EXPERIMENT

PURPOSE. To determine the effects of cue deprivation and cue supplementation on the acquisition of a simple balancing skill.

EQUIPMENT. Stabilometer (see "Knowledge of Results" chapter), blindfold, and external cueing device. (See Appendix for illustration and explanation.)

PROCEDURE. Form three groups, blindfolded (B), control (C), and supplementary (S). All subjects will perform ten thirty-second trials on the stabilometer with thirty seconds rest between trials. Subjects in the *B* group will balance while blindfolded. Subjects in the *S* group will perform on the stabilometer equipped with the visual cueing device. The control group will balance in the usual fashion.

RESULTS.

1. Record the time on balance scores for each group on the data sheet provided.
2. Compute the mean scores for each trial across subjects in the three groups and plot the learning curves on the sheet provided.
3. Statistically determine by means of a one-way ANOVA if there are significant differences in the overall performance of the groups. Should a significant F ratio be obtained, do a follow-up analysis using the Duncan multiple range test.

FIELD EXPERIMENT

PURPOSE. To examine the effects of a supplementary visual cue on golf putting performance.

EQUIPMENT. Six golfballs, a putter, and a forty-eight-inch archery target face. Adhesive tape can be used for the cue.

LABORATORY EXPERIMENT : CUE SUPPLEMENTATION AND DEPRIVATION DATA SHEET

Group B		Trials											
Subjects		1	2	3	4	5	6	7	8	9	10	ΣX	ΣX^2
1													
2													
3													
4													
5													
N=	$\Sigma X=$ $\bar{X}$											$\Sigma\Sigma X=$ $\bar{X}_b=$	$\Sigma\Sigma X^2=$

Group S		Trials											
Subjects		1	2	3	4	5	6	7	8	9	10	ΣX	ΣX^2
1													
2													
3													
4													
5													
N=	$\Sigma X=$ $\bar{X}$											$\Sigma\Sigma X=$ $\bar{X}_s=$	$\Sigma\Sigma X^2$

Group C		Trials											
Subjects		1	2	3	4	5	6	7	8	9	10	ΣX	ΣX^2
1													
2													
3													
4													
5													
N=	$\Sigma X=$ $\bar{X}$											$\Sigma\Sigma X=$ $\bar{X}_c=$	$\Sigma\Sigma X^2=$

FIELD EXPERIMENT : Cue Supplementation Data Sheet

Cue	Trials											
Subject #	1	2	3	4	5	6	7	8	9	10	ΣX	ΣX²
1												
2												
3												
4												
5												
6												
N=								$\Sigma\Sigma$X= $\bar{X}=$		$\Sigma\Sigma$X²=		

Non-Cue	Trials											
Subject #	1	2	3	4	5	6	7	8	9	10	ΣX	ΣX²
1												
2												
3												
4												
5												
6												
N=								$\Sigma\Sigma$X= $\bar{X}=$		$\Sigma\Sigma$X²=		

PROCEDURE. Form two groups, cue and non-cue. Subjects will putt six balls in each of ten trials at an archery target face whose center is ten feet from the starting line. In both conditions, all subjects should address the ball with their nonpreferred side. Under the cue condition, a two-foot strip of tape will be placed along the line of travel of the ball so that it extends one foot behind and one foot in front of the initial position of the ball. At the point five feet from the exact center of the target and directly in line with the initial position of the ball, place an additional six-inch strip of tape. Subjects should be instructed to use the tape cues to facilitate a straight and consistent backswing and to provide a reference

FIELD EXPERIMENT : Learning Curves

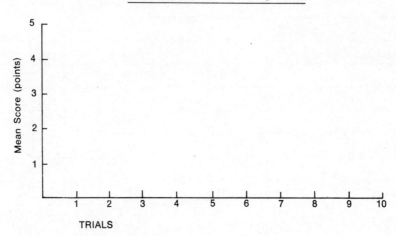

TRIALS

LAB EXPERIMENT : Learning Curves

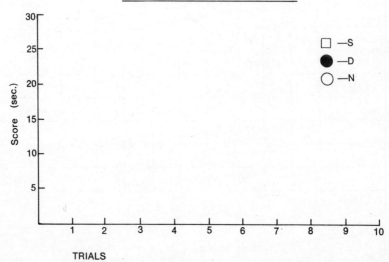

TRIALS

aiming point. Subjects in the non-cue group should perform with the tape removed. No practice or warm-up should be given.

RESULTS.

1. Each ball rolling to a stop on the target face shall be scored as follows: 5 points—gold, 4 points—red, 3 points—blue, 2 points —black, and 1 point—white.

2. Sum the scores for each trial (six putts) and record on the field experiment data sheet.

3. Derive the mean scores for each trial for both groups and plot learning curves on the sheet provided.
4. Statistically compare the group data by using a *t*-test for independent means.

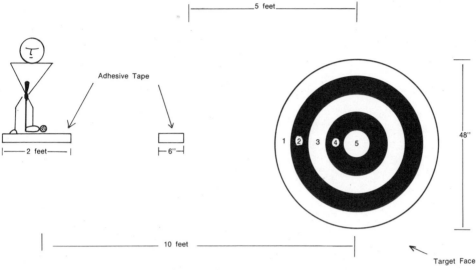

CUEING FOR GOLF PUTTING PERFORMANCE

Figure 16-4:

APPENDIX

Constructed Equipment: The stabilometer is described in the chapter on knowledge of results. The cueing device can be constructed with the following materials: fifteen feet of cotton clothesline; two screw eyes; a mayonnaise jar lid; a heavy rubber band(s); a cardboard pointer, and a reference scale. Position the stabilometer three feet from a bare wall or door and attach the jar lid so it rotates freely. Small washers on both sides of the lid will facilitate rotary movement and reduce play. As shown in the illustration, the clothesline should be attached to the extreme ends of the surface of the stabilometer balance platform and form a complete circuit through the screw eyes and around the jar lid. Insert a heavy rubber band as shown to maintain some tension on the cord. Tape or otherwise secure a pointer on the jar lid so that it is exactly perpendicular to the balance board when the board is parallel to the floor. Finally, construct a scale approximating degrees off balance and place it behind the pointer. The pointer should be re-calibrated before each subject. The stabilometer should be maintained in the same position throughout the experiment.

The layout of the field experiment is illustrated in Figure 16-4. Under the non-cue situation the adhesive tape should be removed. If possible, a carpeted surface should be used.

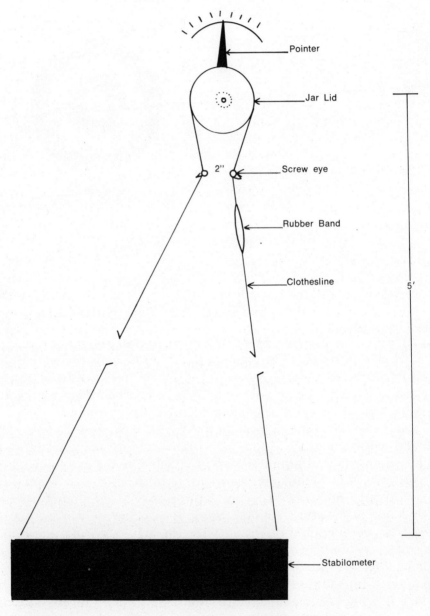

Visual cueing device to be used with stabilometer.

Chapter 17

HUMAN ABILITIES
AND PERFORMANCE

INTRODUCTION

THE IMPORTANCE OF HUMAN abilities in motor performance and in motor learning is generally acknowledged. Whether an individual begins the learning of a new task at a higher or at a lower level than others may be partly explained by his entering abilities developed through mechanisms of interaction between genes and environment. His level of entering abilities may also be a determinant of his own optimal level of performance and of the difficulties he encounters at different stages of learning a given task.

The study of human abilities has been the concern of researchers for many years. Originally, an attempt was made to find dimensions of human abilities and to describe them. In 1957, Cronbach differentiated two disciplines of psychology: differential and experimental. However, increasing attention is being given to the relationship between individual differences and learning. The emergence of this trend may be explained by the transformation of the educational system from a mechanism for successive screenings into an institution to develop the abilities of all youth (Tyler, 1972). Of particular concern to psychomotor oriented researchers are human abilities related to motor performance and to motor learning.

A look at the existing scientific literature suggests that the factor analytical approach has been dominant in spite of recognized shortcomings in various representative techniques. However, it has contributed to the knowledge we have available presently about human abilities and motor learning. Fleishman and his collaborators are among those who have the more extensively studied abilities related to psychomotor skills.

With respect to the definition of human abilities and interpretation of related findings, a lack of agreement seems prevalent at the present time, although they are not incompatible as such (Ferguson, 1954). For instance, two models which attempt to explain changes in behavior during training were presented by Alvares and Hulin (1972). One model assumes that the abilities which contribute to task performance change systematically over time, while the second model assumes that practice on the criterion task systematically affects the ability levels of the subjects. They are referred to as the changing task model and the changing subject model. These authors showed preference for the changing subject model and they conducted a study which confirmed their preference. On this ground, they criticized Fleishman's interpretations of studies on the basis of the changing task model.

Another area of interest is the study of the differential transfer of abilities at different stages of learning. Ferguson (1954, 1956) put forward two hypotheses: (1) the most important variables exerting transfer effects on subsequent learning would be the entering abilities, and (2) such abilities would exert their effect differentially in any learning situation and at different stages of learning. In a recent study Vachon (1973) found that original practice on two skills related to the final learning task transferred differentially at one stage of final learning and not at another. Although the evidence in favor of the Ferguson hypotheses is scarce at the present time, it seems to be an area which merits attention in research on human abilities and motor learning.

In order not to exaggerate the length of the introduction, the conclusions substantiated by the Fleishman and co-workers' studies are presented only in the next general research findings section. The reader is invited to read publications written by Adams (1957), Alvares and Hulin (1972), Bechtoldt (1962), Ferguson (1954, 1956), Jones (1970), Woodrow (1939), Tyler (1972), and others in order to understand contemporary issues in human abilities and motor learning.

Fleishman has relied on factor analysis in most of his studies. Bechtoldt (1962), Jones (1970), Alvares and Hulin (1972), Fleishman and Fruchter (1967), and many others, have expressed their points of view on the factor analysis approach. For instance, Bechtoldt (1960) mentioned that his reanalyses óf the data obtained by Fleishman offered little or no support for some of Fleishman's hypotheses. This is not surprising since the general equations of factor analysis do not provide a unique solution at the present time (Henrysson, 1960), and each existing computer program on factor analysis seems to have such distinct features as the starting point (correlation matrix or variance covariance matrix), the criterion used (simple structure, varimax, etc.), or the model used (e.g. canonical, principal axis, or alpha factor analysis). A recent study by Baumgartner and Zuidena (1972) confirms the fact that comparable results should not be expected at the present time when a different number of factors are rotated in using different factor analysis programs. The preceding observation indicates a need for more sophisticated computer programs in factor analysis and that any interpretation of factor analysis studies must be made within the acknowledged restraints.

GENERAL RESEARCH FINDINGS

The following findings have been substantiated by Fleishman and his co-workers' where typically a correlation matrix has been factor analyzed by Thurstone's centroid method. Orthogonal rotations of the primary axes were accomplished using Zimmerman's graphical method, and they continued rotation until the criterion of simple structure and positive manifold were closely approximated. In general, variables with loadings of .30 or higher on a factor were considered in the interpretation of factors, in terms of proportion of variance.

Within the limits of the preceding procedures and criteria, the major findings are:

1. *Ability* refers to a relatively permanent trait of the individual which is inferred from the factor analysis of performance of individuals on certain kinds of tasks.
2. *Skill* refers to the level of proficiency on a particular task.
3. Skills involved in complex activities can be described in terms of more basic abilities.
4. Most abilities depend on both genetic and learning factors.
5. Eleven psychomotor abilities and nine abilities in the area of physical proficiency appear to account for the communality in psychomotor tasks.
   Psychomotor abilities: Control precision, multilimb coordination, response orientation, reaction time, speed of arm movement, rate control, manual dexterity, finger dexterity, arm-hand steadiness, wrist-finger speed, and aiming.
   Physical proficiency: Extent flexibility, dynamic flexibility, explosive strength, dynamic strength, trunk strength, gross body coordination, gross body equilibrium, and stamina.
6. Physical Proficiency is not a general ability, but includes a number of relatively independent abilities.
7. Central factors are of importance in physical fitness in addition to specific factors.
8. Some abilities play a differential role at different stages of learning more complex tasks.
9. Nonmotor abilities seem to play a role early in learning, but their importance seems to decrease with practice relative to motor abilities.
10. In psychomotor learning, kinesthetic ability factors play an increasingly important role relative to spatial-visual abilities.
11. As practice proceeds, an increase in a factor specific to the task itself occurs.
12. The task components of a more complex task contribute differen-

tially to different kinds of criterion measures on the complex task.
13. Systematic changes in ability requirements occur as a function of task difficulty.
14. Learning rates are not predictable from a subject's pretask abilities.

REFERENCES

Adams, J. A.: The relationship between certain measures of ability and the acquisition of a psychomotor criterion response. *J Gen Psychol, 56*:121, 1957.

Alvares, K. M. and Hulin, C. L.: An experimental evaluation of a temporal decay in the prediction of performance. *Organizational Behavior and Human Performance, 9*:169, 1973.

Alvares, K. M. and Hulin, C. L.: Two explanations of temporal changes in ability-skill relationships: A literature review and theoretical analysis. *Hum Factors, 14*:295, 1972.

Attridge, B. G. and Sampson, H.: A note on Ferguson's learning ability matrix. *Can J Psychol, 9*:84, 1955.

Baumgartner, T. A. and Zuidena, M. A.: Factor analysis of physical fitness tests. *Res Q Am Assoc Health Phys Educ, 43*:443, 1972.

Bechtoldt, H. P.: Factor analysis and the investigation of hypotheses. *Percept Mot Skills, 14*:319, 1962.

Bechtoldt, H. P.: Motor abilities in studies of motor learning. In Smith, Leon E. (Ed.): *Psychology of Motor Learning*. Chicago, The Athletic Institute, 1970.

Butollo, W. H.: A logistic test model approach to changes of the factorial structure during learning. *J Gen Psychol, 86*:189, 1972.

Buxton, C.: The application of multiple factorial methods to the study of motor abilities. *Psychometrika, 3*:85, 1938.

Dickinson, J.: The role of two factors in a gross motor aiming task. *Br J Psychol, 60*:465, 1969.

Ferguson, G. A.: Human abilities. *Annu Rev Psychol, 16*:39, 1965.

Ferguson, G. A.: On learning and human ability. *Can J Psychol, 8*:95, 1954.

Ferguson, G. A.: On transfer and the abilities of man. *Can J Psychol, 10*:121, 1956.

Fleishman, E. A.: A factor analysis of intra-task performance on two psychomotor tests. *Psychometrika, 18*:45, 1953.

Fleishman, E. A.: Abilities at different stages of practice in rotary pursuit performance. *J Exp Psychol, 60*:162, 1960.

Fleishman, E. A.: Development of a behavior taxonomy for describing human tasks: A correlational-experimental approach. *J Appl Psychol, 51*:1, 1967.

Fleishman, E. A.: Factor structure in relation to task difficulty in psychomotor performance. *Educational Psychological Measurement, 17*:522, 1957.

Fleishman, E. A.: Individual differences and motor learning. In Gagné, Robert M. (Ed.): *Learning and Individual Differences*. Columbus, Ohio, Charles E. Merrill Books, Inc., 1967.

Fleishman, E. A.: Performance assessment based on an empirically derived task taxonomy. *Hum Factors, 9*:349, 1967.

Fleishman, E. A.: Testing for psychomotor abilities by means of apparatus tests. *Psychol Bull, 50*:241, 1953.

Fleishman, E. A. and Bartlett, C. J.: Human abilities. *Annu Rev Psychol, 20*:349, 1969.

Fleishman, E. A. and Ellison, G. D.: Prediction of transfer and other learning phenomena from ability and personality measures. *J Educ Psychol, 60*:300, 1969.

Fleishman, E. A. and Fruchter, B.: Factor structure and predictability of successive stages of learning Morse code. *J Appl Psychol, 44*:97, 1960.

Fleishman, E. A. and Hempel, Jr., W. E.: Changes in factor structure of a complex psychomotor test as a function of practice. *Psychometrika, 9*:239, 1954.

Fleishman, E. A. and Hempel, Jr., W. E.: The relation between abilities and improvement with practice in a visual discrimination reaction task. *J Exp Psychol, 49*:301, 1955.

Fleishman, E. A. and Rich, S.: Role of kinesthetic and spatial-visual abilities in perceptual-motor learning. *J Exp Psychol, 66*:6, 1963.

Fruchter, B. and Fleishman, E. A.: A simplical design for the analysis of correlational learning data. *Multivariate Behav Res, 2*:83, 1967.

Greene, E. B.: An analysis of random and systematic changes with practice. *Psychometrika, 8*:37, 1943.

Henrysson, S.: *Factor Analysis in the Behavioral Sciences.* Stockholm, Almqqvist and Wiksell, 1960.

Hinrichs, J. R.: Ability correlates in learning a psychomotor task. *J Appl Psychol, 54*:56, 1970.

Holding, D. H.: Critique of Bechtoldt's paper. In Smith, Leon E. (Ed.): *Psychology of Motor Learning.* Chicago, The Athletic Institute, 1970.

Inomata, K.: A factor-analytic study of perceptual-motor learning. *Res J Phys Educ, 16*:33, 1971.

Jones, M. B.: A two-process theory of individual differences in motor learning. *Psychol Rev, 77*:353, 1970.

Jones, M. B.: Individual differences. In Singer, Robert N. (Ed.): *The Psychomotor Domain: Movement Behaviors.* Philadelphia, Lea and Febiger, 1972.

McDonald, R. P.: The theoretical foundations of principal factor analysis, canonical factor analysis, and alpha factor analysis. *Br J Math Stat Psychol, 23*:1, 1970.

Miller, E. E.: Military psychology and training. In Singer, Rogert N. (Ed.): *The Psychomotor Domain: Movement Behaviors.* Philadelphia, Lea & Febiger, 1972.

Parker, Jr., J. F. and Fleishman, E. A.: Prediction of advanced levels of proficiency in a complex tracking task. United States Air Force, Wright Air Development Division Technical Report, *59*:225, 1960.

Phillips, B. E.: The relationship between certain phases of kinesthesis and performance during the early stages of acquiring two perceptual-motor skills. *Res Q Am Assoc Health Phys Educ, 12*:571, 1941.

Phillips, M. and Summers, D.: Relation of kinesthetic perception to motor learning. *Res Q Am Assoc Health Phys Educ, 25*:456, 1954.

Tucker, L. R.: Three-mode factor analysis of Parker-Fleishman complex tracking behavior data. *Multivariate Behav Res, 2*:117, 1967.

Tyler, L. E.: Human abilities. *Annu Rev Psychol, 23*:177, 1972.

Vachon, L.: Transferts positife entre l'apprentissage de tâches matrices en fonction de leur niveau respectif de difficulté. *A.C.F.A.S., 40*:49, 1973.

Woodrow, H.: The relation between abilities and improvement with practice. *J Educ Psychol, 29*:215, 1938.

Woodrow, H.: The application of factor analysis to problems of practice. *J Gen Psychol, 21*:457, 1939.

LABORATORY EXPERIMENT

PURPOSE. To determine the relationship between simple reaction time to a visual stimulus and performance on a discrimination reaction task.

EQUIPMENT. A reaction timer and a visual discrimination reaction timer.*

DESIGN. A pretest/posttest one group design is suggested for this experiment.

PROCEDURE. To a group of subjects as large as possible, a *true* reaction time test to a visual stimulus is administered individually to all subjects. The subject should sit at a table in front of the response key. A ready signal presented at different intervals before the presentation of the visual stimulus indicates the subject should depress the response key with the index finger of his nonpreferred hand. At the onset of the visual stimulus, the subject releases the key as quickly as possible. Fifty such trials are administered at the subject's own pace. The sum of the trials is kept as the index of ability level of each subject as measured by this reaction time test.

One day later, at approximately the same hour, the subjects are given individually 210 trials of practice on the following visual discrimination reaction task. It consists of three visual stimuli (S) and three response keys. The position of the visual stimulus determines which one of the three response keys (R) should be depressed as quickly as possible. Let S1, S2, and S3 denote the three stimuli, and R1, R2, and R3 the three responses. One arrangement could be S1R3, S2R2, and S3R1. The visual stimulus S1 requires the depression of the response key R3. If this arrangement is adopted, then the subject at the ready signal places the index of his nonpreferred hand just above the response key R2. And when one stimulus is generated, he depresses as quickly as possible the appropriate key. If the appropriate key is depressed, the visual stimulus will terminate. Before actual testing, each of the three signals associated with the appropriate response will be demonstrated to subjects and five practice trials are given.

The sequence of presentation of the three visual stimuli is decided on a random basis, with the condition that each stimulus will be presented ten times on each set of thirty trials, and the sum of each block of thirty trials will serve as the dependent measures. Seven blocks of trials will represent the acquisition of performance on the discrimination reaction time practice task.

RESULTS.

Use the appropriate computation sheet presented in the statistics chapter and:

---

*Both pieces of equipment are described in the chapter on reaction-time and movement-time.

1. Compute the Pearson product moment correlation coefficient between the reaction time sum and each sum of the visual discrimination reaction time task.
2. Divide your group of subjects into two subgroups, the highest 25 percent and the lowest 25 percent on the reaction time test. Then draw the performance curve of each subgroup on the discrimination reaction time task.
3. Compare the two subgroups on each block of trials on the discrimination reaction time task with the one-way analysis of variance.
4. (Optional) Compute the multiple correlation coefficient between the reaction time sum and the sums of the seven blocks of trials. Square the multiple R and discuss in terms of communality.
5. (Optional) Conduct a principal component analysis on all the sums, e.g. the reaction time sum and the seven discrimination reaction time sums.

FIELD EXPERIMENT

PURPOSE. To investigate the relationship between dynamic balance, static balance, peripheral vision, and performance upon the Balla-Rolla.

EQUIPMENT. A stabilometer, a balance rail, a perimeter, a Balla-Rolla, electric timer, interval timer, stopwatch.

DESIGN. A pretest/posttest one-group design is suggested for this experiment.

PROCEDURE. Performance tests are administered to a group of subjects as large as possible. One day later, practice on a Balla-Rolla is given until a perfect score is obtained once.

1. Dynamic balance test. The subject attempts balancing the stabilometer platform horizontally as long as possible during each of ten trials administered with a thirty-second work/thirty-second rest schedule. The subject is blindfolded during each work period. The total time-on-balance or the total time-off-balance is recorded on an electrical timer to .01 of a second during each work period. An interval timer is used to control the administration of the test. The sum of the scores on the ten trials is computed to represent the subject's dynamic balance ability.
2. Static balance test. The subject, blindfolded, places his preferred foot lengthwise on the rail and his hands on his hips and stands up on the rail. The balance rail consists of a piece of wood mounted to a base board with dimensions 1 1/2 inches high, ¾ inch wide, and 24 inches long. When he has his balance and wants to start the trial, he says: "go." The administrator then begins timing the subject until

any part of his body touches the floor or until he removes either hand from his hips. Ten test trials are administered.

The number of seconds the subject maintains his balance for each trial is recorded separately and added together for the ten trials. A practice trial with eyes open may be given before the test.

3. Peripheral vision test. A perimeter can be purchased or built for the administration of this test. The subject places the left eye support and is asked to fixate his eyes to the fixation point. His right eye is then blindfolded. The subject is also told to indicate to the experimenter when he will see a shade appearing on his left side; then, the experimenter will register the location of the wand on the graduated arc. The task of the experimenter is to move the wand slowly on the graduated arc toward the fixation point. This procedure is repeated for the right eye. The left and the right eye will be alternately tested, until ten trials have been given for each eye. The sum of the scores of the left eye and the sum of the right eye will be first computed separately. Both scores will be added together to represent the subject's peripheral vision ability.

4. Balla-Rolla. The subject, eyes open, will first place his feet on the inclined platform without attempting to balance it. When he is ready, he says "go" and the experimenter records the number of contacts of the two ends of the platform on the floor during a period of thirty seconds. This is followed by a rest period of thirty seconds. Practice is given according to this procedure until the subject succeeds balancing without having the platform touch the floor during a period of thirty seconds. The number of contacts between the platform and the ground is recorded for each trial, and the number of trials necessary to reach the final performance criterion is also tabulated.

The Balla-Rolla consists of a wood platform about three feet long and one foot wide which can be placed upon a wood roll. The subject's task is to place his feet apart, one at each end upon the platform, and to attempt balancing without having the ends of the platform touching the ground. The platform can move from left to right, or vice versa, upon the roll. This apparatus can be purchased in many stores or can be easily built.

RESULTS.

From the compilation sheet, enter the data into the computation sheet presented in the statistic chapter. Then, calculate:

1. The Pearson product moment correlation coefficient between the scores on the dynamic balance test, the static balance test, the peripheral vision test, and the number of trials necessary to reach the final performance criterion on the Balla-Rolla.

2. Plot the performance curve for each subject using the number of contacts made at each trial on the stabilometer.

LABORATORY EXPERIMENT : HUMAN ABILITIES
Sample Data Form for each subject

Name : _____

Subject Number : _____

VISUAL DISCRIMINATION REACTION TASK

Trials 1-30	Trials 31-60	Trials 61-90	Trials 91-120	Trials 121-150	Trials 151-180	Trials 181-210

Sum :

LABORATORY EXPERIMENT : HUMAN ABILITIES
Sample Data Form for each subject

Group : _____ Subject Number : _____

Name : _____ Age : _____ Tel. : _____

Non-preferred hand : _____

Comments :

Simple Reaction Time		
Trials :		Trials :
1		26
2		27
3		28
4		29
5		30
6		31
7		32
8		33
9		34
10		35
11		36
12		37
13		38
14		39
15		40
16		41
17		42
18		43
19		44
20		45
21		46
22		47
23		48
24		49
25		50
Sum :	Sum :	Grand Sum :

3. (Optional) The multiple correlation coefficient between the three tests and the Balla-Rolla can be computed.

4. (Optional) Divide your group of subjects successively into subgroups: the highest ability subgroup (25 percent) and the lowest ability subgroup (25 percent) for each test, and compare the number of trials taken to reach the performance criterion by each subgroup on the Balla-Rolla with a one-way analysis of variance.

FIELD EXPERIMENT : HUMAN ABILITIES
Sample Data Form for each subject

Group : _____ Subject Number : _____

Name : _____ Age : _____ Tel. : _____

Non-preferred hand : _____

Comments :

Trials	Dynamic Balance	Static Balance	Peripheral Vision	
			Left Eye	Right Eye
1				
2				
3				
4				
5				
6				
7				
8				
9				
10				
XXXXXXX XXXXXXX XXXXXXX XXXXXXX XXXXXXX				
SUM				

BALLA-ROLLA

Trial : N. Contacts :	1	2	3	4	5	6	7	8	9	10
Trial : N. Contacts :	11	12	13	14	15	16	17	18	19	20
Trial : N. Contacts :	21	22	23	24	25	26	27	28	29	30
Trial : N. Contacts :	31	32	33	34	35	36	37	38	39	40

Total Number of Trials :

Laboratory Experiment: Abilities Data

Subjects	Reaction Time	Visual Discrimination Reaction Time						
		Trials 1–30	Trials 31–60	Trials 61–90	Trials 121–150	Trials 151–180	Trials 181–210
S_1							
S_2							
S_3							
S_4							
S_5							
S_6							
S_7							
S_8							
S_9							
S_{10}							
S_{11}							
S_{12}							
S_{13}							
S_{14}							
S_{15}							
S_{16}							
S_{17}							
S_{18}							
S_{19}							
S_{20}							

Field Experiment: Abilities Data

SUBJECTS	① Dynamic Balance	② Static Balance	③ Peripheral Vision	④ Balla-Rolla
S_1				
S_2				
S_3				
S_4				
S_5				
S_6				
S_7				
S_8				
S_9				
S_{10}				
S_{11}				
S_{12}				
S_{13}				
S_{14}				
S_{15}				
S_{16}				
S_{17}				
S_{18}				
S_{19}				
S_{20}				

r ①② : ____   r ①③ : ____   r ①④ : ____

r ②③ : ____   r ②④ : ____   r ③④ : ____

Field Experiment: Abilities Data

Number
of
Contracts

Trials

Chapter 18

LEVEL OF ASPIRATION

INTRODUCTION

INDIVIDUALS DIFFER WIDELY not only in their performance levels but also in their expectations of their own performance and in the demands which they make upon themselves. The phrase *level of aspiration* denotes such expectations individuals have of their accomplishment. Frank (1935) defined this concept as "the level of future performance in a familiar task which an individual, knowing his level of past performance in that task, explicitly undertakes to reach." Cratty (1968), considering the aspiration level to be a component of the individual's self-concept, defined it as the feeling a person has concerning his potential for performance. Generally, the concept of aspiration level has been accepted as the individual's own expected level of future performance relative to his past successes and failures in similar tasks.

Much of the general development of the basic tenets of the level of aspiration was done in the 1930's and early 1940's. Attempts were made to determine the various factors which influence the rising and lowering of the aspiration level and to understand the basic conditions of success and failure. More recent research is attempting to explain the effects of complex variables upon the level of aspiration as well as to identify the role of various personality traits, and their effects.

Levels of aspiration are influenced by the person's concept of himself as well as by his estimate of his particular status among his peers. He gains or loses his self-esteem as he succeeds or fails to reach his goals. Some individuals, however, seem to consistently set levels which are not attainable while others set goals which are close to their actual performance. A third group sets levels which are far too low. The ego-involved individuals tend to limit the range of difficulty in an attempt to feel the reward of success. A pole-vaulter for example, expecting to succeed, would set his momentary goal high enough that he might fail. He would take no satisfaction in setting it so low that he could jump it successfully every time. Satisfaction comes when he is able to clear the bar at a new height. Lewin (1944) has suggested that there are really three aspiration levels for every task: (1) what the person says he expects to attain; (2)

what the person really expects, and (3) what the person would like to attain. In general, the level of aspiration is fairly close to the individual's actual performance, but there is a tendency for it to remain above rather than below actual performance. There is a greater tendency, too, for the individual to raise his goal after success and to lower it after failure.

It has been revealed that the experiencing feelings of success or failure depends upon the difficulty of the task. When the task is too easy, the person experiences no sense of success even though he accomplishes the task. Hoppe (1930) considers success as defined by the range of difficulty. Success and failure experiences come in the in-between range: from the point at which success is highly probable, but failure possible, to that point at which failure is highly probable, but success possible.

Group standards are very influential in determining aspiration level. These standards may be of a peer group of which one is a member or the standards of groups differing from one's own in prestige. It has been demonstrated that one's private expectations of his performance are modified by the performance of his social group. Those with scores above average tend to lower while those with scores below the groups' average tend to gain in level of performance expectation.

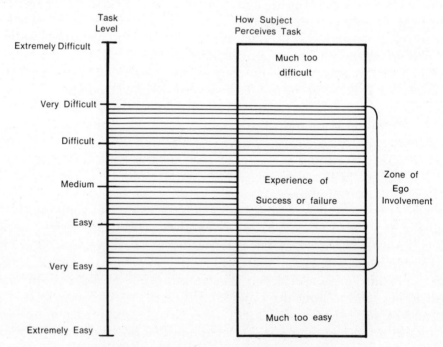

SUCCESS AS RELATED TO TASK DIFFICULTY

Figure 18-1: From Hoppe, F. Erfolg und Misserfolg. *Psychologische Forschrift*, 1930, 14, 1-62 (as it appears in Hilgard, E. R.: *Introduction to Psychology*. New York, Harcourt, Brace and Company, 1953, p. 169.

The influence of social factors has been suggested by the observation that if an individual's score is below the low prestige group, his level of aspiration subsequently increases the most; if above the high prestige group, aspiration level tends to decrease the most.

The level of aspiration a person sets is sensitive to past successes and failures. Past success will tend to make an individual less likely to lower the level of aspiration upon encountering momentary failure. Past failures will make an individual more likely to lower his future performance when encountering failure.

Other factors such as motivation, need for achievement and desire for competition have also been shown to influence one's level of aspiration.

The measurement of aspiration level has depended mainly upon the subject's willingness to express his verbal expectation of what level he expects to attain on his next performance trial. This expressed achievement level is open to a variety of influences such as peer pressure, presence of an audience, desire to succeed, competitive nature of individual, fatigue, boredom, and motivation.

The majority of experiments allows the subject to perform the task several times, receiving feedback, whether instant or delayed, as to his actual level of performance. The subject is then asked to state his level of aspiration for further performance of the task. Sometimes the subject is not told of his actual accomplishment but is given a fictitious score which he believes to be his own. In other situations, subjects may be told how others have scored on a similar task. The experimenter calculates how success or failure in meeting the designated level influences the level of aspiration.

GENERAL RESEARCH FINDINGS

Some of the more conclusive findings in the area of aspiration level are as follows:

1. Success leads to a raising of the level of aspiration whereas failure tends to lower the level.
2. The greater the success, the greater the probability of a rise in the level.
3. When performing motor skills, an individual usually compares his performance with performances of individuals of his own age, sex, and experience.
4. Aspiration level is influenced to a marked degree by past experiences.
5. Aspiration level has been found to be more variable among men, among tense and insecure individuals, and among the young.
6. Social class significantly affects level of aspiration while race alone does not, but together, aspiration level is affected.

7. Level of aspiration is usually modified from time to time in terms of success or failure in attaining goals.
8. Individuals tend to shift their own estimates of aspiration level to those of a reference group performance.

REFERENCES

Aranson, E. and Carlsmith, J. M.: Performance expectancy as a determinant of actual performance. *J Abnorm Soc Psychol, 65*:178, 1962.

Cottrell, N. B.: Performance expectancy as a determinant of actual performance. *J Pers Soc Psychol, 2*:685, 1965.

Cratty, B. J.: *Psychology and Physical Activity.* New Jersey, Prentice-Hall, Inc., 1968.

Feather, N. T. and Saville, M. M.: Effects of amount of prior success and failure on expectations of success and subsequent task performance. *J Pers Soc Psychol, 5*:226, 1967.

Frank, J. D.: Individual differences in certain aspects of the level of aspiration. *Am J Psychol, 47*:119, 1935.

Harari, H.: Level of aspiration and athletic performance. *Percept Mot Skills, 28*:519, 1969.

Hilgard, E. R.: *Introduction to Psychology.* New York, Harcourt, Brace and World, Inc., 1957.

Inglis, J.: Abnormalities of motivation and ego functions. In Eysenck, H. J. (Ed.): *Handbook of Abnormal Psychology.* New York, Basic Books, Inc., 1961.

Leshman, S. S.: Effects of aspiration and achievement on muscular tension. *J Exp Psychol, 61*:133, 1961.

Locke, E. A.: The relationship of intentions to level of performance. *J Appl Psychol, 50*:50, 1966.

Locke, E. A. and Bryan, J. F.: Cognitive aspect of psychomotor performance: The effects of performance goals on level of performance. *J Appl Psychol, 50*:286, 1966.

Rotter, J. B.: *Social Learning and Clinical Psychology.* New Jersey, Prentice-Hall, 1954.

Ussery, J.: Pacing a team to the championship in track. *Coaching Clinic, 6*:10, 1968.

Ward, W. D. and Sandvold, K. D.: Performance expectancy as a determinant of actual performance: A partial replication. *J Abnorm Soc Psychol, 67*:293, 1963.

Worell, L.: Level of aspiration and academic success. *J Educ Psychol, 50*:47, 1959.

LABORATORY EXPERIMENT

PURPOSE. To study the effect of success or failure upon the level of aspiration and performance.

EQUIPMENT. Pursuit rotor set at 60 RPM.*

DESIGN. Three groups, one control and two experimental. One of the two experimental groups will randomly be designated the success group, the other the failure group.

NOTE: No communication regarding the experiment is to be allowed among the subjects, nor will they know which is the experimental or control group.

PROCEDURE. Each subject will have ten thirty-second practice trials

---

*Pursuit rotors are explained in the chapter on massed and distributed practice.

interspersed with twenty-second rest periods. Knowledge of results will be given after each of these ten warm-up trials with the score being determined by the length of time in contact with the disc.

The control group will be given ten thirty-second trials on the pursuit rotor interspersed with twenty-second rest periods following one practice trial. The actual performance score is to be provided to the subjects after each trial. The expected score on the next trial will be recorded before the trial is attempted. For the expected score, the subject will be asked to estimate his performance score on the succeeding trial.

The failure group will receive ten thirty-second trials interspersed with twenty-second rest periods following one practice trial, with knowledge of results given after each trial. The expected score on the next trial will be recorded before the trial is attempted. After trials six, seven, eight, and nine, a false report (a lower score than actually attained, say, two seconds) will be given regardless of performance. The same procedures will be administered to the success group as for the failure group except a success report (a higher score than actually attained, say, two seconds) will be given.

RESULTS.

1. Record resultant data on the master sheet provided. The expected score should appear over the obtained score in a ratio fashion in the appropriate box under each trial.
2. Graph: (a) The expected and obtained score for each group on one graph and, (b) the discrepancy between the expected and obtained scores for each group.
3. Test mean performance differences on the obtained scores among the three groups using the analysis of variance statistic.
4. Compute correlations between estimated scores and obtained scores for each group (if N is large enough), using the mean of the estimated scores and the mean of the obtained scores across ten trials. All groups could be combined for this analysis as well.

FIELD EXPERIMENT

PURPOSE. To study the effects of success or failure on the level of aspiration and performance.

EQUIPMENT. Ten shuffleboard discs, stopwatch, shuffleboard pole, and a roll of two inch colored masking tape.

ACTIVITY. Adapted shuffleboard. (See diagram.)

DESIGN. Similar to laboratory experiment.

PROCEDURE. All subjects will shoot ten practice discs on the adapted shuffleboard court. Knowledge of results will be given after each shot. Discs are to be removed from the court after each shot. Subjects are not to leave the start position until all discs are shot. Discs touching lines will be counted as a lower score.

For the control group, ten additional discs (trials) following one practice trial will be pushed down the court by each subject with a fifteen-second rest between each disc. The subjects will report their expected score on the next trial which will be recorded before that trial is attempted. Their actual obtained score will be reported to them and recorded after each disc (trial).

The failure group will follow a similar procedure as for the control group except that after discs (trials) six, seven, eight, and nine, a false report (a lower score) will be given regardless of their actual performance. Actual obtained scores will be recorded as well as expected scores.

Similar procedures will be followed for the success group except that a success report (a higher score) will be given regardless of actual performance.

RESULTS.

1. Record resultant data on the master sheets provided. The expected scores should appear over the obtained scores in a ratio fashion under each trial.
2. Graph: (a) expected and obtained scores for each group, (b) the discrepancy between expected and obtained scores for each group.
3. Test the mean differences of the obtained scores among the three groups using the analysis of variance statistic.
4. Compute correlations between estimated scores and obtained scores for each group (if N is large enough), using the mean of the estimated scores and the mean of the obtained scores across ten trials. All groups could be combined for this analysis as well.

APPENDIX

PURCHASED EQUIPMENT. Pursuit rotor: see Appendix on massed versus distributed practice.

The Pennsylvania Bi-Manual Worksample, American Guidance Service, Inc., Circle Pines, could also be used as a neutral test.

The Purdue Pegboard test, also a suitable test, may be purchased from the Lafayette Instrument Company, P. O. Box 1279, 52 By-Pass, Lafayette, Indiana.

CONSTRUCTED EQUIPMENT. Level of Aspiration Board:* The board is constructed of 1½ inch plywood, with dimensions of eight inch by thirty-six inches. A trough one-fourth inch deep is routed length-wise down the center of the board leaving a one-half inch solid end as a backstop. Two

---

*From Rotter, J. B.: *Social Learning and Clinical Psychology.* Englewood Cliffs, New Jersey, Prentice-Hall, 1954, p. 129.

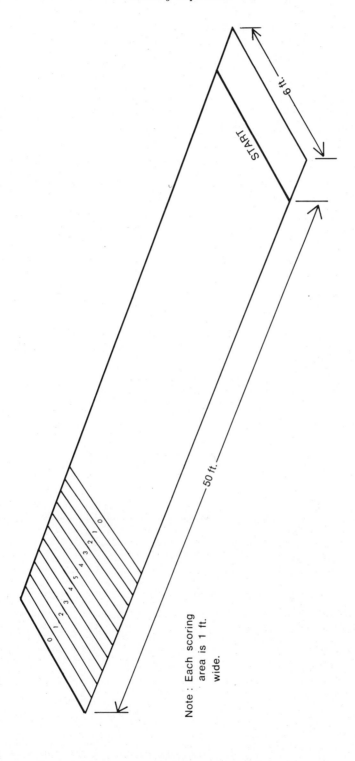

Note : Each scoring area is 1 ft. wide.

LABORATORY EXPERIMENT : Level of aspiration data sheet

Control Group		Trials													
Subjects	PRE	1 E O	2 E O	3 E O	4 E O	5 E O	6 E O	7 E O	8 E O	9 E O	10 E O	ΣX E	ΣX O	D (E -
1														
2														
3														
4														
5•														

ΣΣX=

Failure Group		Trials													
Subjects	PRE	1 E O	2 E O	3 E O	4 E O	5 E O	6 E O	7 E O	8 E O	9 E O	10 E O	ΣX E	ΣX O	D (E -
1														
2														
3														
4														
5														

ΣΣX=

Success Group		Trials													
Subjects	PRE	1 E O	2 E O	3 E O	4 E O	5 E O	6 E O	7 E O	8 E O	9 E O	10 E O	ΣX E	ΣX O	D (E -
1														
2														
3														
4														
5														

ΣΣX=

FIELD EXPERIMENT : Level of aspiration data sheet

Control Group		Trials												
Subjects	PRE	1 E O	2 E O	3 E O	4 E O	5 E O	6 E O	7 E O	8 E O	9 E O	10 E O	∑X E	∑X O	D (E - O)
											∑∑X=		

Failure Group		Trials												
Subjects	PRE	1 E O	2 E O	3 E O	4 E O	5 E O	6 E O	7 E O	8 E O	9 E O	10 E O	∑X E	∑X O	D (E - O)
											∑∑X=		

Success Group		Trials												
Subjects	PRE	1 E O	2 E O	3 E O	4 E O	5 E O	6 E O	7 E O	8 E O	9 E O	10 E O	∑X E	∑X O	D (E - O)
											∑∑X=		

LABORATORY EXPERIMENT: PERFORMANCE CURVES

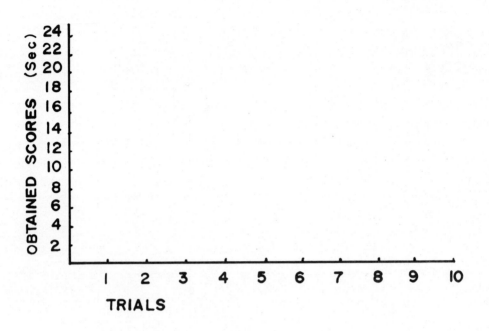

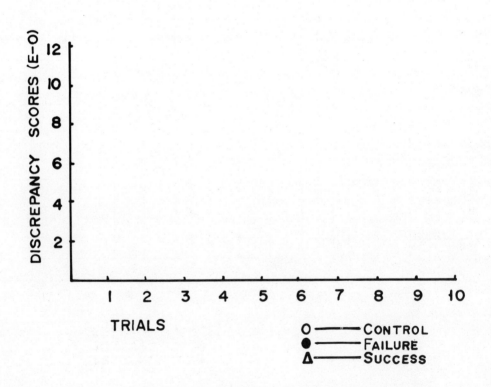

FIELD EXPERIMENT: Performance Curves

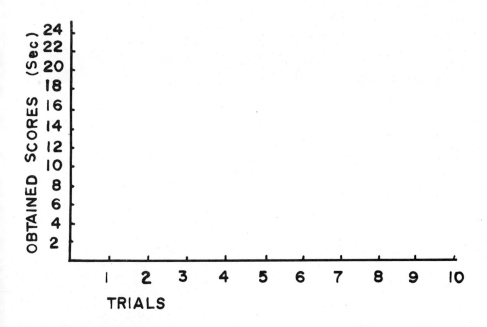

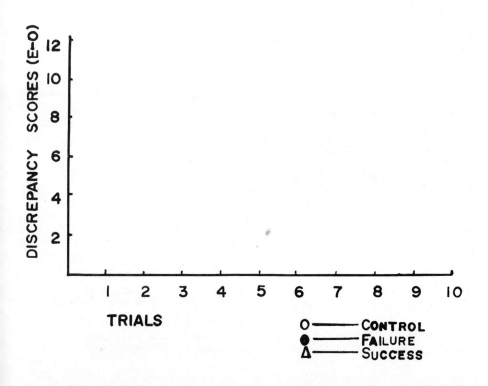

O———— Control
●———— Failure
Δ———— Success

PENNSYLVANIA BI-MANUAL WORKSAMPLE.

Figure 18-7: This task combines the basic elements of a relatively simple work situation. The examinee, seated before the 8″ x 24″ board, grasps a nut between thumb and index finger of left hand, and a bolt with thumb and index finger of right hand; he turns the bolt into the nut, and places in holes in the board. There are one hundred nut-and-bolt combinations. Twenty of these are for practice work and eighty are to be done under timing. Thus, the test combines: finger dexterity of both hands, whole movement of both arms, eye-hand coordination, bi-manual coordination, and ability to use both hands in **cooperation.**

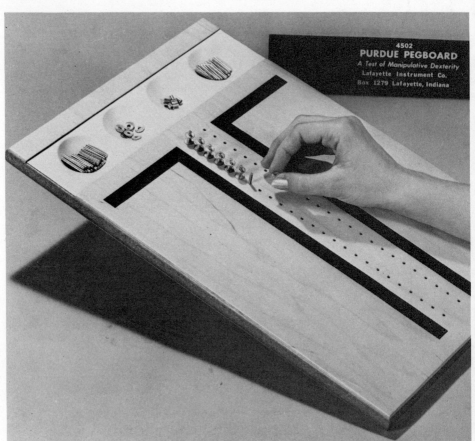

PURDUE PEGBOARD TEST

Figure 18-8: The Purdue Pegboard is an apparatus test of finger manipulation and assembly. It has found wide acceptance in industry because of its diagnostic reliability and validity.

Two problems of manual dexterity are included: (1) the sequential insertion of pegs, and (2) the assembly of pegs, collars and washers.

identical numerical scales are attached on either side of the trough at one end. Each scale is numbered zero to ten and down to zero again with each number area being three-fourths inch wide. A starting point is marked two inches from the opposite end. The marble is pushed down the trough by means of a pencil-like wooden pole twelve inches long.

The subject predicts the numerical score area where the marble will finally stop as he pushes it along the trough with the pole.

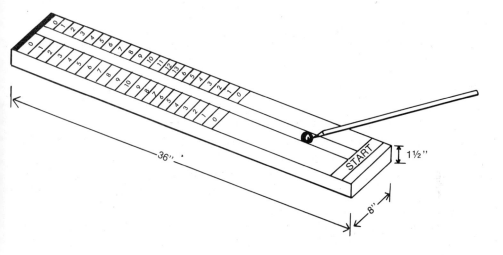

Chapter 19

FATIGUE

INTRODUCTION

FATIGUE HAS BECOME an overworked and an often misunderstood parameter of human performance. The major problem is that its meaning has changed over the years. To the scientific researcher, fatigue has had a specific connotation related to a particular area of interest. To the layman, its meaning and consequences may be entirely different. The interpretation has therefore ranged from the inability of men to work due to the interference of fatigue, to general conditions of bridge structures and airplane frames.

To Bartley (1965), who has spent a lifetime studying this phenomenon, fatigue inferred what people originally meant when they said they were tired. "Fatigue is then an experienced self-evaluation. It is the aversion to activity, a condition of existence expressed in bodily feelings, a self-felt assessment of inadequacy, and the experience of futility, etc., with the desire to escape . . . . The situation where the person is 'fed-up,' bored or annoyed, where the person's thinking becomes disorganized (mental fatigue) and where the person is uncomfortable after excessive muscular activity, it is this feeling of inability to carry on that is the core of the matter and it is this that is essentially fatigue" (Bartley, 1965). The implication is that there is a relationship between how a person feels and the amount of exertion. The greater the effort, the greater the tiredness. An association between fatigue and work output developed and "when fatigue was taken into the laboratory to be studied, decrement in work output became a synonym and finally a definition of fatigue" (Bartley, 1965).

Physiologists are more apt to view fatigue as a measurable decrement in performance or capacity for work, due to chemical changes in the muscle tissue. Karpovich (1963) feels that fatigue is caused by expended bodily energy. It is therefore chemical in character and may result from a depletion of energy stores in the body, accumulation and the hindrance

238

of waste products, and a breakdown in homeostasis. Local poisoning in the living cells of the body has also been suggested as being responsible for fatigue.

Fatigue also has a psychological connotation. Psychological fatigue is most often thought of as mental fatigue which is often due to boredom because of a lack of interest in a routine task. Mental fatigue can be elicited by such factors as temperature and humidity, lack of sleep, drugs, emotions, kind of work, time of day, and insufficient blood supply. The psychologist, however, may also view the effects of fatigue as a reduction in some intellectual productivity.

Impairment has often been considered by many researchers as synonymous with work decrement and fatigue. However, Bartley feels that "impairment is the reduced ability of the cells to function due to the accumulation of waste products of activity, whereas work decrement is the measureable drop in activity of muscles measured in energistic terms" (Bartley, 1957). Impairment does not necessarily follow fatigue as inactivity may lead to fatiguing boredom while changing activities are less likely to create fatigue.

It is generally accepted that any factor such as fatigue that hinders motor performance will also hinder motor learning. The elicitation of fatigue has taken several forms such as severe exercise, sleep deprivation, and simple repetitive and boring tasks. Even anticipation of boring tasks can be fatiguing or can produce a state of fatigue before the task is begun, whereas anticipation of an interesting, more demanding task may produce an exhilarating effect. Phillips (1962) demonstrated that fatigue may impair the performance of a learning task without reducing the amount of learning of that task. The quality of the performance may therefore be impaired without actual motor learning impairment even though the fatigue-producing factor may be relatively heavy and of considerable duration.

Few studies have attempted to evaluate the effects of fatigue on motor learning mainly due to the ambiguity of the phenomenon.

Physiological indices of fatigue may be measured objectively by such factors as increases in instability of neuromuscular coordination, blood lactic acid, reaction time, and decreases in strength, blood glucose, and muscle glycogen.

Psychological indices often employ subjective self-reporting scales as to the monotony of the task or how an individual feels with choices ranging from "worn out, too tired to do anything," to "not tired at all, fresh enough to start a full day."

However, the effect of induced fatigue on motor learning has most often been determined by the increase or decreases in performance of some novel task.

GENERAL RESEARCH FINDINGS

1. Fatigue may impair performance of a motor task without a reduction in the amount of learning, depending on the extent of fatigue.
2. Due to physiological and psychological factors, individuals vary as to the degree of physical and/or mental work that would have a fatiguing effect on them even under identical conditions.
3. Fatigue is nontransferable from one specific body part to another.
4. The onset of fatigue caused by a given task may be postponed through training.
5. Work performances of a long-term nature because of associated boredom are more detrimentally affected by fatigue than are discrete short-term tasks.
6. Fatigue is caused by a number of physiological and psychological variables which overlap and interact.

REFERENCES

Alderman, R. B.: Influence of local fatigue on speed and accuracy in motor learning. *Res Q Am Assoc Health Phys Educ*, *36*:131, 1965.

Barnett, M. L., Ross, D., Schmidt, R., & Todd, B.: Motor skills learning and specificity of training principle. *Res Q Am Assoc Health Phys Educ*, *44*:440, 1973.

Bartley, S. H.: Fatigue and inadequacy. *Physiol Rev*, *37*:301, 1957.

Bartley, S. H.: *Fatigue: Mechanisms and Management*. Springfield, Illinois, Charles C Thomas Pub., 1965.

Bartley, S. H.: Some things to realize about fatigue. *J Sports Med Phys Fitness*, *4*:153, 1964.

Bartz, D. W. and Smith, L. E.: Effect of moderate exercise on the performance and learning of a gross motor skill. *Percept Mot Skills*, *31*:187, 1970.

Benson, D. W.: Influence of imposed fatigue on learning a jumping task and a juggling task. *Res Q Am Assoc Health Phys Educ*, *39*:251, 1968.

Carron, A. V.: Motor performance and learning under physical fatigue. *Med Sci Sports*, *4*:101, 1972.

Carron, A. V.: Physical fatigue and motor learning. *Res Q Am Assoc Health Phys Educ*, *40*:682, 1969.

Carron, A. V. and Ferchuk, A. D.: The effect of fatigue on learning and performance of a gross motor task. *J Motor Behav*, *3*:62, 1971.

Cotten, D., Thomas, J., Spieth, W. and Biasiotto, J.: Temporary fatigue effects in a gross motor skill. *J Motor Behav*, *4*:217, 1972.

Godwin, W. and Schmidt, R.: Muscular fatigue and discrete motor learning. *Res Q Am Assoc Health Phys Educ*, *42*:374, 1971.

Grose, J. E.: Depression of muscle fatigue curves by heat and cold. *Res Q Am Assoc Health Phys Educ*, *29*:19, 1958.

Gutin, B.: Effect of systemic exertion on rotary pursuit and maze performance and learning. Paper presented at the Second International Congress of Sport Psychology. Washington, D. C. 1968.

Haider, M. and Dixon, N. F.: Influence of training and fatigue on the continuous recording of a visual differential threshold. *Br J Psychol*, *52*:227, 1961.

Hammerton, M. and Teikner, A. H.: Physical fitness and skilled work after exercise. *Ergonomics*, *11*:41, 1968.

Holland, G. J.: Effects of limited sleep deprivation on performance of selected motor tasks. *Res Q Am Assoc Health Phys Educ*, *39*:285, 1968.

Hueting, J. E.: and Sarphati, H. R.: Measuring fatigue. *J Appl Psychol*, *50*:535, 1966.

Karpovich, P. V.: *Physiology of Muscular Activity*. Philadelphia, W. B. Saunders Co., 1963.

Kroll, W.: Isometric fatigue curves under varied interval recuperation periods. *Res Q Am Assoc Health Phys Educ*, *39*:106, 1968.

Levitt, S. and Gutin, B.: Multiple choice reaction time and movement time during physical exertion. *Res Q Am Assoc Health Phys Educ*, *42*:405, 1971.

McGlynn, G. H.: Effect of an isometric exercise on force and fatigue in a skeletal muscle. *Res Q Am Assoc Health Phys Educ*, *39*:131, 1968.

Meyers, C. R., *et al.*: Effect of strenuous physical activity upon reaction time. *Res Q Am Assoc Phys Educ*, *40*:332, 1969.

Myers, S. J. and Sullivan, W. P.: Effect of circulatory occlusion on time to muscular fatigue. *J Appl Physiol*, *24*:54, 1968.

Nunney, D. N.: Fatigue impairment, and psycho-motor learning. *Percept Mot Skills*, *16*:369, 1963.

Phillips, W.: The effect of physical fatigue on two motor learning tasks. Unpublished doctoral dissertation, University of California, 1962.

Pierson, W. R.: Fatigue work decrement and endurance in a simple repetitive task. *Br J Med Psychol*, *36*:279, 1963.

Ross, S., Hussman, T., and Andrews, T.: Effects of fatigue and visual functions. *J Appl Psychol*, *38*:119, 1954.

Schmidt, R. A.: Performance and learning a gross motor skill under conditions of artificially-induced fatigue. *Res Q Am Assoc Health Phys Educ*, *40*:185, 1969.

Walster, B. and Aronson, E.: Effect of expectancy of task duration on the experience of fatigue. *J Exp Soc Psychol*, *3*:41, 1967.

Welch, M.: Specificity of heavy work fatigue: Absence of transfer from heavy leg work to coordination tasks using the arms. *Res Q Am Assoc Health Phys Educ*, *40*:402, 1969.

Wilkinson, R. T.: After effect of sleep deprivation. *J Exp Psychol*, *66*:439, 1963.

LABORATORY EQUIPMENT

PURPOSE. To determine the effects of localized fatigue upon the learning and performance of a motor task.

EQUIPMENT. A pursuit rotor* and ten and fifteen pound dumbbells.

DESIGN. Subjects randomly assigned to two groups, one experimental and one control.

PROCEDURE. The object of the task is to maintain the stylus in contact with the small disk on the revolving circular platform for the entire length of the trial. The speed of the turntable is predetermined, usually

---

*Pursuit rotors are explained in the chapter on Massed and Distributed Practice.

at 60 RPM's. A .01 second timer will record the time on target during the trial for each group.

On Day 1, each subject in the control group without prior warm-up and with his dominant hand will perform ten thirty-second trials on the pursuit rotor, with twenty second rest periods between each trial.

The subjects in the fatigued group will perform arm curls with a dumbbell, ten pounds for females and fifteen pounds for males, using their dominant hand for three minutes. The rate should be one complete curl per second or until they are unable to continue with the cadence.

Subjects will immediately perform ten thirty-second trials on the pursuit rotor with twenty second rest periods.

On Day 2, without prior warm-up each subject in the control group will perform ten thirty-second trials similar to Day 1. Each subject in the fatigued group will perform ten thirty-second trials under similar circumstances as the control group.

RESULTS.

1. Record resultant data on master sheet provided.
2. Plot learning curves.
3. Test for significant mean differences by use of the independent *t*-test statistic:
   a. Compare the mean scores of the control group and experimental group for Day 1.
   b. Compare the mean scores of each group for Day 2.
   c. Compare the mean scores of Day 1 and Day 2 for the control group.
   d. Compare the mean scores of Day 1 and Day 2 for the control group.

FIELD EXPERIMENT

PURPOSE. To study the effects of fatigue upon performance in a sport skill.

ACTIVITY. Performance accuracy.

EQUIPMENT. Ten tennis balls and a target area.

DESIGN. Subjects randomly assigned to two groups, one control, the other experimental.

PROCEDURE. The object of the task is to toss a tennis ball at a target. Follow the procedures and task explanations in the chapter entitled "Knowledge of Results."

Each subject in the control group will, without prior warm-up, perform five trials, each consisting of ten tosses at the target, with ten-second rest periods between trials.

The subjects in the fatigued group will be vigorously exercised by running in place at two beats per second for five minutes or until they are unable to continue running in cadence. Knees are to be lifted approximately to the horizontal while running. Immediately following the exercise, each subject will perform five trials, each consisting of ten tosses at the target, with ten second rest periods between each trial.

RESULTS.

1. Record resultant data on the master sheet provided.
2. Plot learning curves.
3. Compare the mean scores of the control groups and experimental group with the use of a *t*-test statistic.

APPENDIX

PURCHASED EQUIPMENT. The equipment on pp. 247-248 may be purchased from the Lafayette Instrument Company, P. O. Box 1279, Lafayette, Indiana, and used as tasks in studies dealing with fatigue. Ergometers and treadmills would be better than weights or dumbbells to induce fatigue, as experimental control is easier to attain.

LABORATORY EXPERIMENT : FATIGUE DATA SHEET

Control group	DAY 1 TRIALS											DAY 2 TRIALS										
Subjects	1	2	3	4	5	6	7	8	9	10	ΣX	1	2	3	4	5	6	7	8	9	10	ΣX
1																						
2																						
3																						
4																						
5																						

$$\Sigma\Sigma X_1 = \qquad\qquad \Sigma\Sigma X_2 =$$

$$\bar{X}_1 = \frac{\Sigma\Sigma X_1}{n_1} \qquad \bar{X}_{Total} = \frac{\Sigma\Sigma X_1 + \Sigma\Sigma X_2}{n_1 + n_2} \qquad \bar{X}_2 = \frac{\Sigma\Sigma X_2}{n_2}$$

Fatigue Group	DAY 1 TRIALS											DAY 2 TRIALS										
Subjects	1	2	3	4	5	6	7	8	9	10	ΣX	1	2	3	4	5	6	7	8	9	10	ΣX
1																						
2																						
3																						
4																						
5																						

$$\Sigma\Sigma X_1 = \qquad\qquad \Sigma\Sigma X_2 =$$

$$\bar{X}_1 = \frac{\Sigma\Sigma X_1}{n_1} \qquad \bar{X}_{Total} = \frac{\Sigma\Sigma X_1 + \Sigma\Sigma X_2}{n_1 + n_2} \qquad \bar{X}_2 = \frac{\Sigma\Sigma X_2}{n_2}$$

FIELD EXPERIMENT : FATIGUE DATA SHEET

Control Group

Subjects	Trials					ΣX
	1	2	3	4	5	
1						
2						
3						
4						
5						

$$\Sigma \Sigma X =$$

Fatigue Group

Subjects	Trials					ΣX
	1	2	3	4	5	
1						
2						
3						
4						
5						

$$\Sigma \Sigma X =$$

LABORATORY EXPERIMENT

Learning Curve

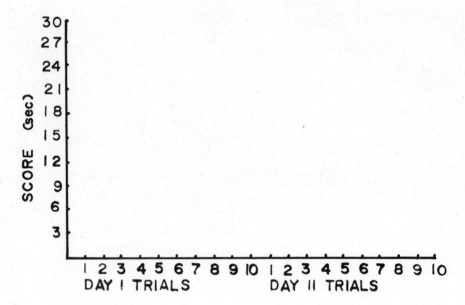

FIELD EXPERIMENT

Learning Curve

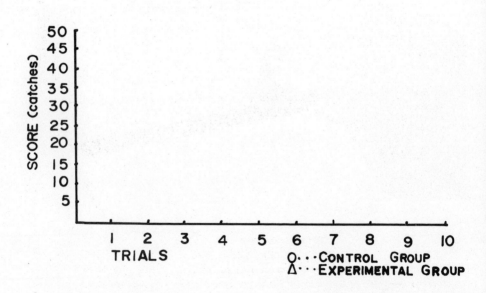

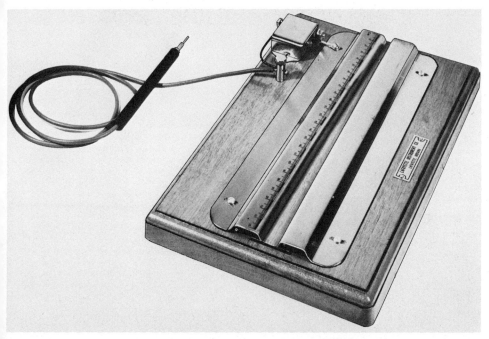

GROOVE TYPE STEADINESS TESTER

Figure 19-4: Calibrated adjustable stainless steel sides produce a slit, the bottom of which is glass to assure smoothness. If the stylus touches the electrified sides, the buzzer is sounded. A counter can be attached to register contact errors if desired.

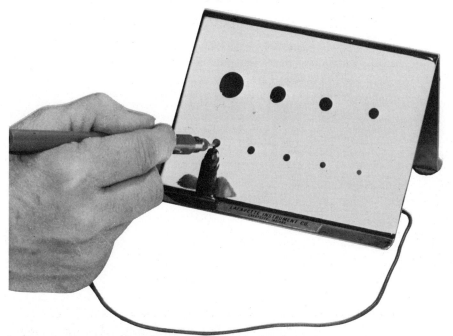

STEADINESS TESTER—HOLE TYPE

Figure 19-5: Conventional hole type with nine graduated holes and a stylus. Terminal provided for completing electric circuit to activate buzzer, counter, or clock. Device is designed to test arm and hand steadiness.

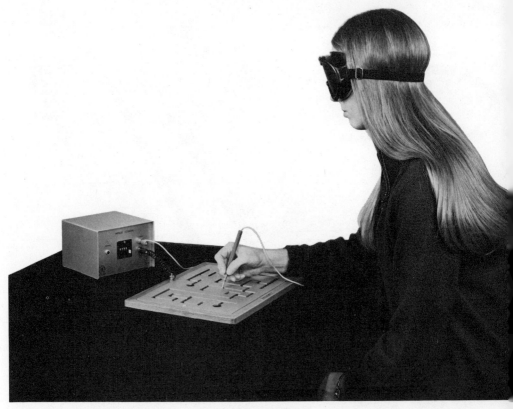

AUTOMATIC TALLY MAZE

Figure 19-6: This durable aluminum maze has the identical pattern of the pencil maze. Provision has been made to automatically tally error scores. Error score can be divided into number of wrong turns made and number of cul-de-sacs entered. Subjects are blindfolded when tracing the maze.

Chapter 20

KINESTHETIC AFTEREFFECTS

INTRODUCTION

THE INFLUENCE OF PREVIOUS posture on subsequent posture has been studied by Selling as early as 1930 (Jackson, 1954). The typical experiment consisted of having the subject hold his two arms horizontally in front of him, then raising one arm to 45 degrees above the horizontal and keeping it there about thirty seconds. Immediately after this, he closed his eyes and tried to bring the elevated arm to the same position as the other. Some upward effect was reported. Most of us have experienced this phenomenon called *kinesthetic aftereffects* in the parlor game which involves pressing one's hands outward on a wall for a few seconds while keeping the arm in a straight position, then stepping away and feeling the arm rise in the air. The interesting phenomenon of an aftereffect phenomenon is the fact that a subject's perception of a stimulus presently confronting him is influenced by a previously fixated stimulus which is now physically no longer present (Immergluck, 1968). Gibson (1966) wrote that aftereffects in perception apply to colors, tastes, smells, feelings of temperature, and also to shape, size, position, and motion. The capacity for adjustment of the perceptual system is then exceeded, and some kinds of feelings accompany this state of affairs.

Aftereffects may be seen as a deficiency of the perceptual process. Their presence may mask the meanings of the afferent messages propelled through the nervous system, resulting in deteriorated performance. It is important for the athlete to be aware of the influence of kinesthetic aftereffects when the proper execution of a movement relies to a great extent upon the feel of actions. Aftereffects may probably explain in part the fact that there may be a difference between what an athlete does and what he thinks he does. It is also important for the coach to properly prepare athletes for a sport contest, e.g. whether he wants to evitate or profit from the aftereffects.

However, this deficiency of the perceptual system is thought to have some positive aspects associated with it. One typical example is the custom of swinging a weighted bat before hitting in baseball in order to swing the regulation bat faster. Whether such practice can contribute to

improved performance or not is not sufficiently substantiated by research findings to draw a conclusion with any high degree of confidence
(Singer, 1972).

Although gaps in knowledge on the phenomenon of kinesthetic aftereffects exist, many studies have been concerned with this area from
different points of view. For instance, Spitz and Lipman (1960) correlated visual and kinesthetic figural aftereffects tests and the obtained
coefficients did not reach the .05 level of significance. However, caution
should be taken in generalizing these coefficients to other studies. They
also reported test-retest tetrachoric correlations of .74 and of .34 when
rest intervals of five minutes or eighteen to twenty minutes were given
between the administration of kinesthetic aftereffects tests. Using a
kinesthetic apparatus with narrow and wide ends, it was also found that
the starting position in this task did not have an effect on kinesthetic
satiation scores.

In 1969, Cratty and Amatelli suggested that figural aftereffects elicited
by gross action patterns were largely independent of kinesthetic aftereffects in the arm-shoulder musculature. From this study and the previous
ones (Cratty and Hutton, 1964; Cratty, 1965), where blindfolded subjects
were guided through curved and straight pathways, verbal reports were
recorded of opposite curvature to the one experienced before in a
straight test pathway given immediately following satiation. These aftereffects seemed to vary with respect to the number of trials in the
inspection task, and twelve trials resulted in a greater percentage of
subjects reporting curvature than eight or sixteen trials (Cratty, 1965).
Kinesthetic aftereffects can also be elicited by walking a ten degree
incline for one to two minutes (Hutton, 1966).

With respect to limb movement or limb posture, Jackson (1954) wrote
that a previous posture of the arm for as little as five seconds influenced
subsequent posture. Nelson and Nofsinger (1965) and Nelson and Lambert (1965) tested subjects for speed of elbow flexion immediately before
and after the application of selected levels of overload. Significant differences were not observed between the conditions, but subjects reported
that they *felt faster* during postoverload trials. Koehler and Dinnerstein
(1946) and Carlson and Campbell (1968) found that the size of the
aftereffect is influenced by the number of repeated exposures to an
inspection object. Devane (1965) obtained similar results in using an
intermittent stimulus. In 1967 Over investigated the magnitude of a
difference between post and preinspection setting of a bar to the apparent horizontal under blindfolded conditions as a function of the angle of
tilt of the bar during the inspection period. Postinspection settings were
found to be displaced from preinspection settings in the direction of the
tilt of the inspection figure at all angles between 15 degrees and 75

degrees. Kinesthetic aftereffects of greatest magnitude were obtained when the inspection figure was tilted 60 degrees from the horizontal. Furthermore, it was observed that the amount of kinesthetic aftereffects varied in function to the rotated (inward vs. outward) position of the arm (Over, 1967).

Charles and Duncan (1959) mentioned that after equal inspection time, the decay function of kinesthetic aftereffects is slower than that of visual aftereffects. Furthermore, Bakan and Thompson (1962) reported that the amount of residual aftereffect is related to the size of the kinesthetic aftereffects induced earlier. Correlations of the residual effect measured one week and one month after a forty-five second stimulation with an inspection object and induced effects were .65 and .75, successively.

Rapoport (1963) studied the duration of the kinesthetic aftereffect with massed practice. Over and Griew (1968) reported no age differences (18 years vs. 75 years) in amount of aftereffects when judgment time to complete the kinesthetic inspection period of a tilted rod was the same for young and old subjects.

Relationships of personality variables and kinesthetic aftereffects were not found by Kidd and Beer (1968). Also, their review of literature indicated similar conclusions. On the other hand, Immergluck (1968) observed that field-independent subjects exhibit potent visual aftereffects on specified perceptual tasks while field dependent subjects show weak visual aftereffects. Furthermore, it was reported that normal subjects under identical test conditions differ with regard to the magnitude of the elicited aftereffect or the speed of its decay.

GENERAL RESEARCH FINDINGS

1. Kinesthetic and visual aftereffects seem relatively independent of each other under normal conditions.
2. Kinesthetic aftereffects may be either short-term or relatively long-term (residuals).
3. The amount of attention given to the initial task, the extent to which a subject kinesthetically perceives, the amount of inspection time in the initial task, and perhaps some personality variables, among others, are factors which seem to determine the amount of kinesthetic aftereffects experienced by a subject.
4. There probably exists an optimum amount of inspection time in the initial task which produces the greatest amount of aftereffects.
5. The most pronounced kinesthetic aftereffects are experienced immediately following the satiation, and they disappear slowly, leaving

a residual aftereffect which may be temporary or relatively permanent.

6. Kinesthetic aftereffects may be associated with a feeling of *better* or *worse*, but performance is probably not affected under normal sport situations.

REFERENCES

Amatelli, F. and Cratty, B.: Figural aftereffects elicited by gross action patterns: the role of kinesthetic aftereffects in the arm-shoulder musculature. *Res Q Am Assoc Health Phys Educ*, 40:1, 1969.

Axelrod, S.: Severe visual handicap and kinesthetic figural aftereffects. *Percept Mot Skills*, 13:2, 1961.

Bakan, P. and Thompson, R.: On the relation between induced and residual kinesthetic aftereffects. *Percept Mot Skills*, 15:2, 1962.

Barlow, H. B. and Hill, R. M.: Evidence for a physiological explanation of the waterfall phenomenon and figural aftereffects. *Nature, 200*:1434, 1963.

Barthol, R.: Kinesthetic figural aftereffects under a drowsy state induced. *Percept Mot Skills*, 11:1, 1960.

Beere, D. and Kidd, A.: Relationship between kinesthetic figural aftereffects and certain personality variables. *Percept Mot Skills*, 26:2, 1968.

Bush A.: Sensorimotor experience and kinesthetic aftereffects. *Percept Mot Skills*, 23:2, 1966.

Cameron, P. and Wertheimer, M.: Kinesthetic aftereffects are in the hands not in phenomenal space. *Percept Mot Skills*, 20:3, Part 2, 1965.

Campbell, S. and Carlson, J.: Influence of repeated testing and of starting position in kinesthetic aftereffects. *Percept Mot Skills*, 27:1, 1968.

Charles, J. P. and Duncan, C. P.: The distance gradient in kinesthetic figural aftereffects. *J Exp Psychol*, 57:164, 1959.

Cratty, B.: Figural aftereffects resulting from gross action patterns: the amount of exposure to the inspection task and the duration. *Res Q Am Assoc Health Phys Educ*, 36:3, 1965.

Cratty, B. and Hutton, R.: Figural aftereffects resulting from gross action patterns. *Res Q Am Assoc Health Phys Educ*, 35:2, 1964.

Day, R. H.: Excitatory and inhibitory processes as the basis of contour shift and negative aftereffects. *Psychologia*, 5:185, 1962.

Day, R. H. and Singer, G.: Temporal determinants of a kinesthetic aftereffects. *J Exp Psychol*, 69:343, 1965.

Deutsch, J.: The Koehler Wallach Theory and the aftereffects of seen movement. *Percept Mot Skills*, 9:4, 1959.

Devane, J.: Kinesthetic aftereffects following intermittent stimulation. *Percept Mot Skills*, 20:1, 1965.

Dinnerstein, A. and Lowenthal, M.: Pain tolerance and kinesthetic aftereffects. *Percept Mot Skills*, 15:1, 1962.

Eysenck, H. J.: Cortical inhibition, figural aftereffects and theory of personality. *J Abnorm Soc Psychol*, 51:94, 1955.

Fobes, J. L. and Perrott, D. R.: Autokinesis as a binaural localization phenomenon: Effects of signal bandwidth. *J Exp Psychol*, 87:2, 1971.

Freedman, S. and Zacks, J.: Active and passive movement in the production of kinesthetic tilt aftereffects. *Percept Mot Skills, 16*:3, 1963.

Ganz, L.: Is the figural aftereffects an aftereffects? a review of its intensity, on set, decay, and transfer characteristics. *Psychol Bull, 66*:151, 1966.

Gibson, J. J.: Adaptation, aftereffects and contrast in the perception of curved lines. *J Exp Psychol, 16*:1, 1933.

Gibson, J. J.: Adaptation, aftereffects and contrast in the perception of tilted lines: II simultaneous contrast and the areal restriction of the aftereffects. *J Exp Psychol, 20*:553, 1937.

Gibson, J. J.: *The Senses Considered as Perceptual Systems.* Boston, Houghton-Mifflin Company, 1966.

Gibson, J. J. and Radner, M.: Adaptation, aftereffects and contrast in the perception of tilted lines: I quantitative studies. *J Exp Psychol, 20*:453, 1937.

Griew, S. and Over, R.: Age, judgment time and amount of kinesthetic aftereffects. *J Exp Psychol, 78*:3, 1965.

Harris, J. R. and Morant, R. B.: Two different aftereffects of exposure to visual tilts. *Am J Psychol, 78*:218, 1965.

Heinemann, E. G.: Figural aftereffects in kinesthetics: Effects of object width and repeated presentation. *Am J Psychol, 61*:51, 1961.

Hochberg, J.: In the importance of movement produced stimulation in prism-induced aftereffects. *Percept Mot Skills, 16*:2, 1963.

Holland, H. G.: L'effet consecutif de spirale. *Psychol Genet,* 1967, p. 303.

Hutton, R. S.: Kinesthetic aftereffects a measure of kinesthetic awareness. *Percept Mot Skills, 23*:3, Part 2, 1966.

Hutton, R. S.: Kinesthetic aftereffects produced by walking on a gradient. *Res Q Am Assoc Health Phys Educ, 37*:368, 1966.

Immergluck, L.: Figural aftereffects, rates of "figure-ground" reversal, and field-dependence. *Psychonomic Science, 6*:45, 1966.

Immergluck, L.: Further comments on is the figural aftereffects an aftereffects? *Psychol Bull, 70*:3, 1968.

Immergluck, L.: Individual differences in figural aftereffects potency: Aftereffects trace versus immediate stimulus context as a determiner of perception. *Psychonomic Science, 10*:203, 1968.

Immergluck, L.: Resistance to an optical illusion, figural aftereffects and field-dependence. *Psychonomic Science, 4*:219, 1966.

Jackson, C. V.: The influence of previous movement and posture on subsequent posture. *Q J Exp Psychol, 6*:72, 1954.

Jaffe, R.: The influence of visual stimulation on kinesthetic figural aftereffects. *Am J Psychol, 69*:70, 1954.

Klein, G. S. and Krech, D.: Cortical conductivity in the brain-injured. *J Pers, 21*:118, 1952.

Koehler, W.: Movement aftereffects and figural aftereffects. *Percept Mot Skills, 20*:2, 1965.

Koehler, W. and Wallach, H.: Figural aftereffects: An investigation of visual processes. *Proc Am Philosophical Soc, 88*:269, 1944.

Lambert, W.; and Nelson, R.: Immediate aftereffects of overload on resisted and non-resisted speeds of movement. *Res Q Am Assoc Health Phys Educ, 36*:3, 1965.

Levanthal, C. M. and Vertheimer, M.: Permanent satiation phenomena with kinesthetic figural aftereffects. *J Exp Psychol, 55*:255, 1958.

Lipman, R. and Spitz, H.: Reliability and intercorrelation of individual differences on visual and kinesthetic figural aftereffects. *Percept Mot Skills, 20*:2, 1965.

Mayer, J.: Influence of inspection of a visually curved field on kinesthetic aftereffects. *Percept Mot Skills, 13*:1, 1961.

Mikaelian, A. H. and Morant, R. B.: Inter-field tilt aftereffects. *Percept Mot Skills, 10*:95, 1960.

Muir, D. and Over, R.: Tilt aftereffects in central and peripheral vision. *J Exp Psychol, 85*:2, 1970.

Nachmias, J.: Figural aftereffects in kinesthetic space. *Am J Psychol, 66*:609, 1963.

Nelson, R.; and Nofsinger, M.: Effect of overload on speed of elbow flexion and the associated aftereffects. *Res Q Am Assoc Health Phys Educ, 36*:174, 1965.

Over, R.: Effects of the angle of tilt of the inspection figure on the magnitude of kinesthetic aftereffects. *J Exp Psychol, 74*:249, 1967.

Pollack, R. H.: Comment on is the figural aftereffects an aftereffects? *Psychol Bull, 68*:59, 1967.

Rapoport, J.: Massed practice and motion aftereffects. *Percept Mot Skills, 17*:1, 1963.

Reinhold, D.: Effect of training on perception of after images. *Percept Mot Skills, 7*:3, 1957.

Ross, P. and Taylor, M.: Tracking rotary motion aftereffects with different illuminations of inspection and test fields. *Percept Mot Skills 18*:3, 1964.

Smith, K. and Wargo, L.: Movement-produced stimulation is important in prism-induced aftereffects. *Percept Mot Skills, 16*:3, 1963.

Standing, L.: Note on central and retinal mechanisms in the aftereffects of seen movement. *Percept Mot Skills, 22*:2, 1966.

Sumi, S.: Paths of seen motion and motion aftereffects. *Percept Mot Skills, 23*:3, Part 1, 1966.

Sweeney, D.: Pain reactivity and kinesthetic aftereffects. *Percept Mot Skills, 22*:3, 1966.

Taylor, M.: Tracking in decay of the aftereffects of seen rotary movement. *Percept Mot Skills, 16*:1, 1963.

Vetter, R.: Retinal after-image of induced movement. *Percept Mot Skills, 26*:2, 1968.

Weitheimer, M.: Figural aftereffects as a measure of metabolic efficiency. *J Pers, 24*:56, 1955.

Weitheimer, M.: The differential satiability of schizophrenic and normal subjects: A test of the deduction from the theory of figural aftereffects. *J Gen Psychol 51*:291, 1954.

Winters, J.: Gamma movement: Apparent movement in figural aftereffects experiments. *Percept Mot Skills, 19*:3, 1964.

LABORATORY EXPERIMENT

PURPOSE. To determine how exposure to two standard blocks of a kinesthetic figural aftereffect apparatus affects accuracy on the comparison block, and to compare the effects of the two standard blocks.

EQUIPMENT. Kinesthetic figural aftereffect apparatus (see Appendix) and a pair of goggles.

DESIGN. A pretest and posttest three-group design consisting of a control group and two experimental groups is suggested. All groups will be submitted identically to the pretest and the experimental groups will be given the exposure task on the posttest.

PROCEDURE.

1. Pretest: The instructions are provided about the task and the order of the experiment, while the subject is blindfolded. The finger guide is placed at the criterion point on the comparison block, and the subject is instructed to place the thumb and large finger of his nonpreferred hand through the finger guide and to grip the block. Then, the subject is asked to inspect (feel) the width of the comparison block at the criterion point for ten seconds, after which he is asked to withdraw his hand. The experimenter moves the finger guide to a predetermined starting position and the subject is asked to position the finger guide at the criterion point. When the subject thinks he has positioned it accurately, he withdraws his hand. Ten trials are administered. No visual presentation of the criterion point nor visual or verbal knowledge of results is given to subjects. The experimenter records the direction and the distance of the subject's positioning performance from the criterion point at each trial. The control group will repeat this procedure on the posttest.

2. Experimental groups posttest: Both experimental groups will follow the same procedures, but one experimental group will be exposed to the test block and the other experimental group will be exposed to the inspection block. Hereafter, these two blocks will be referred to as standard blocks. Subjects will be asked to feel the standard block width for forty-five seconds. Immediately afterwards, the experimenter places the subject's hand on the finger guide of the comparison block located at the criterion point. The subject is asked to feel the width of the block for ten seconds, and after the withdrawal of the subject's hand, the experimenter moves the finger guide to one predetermined starting point. The subject's hand is placed back to the finger guide of the comparison block, and the subject is asked to move the finger guide to the criterion point. Ten trials are given to the subject. The same measurements as in the pretest are taken. The pair of goggles are removed from the subject's eyes after each positioning, taking care to hide the apparatus.

RESULTS.

The compilation sheet provided after the field experiment can serve the purpose of providing you with the preliminary data upon which the following analyses will be done using the appropriate computation sheets provided in the statistic chapter.

1. Compare the three groups on the pretest with the a one-way analysis of variance.

2. Repeat the analysis of variance on the posttest scores of the three groups.

FIELD EXPERIMENT

PURPOSE. To determine if exposure to a weighted baseball bat affects accuracy in positioning a regulation bat.

EQUIPMENT. Positioning target,* regulation baseball bat, blindfolds, a weighted baseball bat, and chalk.

DESIGN. A pretest/posttest two-group design consisting of a control group and an experimental group is suggested. The experimental group will be administered the exposure treatment on the posttest.

PROCEDURE.

1. Pretest: Instructions are given about the task and the order of the experiment. The end of the bat is chalked. The subject holds a regulation bat over his shoulder opposite the wall as in a standard striking position while blindfolded. The experimenter asks the subject to move the regulation bat slowly against the target to a pre-designated point. The subject then attempts to duplicate this point on his own. The experimenter records the location of the bat position to the nearest half inch during ten trials. The subject attempts to replicate the same position during each trial, always starting in the standard striking position. The control group will be submitted again to this treatment on the posttest after a rest of five minutes.

2. Experimental group posttest: Five minutes after the end of the pretest, the subject is given the posttest. He assumes the basic stance while blindfolded. The subject is asked to position first the weighted bat and to maintain positioning during forty-five seconds. The weighted bat is then replaced with a regulation bat, and the subject attempts to position it in each of ten trials to the same target point as in the pretest. The location of each positioning is recorded by the experimenter. The pair of goggles are removed from the subject's eyes during each rest period, taking care to hide the target.

RESULTS.

Find the sum of the ten trials on the pretest and on the regulation bat positioning on the posttest. In using the appropriate computation sheet in the statistical chapter, you can determine the significance of:

1. The difference between the means of the groups on the pretest trials with an analysis of variance or a two-sample t-test

2. The difference between the means of groups on the posttest trials with an analysis of variance or a two-sample t-test.

---

*It is a graduated chalkboard as used for the "Jump and Reach" test.

FIELD EXPERIMENT : KINESTHETIC AFTEREFFECTS DATA SHEET

Control group	Pretest Trials*										Posttest Trials*									
	1	2	3	4	5	6	7	8	9	10	1	2	3	4	5	6	7	8	9	10
S_1																				
S_2																				
S_3																				
S_4																				
S_5																				

Experimental group I	Pretest Trials*										Posttest Trials*									
	1	2	3	4	5	6	7	8	9	10	1	2	3	4	5	6	7	8	9	10
S_1																				
S_2																				
S_3																				
S_4																				
S_5																				

Experimental group II	Pretest Trials*										Posttest Trials*									
	1	2	3	4	5	6	7	8	9	10	1	2	3	4	5	6	7	8	9	10
S_1																				
S_2																				
S_3																				
S_4																				
S_5																				

* Note positioning on the left side of the criterion point with a negative sign and positioning on the right side with a plus sign. Only record deviation from criterion point scores.

APPENDIX

PURCHASED EQUIPMENT. The kinesthetic aftereffect equipment is explained in the chapter entitled "Task Generality versus Specificity."

CONSTRUCTED EQUIPMENT. Kinesthetic aftereffect equipment is also presented in the above chapter. The bat positioning board consists of a test board, which is a chalkboard or a black painted plywood with dimensions four feet by two feet. Marks are placed on the test board at each successive half inch and a number is assigned to each mark corresponding to a given inch.

Chapter 21

OVERLEARNING AND RETENTION

INTRODUCTION

MOTOR SKILLS ARE COMMONLY believed to be very resistant to forgetting. Having learned a particular activity as a child, many years may pass before it is again performed, e.g. bicycle riding. It is generally observed that the later performance of the skill may be a bit rusty but nonetheless of sufficient quality, showing a high degree of retention. Rarely is the same phenomenon observed with verbal material. Memorized prose, geometry theorems, or an old sweetheart's address, all once well-learned, are no longer retained to a high degree, if at all.

Research investigations dealing with retention of motor skills have shown little forgetting to take place during extended time intervals (Myers, 1968; Purdy and Lockhart, 1962; Ryan, 1962, 1965). On the other hand, verbal learning studies employing paired associates or serial anticipation recall almost always show a well documented curve of forgetting (Woodworth and Schlosberg, 1964). Although many variables interact to determine how much is retained after the passage of a specified amount of time, two fundamental considerations seem to be the most tenable explanations.

1. There are fewer similar and thus interfering responses competing with motor skills than with verbal material.
2. Motor skills, e.g. bicycle riding and roller skating, are highly overlearned (overpracticed) whereas specific verbal material receives much less practice and repetition.

In the first case, the concepts of proactive and retroactive interference have received much attention (Schmidt, 1971; Underwood, 1957). A loss in the retention of the material of interest occurs when material of a similar nature is learned immediately beforehand (proactive interference) or immediately after (retroactive interference). The additional material most probably disrupts the memory consolidation process. With respect to motor skills, the high degree of specificity that exists among tasks reduces the possibility that proactive or retroactive effects would interfere to any great extent with retention (Myers, 1968).

Overlearning or practice that continues beyond a criterion success level, is a situation characterictic of many motor skills. The resistance to forgetting that characterizes motor or sports skills can be attributed entirely to overlearning (Melnick, 1971). Overlearning has a favorable effect on verbal material as well; however, the relative durability of the material retained is not as great.

How well a task is learned from an experimental view depends upon the level of performance selected as a criterion for learning, with overlearning consisting of practice beyond that criterion. A representative and logical criterion of learning must be selected. Should the initial criterion of learning be too low, an *underlearning* situation would bias results in favor of overlearning treatments by causing large distorted retention decrements and magnified overlearning gains. If excessive practice is given in order to meet a criterion level set too high, the effectiveness of overlearning treatments would be reduced and any real retention decrements would be masked. The degree of original learning appears to be the most important factor in the retention of motor skills (Fleishman and Parker, 1962; Purdy and Lockhart, 1962), and has received much attention as a strategic variable in determining the ways in which motor skill activities are retained.

Overlearning represents any excess practice of a skill beyond the established criterion of learning. For discrete (distinct response) skills such as basketball foul shooting, the criterion may be the number of attempts necessary in learning to make one basket or a predetermined ratio of baskets made to baskets attempted. A minimum number of errors or time on balance may be designated as criterion learning for the more continuous (variable stimulus) tasks of mirror star tracing and stabilometer performance. When a criterion has been defined, the manipulation of degree of overlearning is accomplished by allowing additional practice. Typically, 50 percent overlearning implies supplementary practice equal to one-half the number of trials (amount of time) previously required to reach criterion; 100 percent overlearning providing an equivalent amount of practice after criterion as was necessary to reach the criterion. Thus, the amount of initial practice can be controlled to produce a quantitative evaluation of the effects of overlearning on retention in a variety of motor skills.

There are several ways in which performance following periods of no practice can be measured. Recognition of previously learned material is a method specific to verbal skills. The typical multiple choice test whereby a student selects a response among several possibilities illustrates recognition as a measure of retention. Recollection is another way in which retention of verbal material is evaluated. The ability to recollect events surrounding the desired response without actually pinpointing it has been used in retention research, particularly in the area of psychoanalysis.

In dealing with motor skills, two ways of assessing the degree of retention are normally used. Recall, used with both verbal and motor skills, is the simplest measure of retention. Filling in the blank of a written test is a measurement of recall. For motor skills a recall measure is usually expressed as the score or degree of success on the first trial of a retention test. Relearning is a measure of retention in which the number of trials necessary to reach former proficiency is determined. Having once learned to ride a bicycle to a criterion level of performance, the ability to ride it on the first try after a period of no practice would constitute the recall score. The amount of time (number of trials) necessary to reach the former level of mastery (criterion) is interpreted as a measure of relearning.

When fewer trials are needed to relearn a skill than were initially required, the difference is referred to as a savings score. Thus, initial acquisition rate is compared to the learning rate of the second exposure, and if the second learning requires fewer trials than the first, a savings has occurred. The often-found reduction in number of trials to reach criterion the second time is attributed to the prior learning experience. In relearning, the savings score can be expressed as a percentage and computed from the following formula:

$$\text{Savings} = 100 \times \frac{\text{original trials} - \text{relearning trials}}{\text{original trials}}$$

GENERAL RESEARCH FINDINGS

1. Motor skills are highly resistant to forgetting with little if any decrement in performance occurring after several months or more of no practice.
2. Overlearning or degree of original learning represents one of the most important factors in the retention of motor skill.
3. Highly difficult and complex tasks seem the least resistant to forgetting. Continuous tasks such as swimming, skating, and tracking are better retained than discrete tasks, e.g. throwing or striking movements.
4. Generally, 50 to 100 percent overlearning appears to be the most efficient for optimum retention. A situation of diminishing returns arises with overlearning is excess of 100 percent.

REFERENCES

Adams, J. A.: The second facet of forgetting: A review of warm-up decrement. *Psychol Bull, 58*.257, 1961.

Ammons, R. B., *et al.*: Long-term retention of perceptual-motor skills. *J Exp Psychol, 55*:318, 1958.

Batson, W. H.: Acquisition of skill. *Psychol Monogr, 21:*1, 1916.

Bell, H. M.: Retention of pursuit rotor skill after one year. *J Exp Psychol, 40*:648, 1950.

Bell, V. L.: Argumented knowledge of results and its effect upon acquisition and retention of a gross motor skill. *Res Q Am Assoc Health Phys Educ, 39*:25, 1968.

Bilodeau, E. A., Jones, M. B., and Levy, C. M.: Long-term memory as a function of retention time and repeated recalling. *J. Exp Psychol, 67*:303, 1964.

Bilodeau, E. A. and Levy, C. M.: Long-term memory as a function of retention time and other conditions of training and recall. *Psychol Rev, 71*:27, 1964.

Carron, A. V.: Effect of ability level upon retention of a balance skill after two years. *Percept Mot Skills, 33*:527, 1971.

Carron, A. V. and Martiniuk, R. G.: An examination of the factors involved in determining learning and forgetting score reliabilities. *J Mot Behavior, 2*:239, 1970.

Carron, A. V. and Marteniuk, R. G.: Retention of a balance skill as a function of initial ability level. *Res Q Am Assoc Health Phys Educ, 41*:478, 1970a.

Duncan, C. P. and Underwood, B. J.: Retention of transfer in motor learning after twenty-four hours and after fourteen months. *J Exp Psychol, 46*:445, 1953.

Eysenck, S. B. G.: Retention of a well-developed motor skill after one year. *J Gen Psychol, 63*:267, 1960.

Fleishman, E. A. and Parker, J. F.: Factors in the retention and relearning of perceptual-motor skill. *J Exp Psychol, 64*:215, 1962.

Gillette, A. L.: Learning and retention. *Arch Psychol, 198*:1, 1936.

Hammerton, M.: Retention of learning in a difficult tracking task. *J Exp Psychol, 66*:108, 1963.

Henshaw, E. M. and Holman, P. G.: A note on overtraining. *Br J Psychol, 20*:333, 1930.

Irion, A. L.: The relation of set to retention. *Psychol Rev, 55*:336, 1948.

Jahnke, J. C.: Retention in motor learning as a function of amount of practice and rest. *J Exp Psychol, 55*:270, 1958.

Jahnke, J. C. and Duncan, C. P.: Reminiscence and forgetting in motor learning after extended rest intervals. *J Exp Psychol, 52*:273, 1956.

Kruger, W. C. F.: The effect of overlearning on retention. *J Exp Psychol, 12*:71, 1929.

Kruger, W. C. F.: Further studies in overlearning. *J Exp Psychol, 13*:152, 1930.

Leavitt, H. J. and Schlosberg, H.: The retention of verbal and motor skills. *J Exp Psychol, 34*:404, 1944.

Lersten, K. C.: Retention of skill on the rho apparatus after one year. *Res Q Am Assoc Health Phys Educ, 40*:418, 1969.

Llewellyn, J. H.: Effects of two levels of overlearning on retention of gross motor skill by institutionalized educable mental retardates and normal students. Unpublished doctoral dissertation. Florida State University, Tallahassee, 1972.

McGeoch, J. A.: Forgetting and the law of disuse. *Psychol Rev, 39*:352, 1932.

McGeoch, J. A. and Melton, A. W.: The comparative retention values of maze habits and of nonsense syllables. *J Exp Psychol, 12*:392, 1929.

Melnick, M. J.: Effects of overlearning on the retention of a gross motor skill. *Res Q Am Assoc Health Phys Educ, 42*:60, 1971.

Mengelkoch, R. F., Adams, J. A., and Gainer, C. A.: The forgetting of instrument flying skills. *Hum Factors, 13*:397, 1971.

Meyers, J. L.: Motor learning and retention: influence of practice and remoteness on individual differences. *Res Q Am Assoc Health Phys Educ, 39*:314, 1968.

Meyers, J. L.: Retention of balance coordination learning as influenced by extended lay-offs. *Res Q Am Assoc Health Phys Educ, 38*:72, 1967.

Neuman, E. and Ammons, R. B.: Acquisition and long-term retention of a simple serial perceptual-motor skill. *J Exp Psychol, 53*:159, 1957.

Purdy, B. J. and Lockhart, A.: Retention and relearning of gross motor skills after long periods of no practice. *Res Q Am Assoc Health Phys Educ, 33*:265, 1962.

Reynolds, B. and Bilodeau, I. McD.: Acquisition and retention of three psychomotor tests as a function of distribution of practice during acquisition. *J Exp Psychol, 44*:19, 1952.

Rivenes, R. S. and Mawhinney, M. M.: Retention of perceptual motor skill: an analysis of new methods. *Res Q Am Assoc Health Phys Educ, 39*:684, 1969.

Rubin-Rabson, G.: Studies in the psychology of memorizing piano music. VII: A comparison of two forms of mental rehearsal and keyboard overlearning. *J Educ Psychol, 32*:593, 1941a.

Rubin-Rabson, G.: Studies in the psychology of memorizing piano music. VIII: A comparison of three degrees of overlearning. *J Educ Psychol, 32*:688, 1941b.

Ryan, E. D.: Retention of stabilometer and pursuit rotor skills. *Res Q Am Assoc Health Phys Educ, 33*:593, 1962.

Ryan, E. D.: Retention of stabilometer performance over extended periods of time. *Res Q Am Assoc Health Phys Educ, 36*:46, 1965.

Schmidt, R. A.: Experimental psychology. In Singer, R. N. (Ed.): *Psychomotor Domain: Movement Behavior.* Philadelphia, Lea & Febiger, 1972.

Schmidt, R. A.: Retroactive interference and level of original learning in verbal and motor tasks. *Res Q Am Assoc Health Phys Educ, 42*:314, 1971.

Underwood, B. J.: Interference and forgetting. *Psychol Rev, 64*:49, 1957.

Van Dusen, F. and Schlosberg, H.: Further study of the retention of verbal and motor skills. *J Exp Psychol, 38*:526, 1948.

Woodworth, R. S. and Schlosberg, H.: *Experimental Psychology.* New York, Holt, Rinehart and Winston, 1964.

LABORATORY EXPERIMENT

PURPOSE. To examine the effects of 100 percent and 0 percent overlearning on the retention of a motor skill following one week of no practice.

EQUIPMENT. Pursuit rotor* and .01 second timer.

PROCEDURE. Assign a minimum of three subjects to each of two groups and randomly designate the groups as 0 percent and 100 percent overlearning. All trials on the pursuit rotor will be on a 20/15-second practice/rest ratio, with the rotor set at 60 RPM.

The criterion of learning will be the number of trials necessary to reach a cumulative total of twenty-five seconds time on target, i.e. the timer should not be reset between trials and the total number of trials needed

---

*The pursuit rotor is explained in the chapter entitled "Massed and Distributed Practice."

will include the trial in which criterion is met. Immediately after each member of the 100 percent overlearning group reaches criterion, he shall be given additional practice trials equal to the number of trials required to initially reach criterion. The 0 percent group will not be given any further practice. A retention test should be given one week later. Follow the same procedures for the retention test by recording the total number of trials necessary to regain criterion proficiency.

RESULTS.

1. Record the resultant data on the sheet provided.
2. Compute a *t*-test for independent samples on the mean number of relearning trials necessary to reach criterion for each group.
3. Calculate the percentage savings score for each group by applying the formula presented in the introduction of this chapter, and analyze the data with a *t*-test.

FIELD EXPERIMENT

PURPOSE. To determine the effects of 100 percent and 0 percent overlearning on the retention of novel motor skill after one week of no practice.

EQUIPMENT. A standard croquet mallet, six wooden balls, a forty-eight inch archery target face, and nails or tape sufficient to secure the target flat to the ground or other level non-smooth surface, e.g. carpet or a golf putting green.

PROCEDURE. A minimum of three subjects are to be assigned to each of two groups with the 100 percent and 0 percent overlearning conditions decided randomly. The center of the target shall be located eight feet from a restraining line behind which the subject will stand with his back to the target and his heels resting on the line. Gripping the croquet mallet with two hands, each subject will strike a ball in such a way so it will come to rest on the target face. (See illustration.) The initial position of the ball should be on the restraining line between the legs. A trial will consist of three successive hits with the score determined by the resting position of the ball on the target; 9 points—gold, 7 points—red, 5 points—blue, etc. Subjects not practicing should remove each ball from the target returning it to a position readily available to be hit again.

The criterion of learning is two successive trials in which the subject scores twelve or more points. Blocks of ten trials separated by one-minute rest periods should be administered until each subject attains criterion. For the overlearning group additional trials equal to the number required to reach criterion should be given immediately and conducted on the same work/rest ratio. One week later all subjects should be retested in

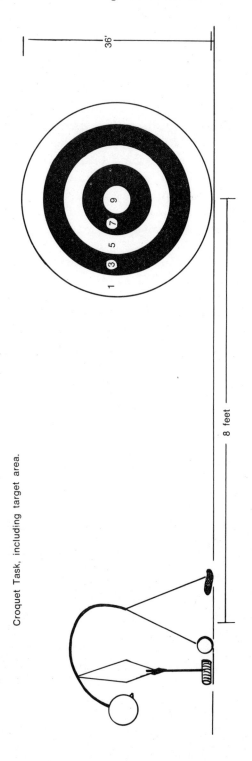

Croquet Task, including target area.

the same sequential order of performance and to the original criterion level of proficiency. Data sheets are to be maintained for each subject recording total number of points required to reach criterion and the total score obtained for each trial.

RESULTS.

1. Record the number of points made for each three balls hit (one trial) on the initial acquisition data sheet provided. Remember that no more trials are to be administered when the criterion of twelve or more points on two successive trials has been met.

2. Record in the space provided the number of overlearning trials given to the 100 percent overlearning group.

3. For each subject sum the total number of points necessary to reach criterion and record in the space provided on the initial acquisition sheet.

4. During the retention period follow the same procedures as in (1) and (3) above and record data on the retention sheet provided.

5. Determine the effects of overlearning on recall by using a t-test for independent means. The mean sums of points for the first retention trial should be compared to the last trial of practice before criterion was obtained. Note: the scores received during overlearning are not considered in the data analysis.

6. To determine relearning, the mean number of points for each group that was necessary to again reach criterion should be statistically compared to the mean number of points required in initial acquisition. Using the formula given in the introduction of this chapter, a percentage savings can be expressed for the two groups.

LABORATORY EXPERIMENT : OVERLEARNING AND RETENTION DATA SHEET

0% Overlearning

Subject #	# original trials to criterion	# overlearning trials	# relearning trials to criterion	X	X^2
1		0			
2		0			
3		0			
4		0			
5		0			
6		0			
N=				$\Sigma X=$	$\Sigma X^2=$
			$\overline{X} = \dfrac{\Sigma X}{N} =$		$(\Sigma X)^2=$

100% Overlearning

Subject #	# original trials to criterion	# overlearning trials	# relearning trials to criterion	X	X^2
1		0			
2		0			
3		0			
4		0			
5		0			
6		0			
N=				$\Sigma X=$	$\Sigma X^2=$
			$\overline{X} = \dfrac{\Sigma X}{N} =$		$(\Sigma X)^2=$

FIELD EXPERIMENT : OVERLEARNING AND RETENTION DATA SHEET

Initial Acquisition

0% Overlearning

Subject #	Trials 1 2 3 4 5 6 7 8 9 10 11 12 13 14 15 16 17 18 19 20 21 22 23 24 25	# overlearning trials	total points to criterion (X)	X²
1		0		
2		0		
3		0		
4		0		
5		0		
6		0		
N=			$\Sigma X =$	$\Sigma X^2 =$ $(\Sigma X)^2 =$

$\bar{X} = \dfrac{\Sigma X}{N} =$

$\bar{X}$ last trial before criterion reached $= \dfrac{\Sigma X \text{ last trial points}}{N}$

100% Overlearning

Subject #	Trials 1 2 3 4 5 6 7 8 9 10 11 12 13 14 15 16 17 18 19 20 21 22 23 24 25	# overlearning trials	total points to criterion (X)	X²
1		0		
2		0		
3		0		
4		0		
5		0		
6		0		
N=			$\Sigma X =$	$\Sigma X^2 =$ $(\Sigma X)^2 =$

$\bar{X} = \dfrac{\Sigma X}{N} =$

$\bar{X}$ last trial before criterion reached $= \dfrac{\Sigma X \text{ last trial points}}{N}$

FIELD EXPERIMENT: OVERLEARNING AND RETENTION DATA SHEET

Retention

0% Overlearning

Subject #	Trials 1 2 3 4 5 6 7 8 9 10 11 12 13 14 15 16 17 18 19 20	Total Points to Criterion (X)	X^2
1			
2			
3			
4			
5			
6			
N=	$\overline{X}$ first recall trial $= \dfrac{\Sigma X \text{ trial 1}}{N} =$	$\overline{X} = \dfrac{\Sigma X}{N} =$ $\Sigma X^2 =$	$\Sigma X^2=$ $(\Sigma X)^2 =$

100% Overlearning

Subject #	Trials 1 2 3 4 5 6 7 8 9 10 11 12 13 14 15 16 17 18 19 20	Total Points to Criterion (X)	X^2
1			
2			
3			
4			
5			
N=	$\overline{X}$ first recall trial $= \dfrac{\Sigma X \text{ trial 1}}{N} =$	$\overline{X} = \dfrac{\Sigma X}{N} =$ $\Sigma X =$	$\Sigma X^2=$ $(\Sigma X)^2 =$

SHORT-TERM MEMORY

INTRODUCTION

THE STUDENT IN PHYSICAL education is often required to perform a skill following a demonstration by the instructor. He may also be asked to repeat the performance of a skill after having done the skill with assistance from the teacher. In both instances, the student must remember either the demonstration or how he did the skill the first time under the teacher's guidance before he can perform the skill again. These situations help to point out the involvement of memory, in particular, short-term memory, in the learning of motor skills.

Short-term memory (STM) is generally accepted as being a separate and different system from long-term memory (LTM). Most of the experimental research in STM has considered primarily the short-term retention of verbal items, such as paired-associates. Thus the theoretical understandings of STM are primarily based on verbal STM. A memory model which includes STM was presented by Atkinson and Shiffrin (1971) and is reproduced here to facilitate an understanding of STM as a part of the overall memory system:

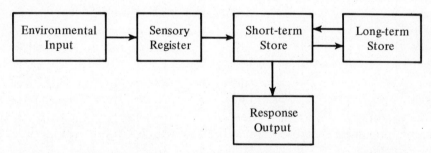

In this model, information which reaches the short-term store (STS) remains there for a time which arbitrarily has been considered to be no more than thirty seconds. The STS is a person's working memory. The only means of maintaining a limited amount of information in the STS is by rehearsal. Information may also be transferred from the STS to the long-term store (LTS), which is a fairly permanent repository for information. If the person wishes to use this information, it must be searched for and retrieved from the LTS and brought into the STS or the working memory. Thus it can be seen that the STS plays an important role in human memory.

A basic question that must be considered is how information in the STS is lost or forgotten. Theoretical considerations have involved two basic explanations: (1) trace-decay— the information completely decays and is lost within a short amount of time, approximately thirty seconds, and (2) interference—the information is lost due to competing responses within the store itself. If these competing responses occur prior to the acquisition of the information, it is called proactive interference (PI). If the competing responses occur after the acquisition of the information, it is called retroactive interference (RI). There is a question, therefore, that has been investigated: is information forgotten because of time alone, or because of interference, or because of a combination of these factors?

The answers to these questions were not investigated in the motor learning area until 1966 when Adams and Dijkstra attempted to relate the findings of verbal STM studies to motor STM. It appears from the results of this study and those which followed that the application of the theory of forgetting from STM may not be the same for verbal learning as it is for motor learning. According to a review of the literature on this topic by Milone (1971), that for verbal STM, the interference theory is almost universally accepted and the burden of proof rests with the trace-decay adherents, while for motor STM the opposite seems to be true.

Interference effects have been found in motor STM theory by some researchers (e.g. Ascoli and Schmidt, 1969; Milone, 1971; Patrick, 1971). To incorporate these findings with the generally held position of the trace-decay theory, Pepper and Herman (1970) developed a proposed system for motor STM to provide a workable theory of forgetting. This theory involves a *dual process theory* for motor STM and incorporates both decay and interference features. Thus, for motor STM it appears that neither decay nor interference alone can account for forgetting but both must considered. It should be mentioned, however, that this explanation is not universally accepted. The effect of interference on motor recall remains questionable and is the subject of much current research.

GENERAL RESEARCH FINDINGS

Some of the more conclusive findings in the study of motor STM are:
1. Forgetting from STM occurs relatively rapidly as a function of time.
2. Successive repetitions of the original response result in improved short-term retention.

3. Interpolated activities do not appear to have the same effect on motor STM as on verbal STM.

REFERENCES

Adams, J. A.: A closed-loop theory of motor learning. *J Motor Behav, 3*:111, 1971.

Adams, J. A.: *Human Memory.* New York, McGraw-Hill, 1967.

Adams, J. A. and Dijkstra, S.: Short-term memory for motor responses. *J Exp Psychol, 71*:314, 1966.

Ascoli, K. M. and Schmidt, R. A.: Proactive interference in short-term motor retention. *J Motor Behav, 1*:29, 1969.

Atkinson, R. C. and Shiffrin, R. M.: The control of short-term memory. *Sci Am, 225*:82, 1971.

Brown, J.: Some tests of the decay theory of immediate memory. *Q J Exp Psychol, 10*:12, 1958.

Keppel, G. and Underwood, B. J.: Proactive inhibition in short-term retention of single items. *Journal of Verbal Learning and Verbal Behavior, 1*:153, 1962.

Milone, F.: Interference in motor short-term memory. Unpublished master's thesis, The Pennsylvania State University, 1971.

Montgomery, J. M.: Interaction of movement length and interpolated activity in short-term motor memory. Paper presented at the Second Canadian Psycho Motor Learning and Sports Psychology Symposium. University of Windsor, October 1970.

Norrie, M. L.: Short-term memory trace decay in kinesthetically monitored force production. *Res Q Am Assoc Health Phys Educ, 39*:640, 1968.

Patrick, J.: The effect of interpolated motor activities in short-term memory. *J Motor Behav, 3*:39, 1971.

Pepper, R. L. and Herman, L. M.: Decay and interference effects in the short-term retention of a discrete motor act. *J Exp Psychol, 83,* 1970, (Monograph Supplement 2).

Peterson, L. R. and Gentile, A.: Proactive interference as a function of time between tests. *J Exp Psychol, 70*:473, 1965.

Peterson, L. R. and Peterson, M. J.: Short-term retention of individual verbal items. *J Exp Psychol, 58*:193, 1959.

Posner, M. I.: Short-term memory systems in human information processing. *Acta Psychol, 27*:267, 1967.

Posner, M. I. and Konick, A. F.: Short-term retention of visual and kinesthetic information. *Organizational Behavior and Human Performance, 1*:71, 1966.

Schmidt, R. A.: Proactive inhibition in retention of discrete motor skill. Paper presented at the Second International Society of Sports Psychology, Washington, D. C., October 1968.

Schmidt, R. A.: Retroactive interference and amount of original learning verbal and motor tasks. *Res Q Am Assoc Health Phys Educ, 42*:314, 1971.

Schmidt, R. A.: Experimental psychology. In R. N. Singer (ed.): *The Psychomotor Domain: Movement Behavior.* Philadelphia, Lea & Febiger, 1972.

Schmidt, R. A. and Ascoli, K. M.: Attention demand during storage of traces in motor short-term memory. *Acta Psychol, 34*:497, 1970.

Schmidt, R. A. and Ascoli, K. M.: Intertrial intervals and motor short-term memory. *Res Q Am Assoc Health Phys Educ, 41*:432, 1970.

Stelmach, G. E.: Prior positioning responses as a factor in short-term retention of a simple motor task. *J Exp Psychol 81*:523, 1969a.

Stelmach, G. E.: Short-term motor retention as a function of response similarity. *J Motor Behav, 1*:37, 1969b.

Sulzer, J. L.: Manual lever D: A basic psychomotor apparatus for the study of feedback. *Percept Mot Skills, 16*:859, 1963.

Williams, H. L., Beaver, W. S., Spence, M. T., and Rundell, O. H.: Digital and kinesthetic memory with interpolated information processing. *J Exp Psychol, 80*:530, 1969.

Williams, I. D.: The effects of practice trials and prior learning on motor memory. *J Motor Behav, 3*:289, 1971.

LABORATORY EXPERIMENT

PURPOSE. The purpose is to consider the effect of time and interference on the retention of a motor task.

EQUIPMENT. At least four different pieces of equipment can be adapted to use for this experiment. One needs to be purchased: the Kinesthesiometer (model 1770, Lafayette Instrument Co.); two may be built: a lever (described by Sulzer, 1963), and a slide on a metal bar (described by Adams and Dijkstra, 1966); the fourth is simply a paper, pencil, and ruler set-up. The following experiment is described using the Kinesthesiometer.

This piece of equipment will need to be modified by drilling one hole into the masonite base at the starting position or 0 degrees. A pencil or dowling rod will work well as a stop, although either must be long enough to stop the movement of the Kinesthesiometer.

Other equipment needed will be a blindfold and a stopwatch.

PROCEDURE. Randomly assign class members to one of four groups. The distinctions between the groups will be the nature of the interpolated activity to be engaged in during the retention interval and the length of the retention interval.

Motor Interpolated Activity

	NO	YES
5"		
30"		

Retention Interval (Sec.)

These steps should be followed for the experiment:
1. Cover the scale on the Kinesthesiometer with a piece of paper so that the subject cannot see it before he begins.

2. Ask the subject to be seated and to place his preferred arm, palm down, in the tray of the Kineothesiometer. Be sure that the knob at the end of the tray is between his middle and ring finger.
3. As soon as the subject is comfortable, blindfold him. Be certain that he cannot see under the blindfold.
4. Permit one practice trial, using the condition to which the subject is assigned. Place a stop at the 50 degree angle. (Holding a pencil there will do.) The subject should be instructed that on the command "Move," he is to move his arm until it stops. He should remain at that position for two seconds and then return to the starting position. Begin timing of the retention interval as soon as he returns to 0 degrees. If the subject is in an interpolated activity group, he should begin that activity immediately. The activity should continue until the time of the retention interval has elapsed. Instruct the subject to recall the original criterion position, this time without the use of a stop. When he feels he has reached that position, he should respond with "There." Record the response on your data sheet as a practice trial. If he was beyond the position, the score is recorded as + the number of degrees beyond the correct position. If he was short of the correct position, score it as − the number of degrees short.

   The interpolated activity will consist of the subject moving from the starting position to the various stops in the following sequence: five second retention interval: 0 degrees-75 degrees-0 degrees thirty second retention interval: (one movement each five seconds) 0 degrees-75 degrees-20 degrees-50 degrees-0 degrees-20 degrees-0 degrees
   movements: R L R L R L
   You may devise your own sequence of positions for the remaining trials. Each movement should be in the R-L-R sequence. Place a stop at the appropriate angle prior to each movement and remove the stop at his present position (except for 0 degrees; always keep that stop in place).
5. Begin the series of five trials with a one minute rest between trials. A trial is considered as:
   Move to criterion position—return to start—retention interval —recall criterion position.
   The following criterion positions for each trial may be used:

Trial 1:	20 degrees
Trial 2:	75 degrees
Trial 3:	50 degrees
Trial 4:	60 degrees
Trial 5:	15 degrees

RESULTS.

1. Add the number of degrees the subject was long or short of the criterion position, ignoring the signs. This will indicate the absolute error for the subject.
2. Take the absolute error for each subject in the group and calculate the mean for that group. With these four means, an ANOVA may be applied to determine if any significant differences between the groups existed. This calculation is described in Chapter 1.
3. Plot the mean error scores for each group on the graph provided.

FIELD EXPERIMENT

PURPOSE. The purpose is to consider the effect of time on the retention of a motor task.

EQUIPMENT:

bow (twenty or twenty-five pound bow)
yardstick
chalkboard and chalk
stopwatch
blindfold

PROCEDURE.

1. Mark-off a thirty-six-inch horizontal line in inches on a chalkboard. The height of the line should be about shoulder height of an average size person. The inch lines should be vertical lines and should be about twelve inches in length on each side of the horizontal line.
2. Randomly assign two students to each of three groups: five second, twenty second, or forty-five second retention interval groups.
3. Blindfold the subject and move him to a position between you and the chalkboard so that his right side is facing the chalkboard.
4. Ask the subject to make a fist and extend his left arm; move him so that the end of his fist is in line with the beginning point of the thirty-six-inch line.
5. Hand the subject the bow; help him to hold it in a correct shooting position, left arm straight and right hand on the string (index, middle, and ring fingers only on the string).
6. Explain to the subject that he is to draw the string until it stops, hold it there for two seconds, and then return (do not release) the string to its original position. (Use your arm as the stop in this experiment.) After a certain amount of time (depending on the group), he will hear the command "Draw" and he is to draw the string to the same position. (He is to indicate that he is at the position by saying "There.")

7. Permit the subject one practice trial at twelve inches. Use the retention interval according to his group.
8. Begin a series of five trials with a one-minute rest between trials. A trial is considered as:
Draw to the criterion position—return to the starting position - retention interval—recall the criterion position.

LABORATORY EXPERIMENT : STM DATA SHEET

GROUP I: 5 - sec. RI No Interp. Activ.	TRIALS						
SUBJECT	1	2	3	4	5	ΣX	
1.							
2.							
							$\bar{X}_I =$

GROUP II : 5 - sec. RI Interp. Activ.	TRIALS						
SUBJECT	1	2	3	4	5	ΣX	
1.							
2.							
							$\bar{X}_{II} =$

GROUP III : 30 - sec. RI No Interp. Activ.	TRIALS						
SUBJECT	1	2	3	4	5	ΣX	
1.							
2.							
							$\bar{X}_{III} =$

GROUP IV. 30 - sec. RI Interp. Activ.	TRIALS						
SUBJECT	1	2	3	4	5	ΣX	
1.							
2.							
							$\bar{X}_{IV} =$

Trial 1:   five inches
Trial 2:   twenty inches
Trial 3:   thirty inches
Trial 4:   fifteen inches
Trial 5:   ten inches

9. Record the number of inches the subject is long or short of the criterion distance. Make a chalkmark at the position he indicates as "There." This will facilitate scoring and will allow the subject an opportunity to relax his arm as soon as he says "There."

RESULTS.

1. Add the number of inches the subject was long or short of the criterion position. Determine the subject's absolute error by ignor-

FIELD EXPERIMENT : STM DATA SHEET

TRIAL	GROUP I (5 sec.)			GROUP II (20 sec.)			GROUP III (45 sec.)		
	SUBJECT	ABSOLUTE	ALGEBRAIC	SUBJECT	ABSOLUTE	ALGEBRAIC	SUBJECT	ABSOLUTE	ALGEBRAIC
1	1			3			5		
2									
3									
4									
5									
		$\Sigma X =$	$\Sigma X_a =$		$\Sigma X =$	$\Sigma X_a=$		$\Sigma X =$	$\Sigma X_a=$
1	2			4			6		
2									
3									
4									
5									
		$\Sigma X =$	$\Sigma X_a =$		$\Sigma X =$	$\Sigma X_a =$		$\Sigma X =$	$\Sigma X_a =$

GROUP MEANS

Absolute error   Algebraic error

Group I

Group II

Group III

Note : ΣX = Sum of trials using absolute error (ignore + or − signs to obtain sums)

ΣX_a = Sum of trials using algebraic error (include + and − signs to obtain sums)

ing the signs of + and −. Determine the subject's algebraic error by adding the inches according to the signs. Each subject therefore will have two scores: absolute error and algebraic error.

2. Plot the mean error scores for each group on the graphs provided.
3. Using the absolute error scores for each subject, calculate the group means. Do the same for algebraic error. Using an ANOVA, indicate whether or not differences exist for absolute error. Follow the same procedure for algebraic error. (You may wish to consult the Pepper and Herman (1970) article to better understand the importance of the algebraic error and its relation to motor STM.)

LABORATORY EXPERIMENT : STM DATA

GRAPH OF ABSOLUTE ERROR

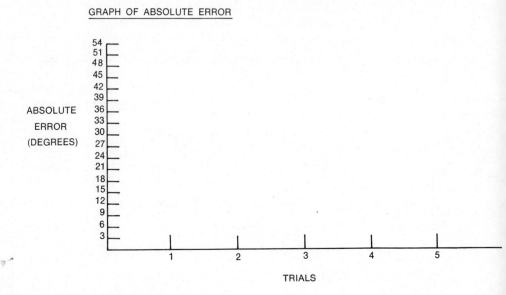

FIELD EXPERIMENT : STM DATA

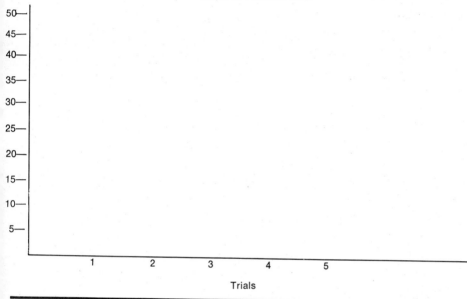

Graph of Absolute Error

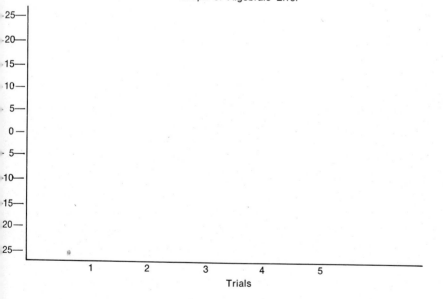

Graph of Algebraic Error

APPENDIX

PURCHASED EQUIPMENT. The Kinesthesiometer may be purchased from the Lafayette Instrument Co., P. O. Box 1279, Lafayette, Indiana.

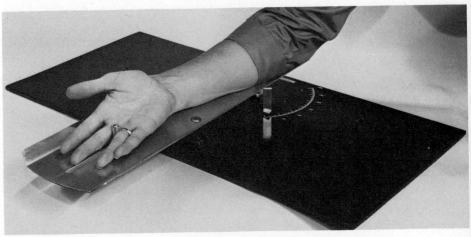

KINESTHESIOMETER

Figure 22-7: This instrument is available for the study of kinesthesis. Units of measurement are given as degree of displacement. Full 180 degrees of movement are provided for. Adjustable finger guides and elbow saddle increase comfort of subject while keeping his arm in place. This instrument can be used with equal facility to study active movement or passive movement or for comparing the two modes of movement.

CONSTRUCTED EQUIPMENT.

1. Lever. The description that follows is taken from an article by Sulzer (1963):

The upper drawing shows E's side of the lever. Essentially, the apparatus consists of a movable lever mounted within a box, with overall dimensions of 23 x 17 x 13 inches. The eleven inches from the back of the box to the center of the lever allows S a comfortable grip without being able to see hand and forearm. The radius is approximately eleven inches from the center of the shaft to the rubber grip at the top. The total response range is 108 degrees or twenty-one inches of arc. A cut-out in the panel enables E to see S's hand throughout the entire response range.

The scale from which the amplitude of response is measured was reproduced by offset lithography on white card stock, with one tick for each degree of arc. Only the ticks were printed so that E might use whatever scale numbers suited his purpose. Different scales can readily be mounted by removing the stop plate and retaining screws. The stop plate is an .062 inch aluminum strip 1.0 inches wide and is cut to an outside radius of 5.0 inches. In this plate 1/16th inch holes are drilled at each degree of arc so that E can insert a steel pin and stop the pointer and lever at any predetermined place. At the starting position is a removable pin against which the back of the pointer rests. The starting position can be varied by changing the position of this pin. Thus, if desired, S can be required to move the lever to a constant target from a varying starting position or can be asked to displace the lever by a constant amount from different starting positions (Sulzer, 1961).

A detail of the individual parts is shown in the lower drawing. The lever is a 3/8 inch steel rod which is threaded into the shaft mounting. The shaft runs completely through *E*'s display panel to his scale. The pointer is securely held to the shaft by means of two large hex nuts. At the other end, the shaft passes through a brass plate which causes a drag on the shaft. The amount of force required to move the lever can be varied by means of a wing nut which opens or closes the brass drag plate. The lever moves through the complete arc with virtually no chatter over a wide range of drag settings.

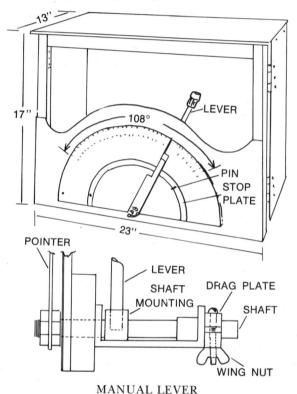

MANUAL LEVER

Figure 22-8:

2. Metal Slide. (Adams and Dijkstra, 1966)

The apparatus is a metal bar that is 75 cm long and is scaled in millimeters. On this bar are two freely moving sliding elements. One slide has a set screw which *E* uses to lock the slide in place for defining the length of a response required of *S* on a trial. The other slide has a knob on top for fingertip grasping and is used by *S* in responding. The apparatus is fixed to a table top at right angles to *S* (for a right-left movement), with *S* sitting on one side of the table and *E* on the other.